SVEN
MY STORY

SVEN-GÖRAN ERIKSSON

headline

First published in the UK in 2013
by HEADLINE PUBLISHING GROUP

1

Cataloguing in Publication Data is available from the British Library

Hardback ISBN 978 1 4722 1150 7
Trade Paperback ISBN 978 1 4722 1325 9

Translated from Swedish into English by Stefan Lovgren

Typeset in Bliss 11/18.25 pt by
Palimpsest Book Production Limited, Falkirk, Stirlingshire

Printed and bound in Great Britain by
Clays Ltd, St Ives plc

Headline's policy is to use papers that are natural, renewable and recyclable
products and made from wood grown in sustainable forests. The logging and
manufacturing processes are expected to conform to the environmental
regulations of the country of origin.

HEADLINE PUBLISHING GROUP
An Hachette UK Company
338 Euston Road
London NW1 3BH

www.headline.co.uk
www.hachette.co.uk

CONTENTS

THE first time I went without a job was after England were knocked out of the 2006 World Cup. Until then, I had always had another job lined up before leaving a post. But everything is different with England. It is a job that holds you hostage, until it spits you out. The World Cup was held in Germany that year. After we lost to Portugal on penalties in the quarter-finals, I travelled with the team back to England. From there, I arranged for a private plane to fly me to Torsby. I wanted to get home, put the defeat behind me, the way I had trained myself to do. It was a bad loss, but life would go on. Except this was different. In club football, there is always a next game, always another season. Not so this time. I'd had my chance. There would not be another. Had I done everything I could?

What made it so disappointing was that I actually thought we could win the World Cup. It was not something I just said to the papers. It had been the plan of the Football Association all along – in 2006 we would be ready. I felt ready. Wayne Rooney had broken a metatarsal bone in his foot just six weeks before the beginning of the tournament. To take him with us, I'd had to fight Sir Alex Ferguson, one of our many battles, and I had won. Rooney was coming. We had no other injuries. Beckham, Gerrard, Owen, Ferdinand, Cole, Terry – they were ready. These were my players. This was my team.

We had sailed through the group stage with ease, winning it without impressing, which had only made me more convinced that this was going to be our year. In the World Cup, you do not want your team peaking too soon. We beat Ecuador in the second round, then faced Portugal in the quarters.

Some people say penalties were inevitable. I don't agree. We would have won that game in regular time if Rooney had not been sent off. Even then, we held out for more than an hour. Most people don't remember that.

When penalties arrived, I was still certain we would prevail, even though England had never won a penalty shootout in a World Cup. I was wrong. And it was partly my fault. After what happened two years earlier, I should have brought in a coach to help us prepare psychologically for penalties. I know that now. At the press conference after the game, I thanked the England supporters. I said I would like to be remembered as an honest man who did his best. Then I went home. And everything went quiet. That is when I began to believe in the curse of the former England manager.

● ● ●

It is early December and the first snow has just arrived, blanketing the ground leading down to the lake. It will be several weeks before Fryken freezes. For now, the waves keep pounding the rocks. It is the only sound you can hear. That was not the case in the summer of 2004, at the height of the Faria business. Back then, the cove below was filled with boats and paparazzi jostling to get a shot, any shot, of me, Swinging Sven. One of them had even rented a crane. My mother got so mad she moved the lunch party inside, even though it was a beautiful summer day.

It has been a month since I left my last job, in Thailand. Some people were surprised I took that assignment, as technical director of a Thai football team. A former England manager working in the Thai Premier League! They said I was finished, that I was going there for the lifestyle, and for the women. The truth is I just wanted to work. So when a wealthy Thai friend of mine who owns a football team in Bangkok offered me a two-month contract as a consultant, I accepted. Why not? I had no other offers.

I like Thailand, despite the problems I had with Thai politics at Manchester City and Leicester. I like the people, the food, the noise. In Bangkok, I had a hotel suite in the busiest part of the city. That is where I like to be, where the commotion is. Of all the places I have lived, my favourite location may have been Manchester. I stayed at a hotel in the city centre there, with all the restaurants and shops downstairs. It was perfect.

Here, at Björkefors, I get restless. I bought this place in 2002, and I must have spent close to £5 million rebuilding and restoring it. It used to be a convalescent home, which is why there is still an elevator in the main house. Before that, it was a private residence. Selma Lagerlöf, one of the most famous citizens of Värmland, wrote the last chapter of *Gösta Berling's Saga* in one of the bedrooms on the third floor. Nineteen years later she won the Nobel Prize for Literature.

There is a separate building with an indoor swimming pool, which I had constructed, along with another house for my parents, Sven and Ulla. They lived there until early last year, when my mother passed away. Now my father stays there only when I am here. Otherwise he lives in Torsby, in his apartment in the centre of town. He likes to spend the afternoons with his newfound friends, betting on the horses. It does not look like the family will be together this Christmas. My girlfriend, Yaniseth, is in Panama. She can't come here because her ex-husband, who lives in Mexico and from whom she's been separated for several years, doesn't want their son to leave the country.

● ● ●

It must have been the spring of 1993, years before I became England manager, when my wife, Anki, and I drove to northern Italy to visit one of the greatest legends of Italian football, Nisse Liedholm. After a glorious career as a player and manager, Liedholm had retired from the game the year before and was now living at the vineyard he had started with his wife in the small village of Cuccaro Monferrato.

I remember the day was cold, and that the road ran through some forest. It did not look like wine country. Perhaps it was fitting that Liedholm's vineyard should appear out of place in these surroundings. He did not belong there, either. Liedholm was not a winemaker, he was a football man. Like me.

I had taken over from him as manager of Roma almost a decade earlier, when he went back to coaching Milan. At the time we may have been the only Swedish football managers working abroad, certainly in Italy.

I had never been able to compare myself to Liedholm as a player. He was an Olympic gold winner with Sweden when he came to Italy in 1949, and went on to play for twelve years with Milan, winning four scudetti. My playing career, in contrast, went as far as Karlskoga in the Swedish second division, although I had a pretty good right foot, but more about that later.

Between us as managers, however, a torch had been passed. Yes, I was still waiting to win my first scudetto, and Liedholm had won two championships. But I was now the manager of Sampdoria, an exciting young team led by superstars such as Roberto Mancini and Ruud Gullit. Liedholm, on the other hand, had called it quits in 1989. Three years later, he changed his mind and returned to manage Verona for a brief spell, with disastrous results. In his last match, his team lost 4–0 to Milan.

One time, Anki and I had watched Liedholm on television as he provided commentary on the weekend's games. On air, he forgot the names of his own players, or got them confused. He was mixing Italian and Swedish. I told Anki that if I ever got to the stage where I could not remember my own players' names, she should force me to quit the game.

When we finally arrived at Villa Boemia, Liedholm's estate, he and his wife Nina, who was a countess, greeted us in the courtyard. They had bought the vineyard twenty years earlier. Liedholm had put all his money into rebuilding the place, and it was stunning. Too stunning. Anki thought it looked artificial, every patch of cement was practically sparkling.

Together with their son Carlo, who was in charge of running the winery, we tasted the wines. After lunch, Nisse, Carlo and I sat down in the garden and the talk turned to football. Liedholm began telling his stories. Did we know that during his first two years as a player for Milan he did not misplace a single pass? When he finally did, the crowd at San Siro had given him a standing ovation that lasted several minutes.

I had heard all the stories, and Carlo had, too. But it did not stop Liedholm from telling them again. He was emotional, and did not entirely make sense. He said he wanted to get back into football.

'Don't you think there is somebody who wants me?' he asked. 'I will take any team, even a youth team.'

I was stunned. Here was Nisse Liedholm, a man who had won everything, and still he was not satisfied. It pained me to see the man I had idolised reduced to a shadow of his former larger-than-life self. But I did not have the heart to tell him it was over. Finally, Carlo turned to his father and said something that I will always remember. 'Papà, basta!' Be quiet, Dad.

It was not said with any apparent malice. But those two short words cut deep into my heart. It would be many years until I understood why.

● ● ●

The phone rings. I have two mobile numbers, one English, one Swedish. This is the English number. It is my lawyer, or one of them. I am involved in at least three legal cases. This is the lawyer representing me in the case of Sven-Göran Eriksson versus Samir Khan, the financial adviser who swindled me out of my fortune.

The truth is, I never cared about money. Not one bit. Some people might find that hard to believe. Suffice to say that Samir Khan caught on pretty quickly. Apparently, I have a beach house in Barbados that he bought for himself with my money. I am told it is next to Wayne Rooney's house. The lawyer informs me that the court date for the case against Khan has been postponed yet again. I know what another postponement means – more legal fees. If only I could sell the London apartment, but that means kicking Nancy out of it first, which brings me to the next legal case – Sven-Göran Eriksson versus Nancy Dell'Olio.

Nancy is my old girlfriend. She was married to someone else when we met, in Rome, during my time at Lazio. She was irresistible then. Until I came to live with her. By the time I left Italy for England, it should have been over but somehow I agreed for her to move with me. I later bought the London apartment without her knowledge, to get away from her. I had done the same thing in Rome. When we finally broke up, I offered her a deal to stay rent-free in that apartment on the condition that she would move out in 2009, or at least that's what I thought we'd agreed. She was still there in 2012. It is complicated.

The third case is Sven-Göran Eriksson versus The Mirror Group Newspapers. At the time of writing, this is a live claim so I am restricted by my lawyers in what I can say, but it seems that Mirror Group Newspapers were secretly hacking my phone during my time as England manager, and that this was how the media found out about me and Ulrika. At one point I suspected my own family of selling information about me but I now think that the media obtained lots of information through hacking my phones. It really upsets me to think about the people close to me whom I wrongly accused of selling information about me.

● ● ●

It is for me to tell my own story. Yet I am not sure this is the time for me to do it. I always believed that you write your story once it is finished. But I am not finished. Besides, how do you do it? Where I come from, we don't talk much about ourselves. We don't reveal what we feel. That would be a sign of weakness. I have never in my life stopped to look back. Perhaps I have been scared of what I would find? There is only one way to find out. Start from the beginning and move forward. Don't fall too deep.

I WILL BE FAMOUS **1**

I was born into secrecy. My father Sven did not dare tell his father Erik or his mother Ester that I had come into this world. An 18-year-old boy getting a lass three years his senior pregnant was not something that was looked upon favourably among the countryfolk in northern Värmland at that time. So my father kept quiet about me. When they called to tell him that I was about to be born, he slipped into the winter night without a word to parents or brothers about my impending arrival.

The journey in neighbour Andersson's taxi cost five kronor (50p). In half an hour he reached my grandmother's house in Sunne where I was born on 5 February 1948. The delivery was complicated. The umbilical cord had wrapped around my neck. A doctor had to be called and for a while they thought I would not make it. But when the sun rose, I was already a few hours old and my father could go to work as usual.

My father's family owned a farm with plenty of land in the village of

Stöpafors, on the western side of Fryken. Sven and his brother Karl-Erik worked as conductors for the bus company, which their uncle owned. It was on the local route that my father had met my mother, Ulla. She worked in a textile store in Torsby and took the bus there and back every day. I don't know what my father did to charm her, but he must have done something right because soon my mother was pregnant with me.

While my father's family were relatively well off by local standards, my mother's were not. Her father had one day up and left his wife and four children, never to return. From the day he disappeared his name was never mentioned again. It was only many years later that I learned he was also called Sven. My mother and her siblings were named Svensson. But when my grandfather disappeared, they all changed their last names to Thudén, my grandmother's maiden name – all but my mother. She kept the name Svensson until she got married. In Sweden, 'Svensson' is the name you use to refer to the average Swede. It is curious that my mother kept the name for so long, because she was hardly a Svensson.

As a young girl, my mother was a very bright student. Her teachers urged her to pursue her education but her mother would not allow her to do that. After sixth grade, she had to start working to earn money. She would be forever resentful that she was not given the opportunity of an education, especially since her younger siblings were allowed to continue with their schooling. Things did not improve when she became pregnant. Two weeks after I was born we moved into a small room that she rented in Torsby.

There we lived, my mother and I, without electricity or running water. I slept on a pull-out kitchen couch, which was not bad because it was placed next to an iron furnace where there was always a fire going, so it was warm. On the floor above us lived my second cousins and on the floor below Maja, a seamstress, had a room. I helped her with her sewing by pumping the foot pedals of her Singer sewing machine with my hands.

My father claims he told his parents about me soon after I was born. Nevertheless, he stayed at their house until I was two years old before moving in with us. My parents got married then. After that, my mother was allowed to come to Stöpafors, but it probably took a while before she was fully accepted by my father's parents. In the beginning, she mostly stayed in the kitchen while she was there.

Soon after that my father went away for his military service. I remember how he put me on my mother's bed to say goodbye. My father doesn't believe that I could remember it. He thinks that I must have seen an old photograph. But I remember that his uniform was grey and the fabric was rough. It could not have been easy for my mother to be left alone again, but she was thick-skinned. She did everything for me. One day her son would show the world what she was never able to show herself. I was going to be her revenge on life.

●　●　●

After my father completed his military service, we moved into an apartment with one room and a kitchen at Östmarksvägen in Torsby. Dad went from bus conductor to driver. His uncle Gottfrid Jönsson also drove the bus. Sometimes Gottfrid let me sit on his lap when he drove the 22-mile route from Torsby to Sunne. Having a four-year-old boy steer the bus did not seem to bother the passengers.

My mother, however, worried about everything. In Värmland, we have a saying that goes: 'Everything will work out . . . and if it doesn't, it doesn't matter.' My mother was a Värmland-native through and through, but her outlook on life was far from easy-going.

My mother believed in God. At home we said grace before dinner and she would read the Lord's Prayer to me every night. Mainly, our religion was about how you behaved. You had to respect everyone, be polite and greet people properly. I had to wait to take a biscuit until all the grown-ups had been served; otherwise I would be in big trouble. My grandmother, Edla, was kind, but very strict. I guess she had to be as a single mother of four children. My mother took after her mother that way.

My father, on the other hand, was not the religious type. When he was little, the village pastor would come to the family home in Stöpafors to test him on the Bible. That did not go well. My father was not able to learn anything by heart. He did not care much for schoolwork. After sixth grade, unlike my mother, he was relieved never to have to set foot in school again. He thought school was a waste of time.

Clearly, I had to take my own schooling seriously. My mother would not have tolerated anything else. I was a quiet student who did as he was told. I got very good grades. There is not a whole lot else to tell about my early education. To be honest, the schooling was not something that interested me or most of the other boys in the area. Our lives were all about sports.

● ● ●

'Next jumper: Sven-Göran "two pancakes high" Eriksson!' the speaker called out. It was my first ski-jumping competition, held in the small town of Grums. I was eight, maybe nine, years old and small for my age, which the speaker pointed out with that pancake remark. I had trained all winter with my ski-jumping club SK Bore at the 25-metre jumping hill in Torsby. I borrowed the skis. They were huge, wooden planks, so heavy that I could hardly carry them, one at a time, up the steep steps leading up to the top. The first time I jumped I was terrified. I remember Arne just holding me while I sat up there on top with my skis on.

'Should I let you go?' he asked.

'No,' I answered, but of course he let me go anyway. So I went.

I survived my first jump, and I think I did okay in my first competitive jump, too. After that, it was all ski-jumping during the winter months. Anders 'Pewe' Persson, who was two years older than I was, organised taxis to competitions. Sometimes we trained in Sysslebäck, which had a 70-metre-tall jumping hill. Pewe was one of the best youth jumpers in Sweden but the first time my father came to see me jump, Pewe fell and suffered a concussion.

Ski-jumping was not a particularly safe sport. It required courage, which I did not lack, but also strength and technique. You had to be able to push your body foward during the jump. One time I crashed and hit my lower back so badly I could not sit down for a week. But that was nothing compared to what happened to one of the other boys, Kullbleck. He fell during training on the big hill in Sysslebäck. The snow conditions were fast that day, too fast for Kullbleck, who was not able to stand up properly during the jump. When he landed, his knee hit his chin. Pewe ran down to check on him. It was not good. Kullbleck had bitten off half his tongue. Pewe kept calm, though. 'Close your mouth,' he said. 'We're going to the hospital.' In northern Värmland we didn't make a big fuss about things.

When we were not jumping, we played ice hockey or went cross-country skiing, but when eventually winter gave way to spring, football took over. In school, we played during every recess – Torsten Kjellgren and me against everyone else. We still won. Our natural meeting place was the Björnevi football ground. As soon as the snow melted, and sometimes even before then, Björnevi filled up with football-playing boys of all ages. The girls did not really play back then.

We played quite a bit at home, too, even though the garden sloped so much that the ball constantly rolled out into the street. There were several families living in the building. Klara Norlén lived in one apartment. Her son, Göte, was my father's age and he worked for the Transportation Board. He was a former player for the Torsby senior team and always played football with us kids at home. He was also a musician and when he got home from work, he first had to practise his clarinet. It was torment having to wait for him to finish before we could start playing football.

Usually, we played with just one goal. One of us was the goalkeeper and another one played defence. I was normally the centre forward and Göte hit crosses that I was supposed to head into goal. There was just one problem – the goal stood next to a shed where Göte's mother stored milk and cheese. We had no refrigerators at the time. Sometimes the ball hit the wall of the shed so hard that the milk pot got knocked over and shattered. When that happened, Göte ran into the woodshed to hide before his mother came running out, yelling how she had told us a thousand times to go and play football somewhere else.

Göte gave me Gunnar Nordahl's autobiography, *Gold and Green Pitches*. Nordahl was Sweden's first professional football player. He signed for AC Milan in 1949 and became one of the top goalscorers of all time in the Italian Serie A. I stayed up at night to read about his miraculous achievements at the San Siro. Italy felt farther away than the moon.

But Nordahl was not a member of the Swedish national team that made the final of the 1958 World Cup. The tournament was held in Sweden and everyone followed it on the radio or on television. We did not have a television, but someone else must have had one because I distinctly remember watching a fuzzy broadcast of one of the games. Highlights from the matches were shown in the cinema. Kurt 'Kurre' Hamrin was our favourite Swedish player. He was from Stockholm, but he had relatives in Värmland and spent summers there. Of all the players in that World Cup, however, Pelé was, of course, the greatest. To do what he did as a 17-year-old, scoring two goals in the final when Brazil beat Sweden 5–2, was fantastic. After the World Cup, we all wanted to be Pelé.

● ● ●

One night I was sleeping on the kitchen couch when a rat suddenly scurried across my chest, and my mother decided we had to move. My father wanted to buy a car, but my mother insisted that we should build our own house, so that is how it would be. They bought a plot on Åsögatan in Torsby and my mother arranged for the building permit. I was 11 years old when we moved in, at Easter 1959. My parents could not get a single loan that covered the entire cost of building the house, so had to take out a second loan at a higher interest rate. We had moved from one room to four but had no money for furniture. In the beginning, we ate a lot of porridge and pancakes.

Three years earlier, a little brother, Lars-Erik, had arrived. 'Lasse', as he was called, was often sick as a child. He had asthma. To be honest, he did not figure in my life very much. He was eight years younger than I was and so we never played sports together. In the summer, I had to look after Lasse when my parents were at work. It was not a job that I enjoyed. It was, however, because of Lasse that I got my nickname, 'Svennis'. When he was little, he could not say Sven-Göran, so he said 'Tenn-hönan', which rhymes with Sven-Göran in Swedish but translates as 'pewter chicken'. I did not like the name.

'Don't call me Tennhönan,' I said.

'Okay, Tennis,' he replied.

'Don't call me Tennis, either,' I said. 'At least say, Svennis.' And that's how I got the name Svennis.

For several years, my mother had been working at the kiosk that sold sweets, cigarettes and newspapers. She was known as 'Ulla in the kiosk' and had a stern reputation around Torsby. She did not like kids hanging around the kiosk doing nothing. My father had started driving lorries, a job that paid better than driving the bus, but finances were still tight. At least once a month, my parents would make the journey across the border to Norway to buy butter and flour, staples that were cheaper there than in Sweden.

Personally, I was oblivious to any financial hardships that my parents endured. Things always seemed to work out fine. I remember wanting a pair of 'slamkrypare', ankle-high winter boots that had a zipper on top and were very popular at the time. My parents could not afford to buy them for me, but anyway they got me a pair for my birthday. Ahead of the 1960 summer Olympics, my father rented our first television. Two months later he bought it outright. The store owner offered to deduct the rent my dad had paid from the sale price. In Torsby, people helped each other.

When I reached my teenage years, I started working during the summer as a baker's apprentice at the New Bakery in Torsby. The pastry chef at the shop, Sven-Åke 'Åsen' Olsson, was also the coach of Torsby's senior football and hockey teams. The work day at the bakery started at 4 a.m.

and for hours we baked scones and ginger biscuits and talked football. Sometimes Åsen drew tactics in the flour on the baking sheets. In time, those talks grew more and more sophisticated.

After lunch, my work day was over and I headed to Björnevi to play football. I didn't stand out in the team. I was small and skinny, but I ran a lot and worked very hard. When we played matches, my dad always came to watch.

I was stubborn and hated losing. My worst memory from my early playing years was when we made the regional final of the 'Little World Cup', a tournament with teams from all over Sweden. The score was tied after extra time, so the game had to be decided by penalties. At that time, one player took all five penalties. I was chosen. I scored my first four, putting them all in the same corner. The other guy also scored his four. I decided to switch corners for my last penalty. Why, I do not know. I struck it cleanly enough, but the keeper guessed correctly and tipped the shot onto the post. We lost and I cried. I vowed never ever to suffer such a heartbreaking defeat again.

● ● ●

The Torsby senior team played in the Swedish fourth division at that time. The day before each match, Åsen would announce the starting eleven on the public noticeboard opposite my mother's kiosk. I often wondered why he did that. Maybe it was to get the locals involved. If so, it worked. The Torsby residents all flocked to that noticeboard the day before the game to find out whom Åsen had picked. If a surprise name was included, heated discussions ensued. I usually bicycled there to check the line-up. One day my name would be up there on the board.

That day came sooner than I expected. I was 16 years old when the door bell rang one night. It was Åsen. He wanted to tell me and my parents that I had been selected to start the following day's match. 'Okay,' I said, as if it were no big deal. But that night I could barely sleep and in the morning I had to bicycle down to the noticeboard to make sure that my name really was there.

How my debut match went, or even who our opponents were, I don't remember. There must have been those who thought Åsen had lost his mind picking a 16-year-old boy who was still at school for the Torsby senior team. But I must have done reasonably well, because I played regularly after that. I was the youngest player on the team.

By the time I was 18, I was working at the local state insurance office. At Christmas time, all my friends who had gone to work somewhere else returned to Torsby. On Christmas Day we all got together in someone's apartment and drank glögg mixed with vodka, played cards and talked about what we wanted to do with our lives. I was probably slightly intoxicated when I said, 'I will be famous.'

The others laughed. What on earth would I be famous for?

'I haven't decided yet,' I said.

It was really out of character for me to stick my neck out like that. This was Värmland, where no one was better than anyone else. But I knew I was special. My mother had told me so.

TORD

'MONDAY morning' to 'Saturday night'. That's how we ranked girls by their looks. My life was not just about football. I had discovered girls, too. A knockout girl was awarded the honour of being called 'Saturday night'. A 'Monday morning' belonged at the other end of the scale. It may sound a little mean, but it was pretty innocent, and if the girls had ranked us in the same way, most of us would probably not have survived beyond Wednesday.

Unless we had a game the next day, we used to get together at the New Bakery on Saturday nights, sitting in the back room drinking aquavit and soda before going out. There was usually one designated driver for the evening. I had bought a rusty old Opel together with my father, so that designated driver was occasionally me. Sometimes we went to Kongsvinger in Norway, and more than once some of us got pretty smashed during those excursions. If we were going dancing in Ekshärad or Hagfors, the girls would come with us, so things did not get quite as rowdy. No alcohol was available at those dance places so we used to stand in the car park mixing rum and Coke, freezing our butts off in the middle of winter.

I was pretty popular with the girls, although I was no Casanova. Pewe and Anders Hallström were very good dancers. Anders, son of the local tailor, was a sharp dresser. Leif Gunnarsson, our right back, was going out with the district's most beautiful girl, Siv, and everyone wondered how on earth he could have managed it. The problem was Siv never wanted to come dancing with us. She lived halfway to Ekshärad and if we were going there, we had to drop Leif off on the way. Sometimes we sat in the car for fifteen minutes waiting for Leif to persuade Siv to come with us.

In Ekshärad I met Nina Persson, who became my first steady girlfriend. Anders Hallström got together with her sister. Nina was 'Saturday night'. Her father, Rune, was a ceramics artist and well known in northern Värmland. He also ran a local support group for people who had been caught shooting moose illegally. He believed everyone had the right to shoot moose. People needed food. But Rune had a drinking problem and sometimes things got out of hand. One time when Anders and I came to pick up Nina and her sister, Rune was waiting on the veranda with a rifle in his hand.

'Don't you lay a hand on my daughters!' he yelled.

Nina was the first girl I brought home to meet my parents, but in my mother's eyes, no girl was good enough for me. Even Nina. That was something that would never change.

After I did my military service, Nina and I moved to Karlstad. I still worked for the state insurance agency, but in a new office. I commuted to Torsby for training and matches. Nina probably thought that I spent too much time playing football, and our relationship was creaky. It ended completely when she moved to Örebro to study. She married a physical education teacher there.

Work at the insurance office was just as boring as it had been in Torsby. One day I was talking to Bengt Frykman, who worked in radio in Värmland, and he asked me why I would stay in a job that I had no interest in. After hanging up the phone, I walked straight into my supervisor's office and quit my job.

I was 21 years old when I moved back to Torsby and started high school. One person who approved of my decision to continue my education was my mother. To her, there was nothing more important than education. Around this time the kiosk closed. My mother worked in a bookstore for a year or two before she began working the night shift at the local hospital. She was happy for me to move in with her and my dad in the house on Åsgatan. Lasse and I had our own rooms on the second floor.

Living at home, however, did not really work out. My mother still worried about me. I was an adult now, but that did not matter. If I was out late, she would sit up all night to make sure I got home okay. She rarely complained about me, but when Lasse Sundberg and I disappeared for two days without a word – we had gone to Norway to meet some girls – my mother told my father to rebuke me. It was the only time I ever heard my father raise his voice. Either I had to shape up or I had to move out, he said. I moved out.

For some reason, I had got it into my head to study economics. For that, I had to move schools, to Åmål in Dalsland, 93 miles away. It was the first time I had lived outside Värmland. I also had to change football teams. Kurt Rösvall, with whom I had played in Torsby, convinced me to sign for SK Sifhälla, a third-division team in the neighbouring town of Säffle.

No salary was involved but the club gave me a free apartment. I was definitely heading up in the footballing world.

● ● ●

Ann-Christine – everyone called her 'Anki' – was 17 years old, five years younger than I was. I had seen her in school a few times, but I had not talked to her. The Karlberg School in Åmål was a new school with about a thousand students, a lot for such a small town. One day I sat in the cafeteria playing whist with some friends when Anki stopped to watch the card game. She was standing behind my partner, opposite from me. After a while, she started signalling to me what cards to play, based on what cards my partner held. In other words, she helped me. It was called cheating.

It turned out Anki was the daughter of one of the principals at the school, Karl-Erik Pettersson. That may have deterred other potential suitors, but it did not put me off. I invited her to go dancing at the civic hall in Säffle. We kissed on the dance floor and after that we were a couple. At weekends I would collect her in Åmål in my old Saab and drive the 10 miles to my place in Säffle. My apartment was a sparsely furnished one-room place. My mother had arranged for most of the furniture in the apartment.

Anki came from a family of sports enthusiasts. She loved football. She was very mature for her age and we shared the same ambition to travel. My idea of sailing around the world, however, was not received with any enthusiasm. Anki got seasick as soon as she set foot on a boat. To celebrate Midsummer's Eve in 1971, she came with me to Torsby for the first time. I think she had a bit of a culture shock. She had never seen people drink so much. One of my friends asked her if he could offer her a drink. 'Sure,'

Anki said. She probably thought they would at least be sitting at a table, having a proper drink. But instead my friend opened the boot of his car where he kept a drum of moonshine. We called it 'The Forest Star'.

Anki also met my parents. My mother made pizza, which she was probably alone in making among the Torsby residents at that time. As with my previous girlfriends, my mother was friendly but sceptical towards Anki. Despite that, she could not help but talk and talk. My father, Lasse and I had rarely listened to her. I think she told her whole life story to Anki, things that I knew nothing about.

My last year in high school was easy. I was five years older than everyone else and highly motivated. When Anki and I graduated at the same time, I knew that I wanted to continue my studies at university. At the same time, I was a football player. I had not given up hope of one day playing in the Swedish top division, Allsvenskan, or even moving abroad to play professionally. I had to get an education where I was guaranteed a job, but why not stick to sports? I could teach physical education. I decided to apply to the Swedish School of Sport and Health Sciences in Örebro, and was given a place. Now I just had to find another football team to play for.

● ● ●

In 1972, KB Karlskoga played in the second division. Their 34-year-old player-manager, Tord Grip, had three international caps to his name. They were a good team with ambitions of getting into the top flight – exactly the kind of team that I needed to develop my own playing career. I contacted KB and they invited me to come for a trial, so I drove the 28 miles from Örebro, where I was living in student accommodation. It was a drive that I would come to know well.

Tord and I got along right away, but he showed me no partiality. The level of play at KB Karlskoga was a lot higher, and faster, than I was used to. Also, I was playing right back at that time, and KB already had two experienced players for that position. To get into the team would prove much harder than I had ever expected.

My studies at GIH, as the sports university was known, were a lot easier. We had classes from eight in the morning to five in the afternoon – physiology and anatomy and things like that. Anki had got a job at the hospital in Örebro but she didn't like it and instead decided to study to become a teacher. The college was in Karlstad and we agreed to meet at weekends, but that was easier said than done. On Saturdays I played for KB reserves and sometimes made the bench for Sunday games. I don't think I went to Karlstad to visit Anki a single time, and we broke up for a couple of months.

As soon as classes were over for the day, I got into my Renault and drove to Karlskoga for training with the team. I was convinced that my chance would come, which it did in the spring of 1973 when a 25-year-old Torsby boy with professional ambitions finally got to make his debut in the Swedish second division. I must have done a decent job, because after that I got to play regularly. I was looked upon as a distinctly average defender, but someone who rarely made mistakes.

There was nothing wrong with my right foot and no one could fault me for effort. I had also gained strength after spending the winters running up and down a local hill. I did not like to slide tackle, preferring instead to stay on my feet. I was modern that way.

After graduating from GIH, I got a job as a PT teacher at a school on the outskirts of Karlskoga and moved into an apartment in town. Anki had a year of her course remaining but we were back together and at least we would be a little closer to each other. Soon she came to live with me. Our interests were not an exact match. She would come to see me play but she also wanted me to go shopping for antiques with her.

Around this time, the Dutch, and especially Ajax, were revolutionising the game with their so-called 'total football'. Until then, activities on the pitch had revolved around eleven individuals versus eleven individuals. In the 1958 World Cup final, Swedish left back Sven Axbom was left completely on his own to handle Brazil's virtuoso winger Garrincha. Time and again Axbom was turned inside out by Garrincha without ever getting any support from his team-mates. The Dutch tried to change that by prioritising the collective. The team moved together. Attackers became defenders, defenders became attackers. It was something the footballing world had never seen before.

In Karlskoga, we hardly played total football. To our head coach, a Hungarian by the name of Imre Moré, football was still the individual's game. During a match away to Helsingborg, I discovered how Axbom must have felt during the 1958 final. I was left to my own devices to cope with a tricky winger who, despite not being Garrincha, proved way too fast for me. Time and again he blew by me on the right flank.

'Svennis, get closer!' Moré ordered from the sideline.

So I moved closer to the winger, which resulted in their left back sending the ball over me for the winger to chase down.

'Drop deep!' Moré yelled.

So I dropped deep, but that didn't work either. The winger had time to receive the ball and turn upfield to face me. He didn't bother with any trickery, but simply kicked the ball on and ran past me. It was a mess. In the dressing room at half-time, I asked Moré if he had any other ideas about how we could stop him. I had one of my own.

'How about if the centre backs moved out and helped me?' I asked.
Moré had not expected that.

'You know, that's not a bad idea,' he said.

I don't remember if we managed to stem the winger's exploits, but I
began to wonder if there was more to football than 60-yard dashes and
one-on-one duels. There had to be a better way, a way to help each other
and play as a team. I didn't know it then, but for the first time I had
begun thinking like a coach.

● ● ●

By this time, 1975, I had also started to realise that my dream of making
it professionally as a football player would probably not come true. I was
27 years old and an average right back in a mid-table team in the Swedish
second division. When Gunnar Nordahl was the same age, he was on his
way to Milan after making 33 starts for the Swedish national team, scoring
43 goals. Also, I was suffering from an injured ankle that kept me on the
sidelines for some stretches of time.

Late that autumn, I received what was to be the most important phone
call of my footballing life. Tord Grip had left his job as head coach at
Örebro and was taking over at Degerfors.

'Is it now time for you to quit playing?' he asked me. 'Why don't you
come and join me as my assistant coach.'

'Absolutely,' I said, and with that I left my playing career behind me.

FOUR-FOUR-TWO

THERE are towns where football is larger than religion and there are towns where football *is* religion. Then there is Degerfors. This small industrial community is barely big enough to call itself a town, but it is difficult to find a place where football is taken more seriously than in Degerfors. In the middle of the 1970s, 9,000 people lived there, but when the team played at home, their ground, Stora Valla, would fill up with thousands more.

It is also difficult to find a more provincial town in all of Sweden. In Degerfors, outsiders have always been viewed with deep suspicion, even those from other parts of Värmland. Many of the club's best players over the years had been born there, but to achieve success the club had been forced to recruit players from the outside. The farther north they had looked, the more successful the club had been. Tord was from the north and he loved Degerfors. He had played for them for ten years and so, when he got the chance of the head coach's job, he did not hesitate, despite Degerfors being stuck in the third division. The club welcomed him with open arms.

He had no problem convincing me to come but it was more difficult to persuade the Degerfors board that I was the right man for the assistant's job. They wanted him to pick someone local, not a Karlskoga player without any coaching experience. But Tord insisted. He saw something in me and his opinion carried a lot of weight with the old guard at Degerfors.

When Tord and I took over in 1976, the club's glory days seemed a very distant memory. Ten years had passed since Degerfors played top-flight football. But we had a decent team and the aim was to get back to the second division as quickly as possible. Tord had clear ideas on how to achieve that. He wanted to introduce a new system known as 4-4-2, A lot of people were sceptical about it, but not me. I think I saw the future. What I did not realise was that we were on the cusp of the greatest ideological battle in Swedish football history, and although I did not yet have a coaching licence, I would be at its forefront.

● ● ●

In today's football, 4-4-2 is seen as a basic team formation, but in Sweden in the 1970s it was something completely new. The system was based on the English model of four defenders, four midfielders and two forwards. The defence was organised in a straight line, without the sweeper, or *libero*, as the last defender was called. In a 4-4-2 formation, the team was much more compact, with the distance between defensive and attacking lines much shorter than in other systems. Everything was built on organisation and team thinking. You could say it was a revolution against individualism.

Perhaps that is why it appealed to me. As a player I had never been much of an individualist.

Bob Houghton, an Englishman, first introduced 4-4-2 in Sweden. Houghton had taken over as coach of Malmö FF in 1974 and his new system was an immediate success. In his first two years, Malmö won the league. The next year, the same year that Tord and I began coaching Degerfors, another first-division team, Halmstads BK, recruited its own English manager and advocate of 4-4-2 – Roy Hodgson.

Tord wanted to play with attacking full backs. That was also something new. We worked a lot on tactics in training. It took a while for me to earn Tord's trust. In the beginning, I mainly handled the warm-ups but in time Tord gave me more responsibilities. I was ambitious and hungry. I wanted to learn as much as I could and I think Tord appreciated that.

We played well that season and easily won the league, but in the play-offs for promotion to the second division, we fell apart and lost all three games. In the top division, Hodgson won the league in his first year with Halmstad, just like Houghton had done with Malmö. No one paid much attention to the fact that the 4-4-2 system had also taken root in the Swedish third division.

● ● ●

Off the football pitch, my life was in transition, too. Anki and I had got engaged during a trip to Norway. After she graduated with her teacher's degree, she got a job teaching at a school in Karlskoga. We bought a house. I still had my job as a PT instructor. My salary was fairly meagre. As an assistant football coach at Degerfors IF, I earned even less. Things were tight financially.

I had never been good with money. In Säffle, Anki and I sometimes went out to restaurants to eat. I ordered what I wanted, without looking at the price. Anki was dismayed. How could I order the most expensive item on the menu when I had no money? But things always seemed to work out, money-wise. If I was broke, I could always borrow from my mother. When I studied at GIH, I took student loans. Anki didn't do that. She worked extra hours at the hospital. I could not do that. I had the football to focus on.

In February of 1977, the Swedish Football Association offered Tord the position of assistant manager of the Swedish national team. It was a huge opportunity for him and, although torn, he finally came to his senses and took the job. It meant the head coaching job at Degerfors was available. Tord must have put a word in, or maybe it was simply too late for the board to get someone else before the new season started. In Sweden, the season runs from spring to autumn. Whatever happened, I got the job. After one year as an assistant coach, I was suddenly in charge. We were in the third division, but still. I had not yet completed my coaching licence.

The school where I worked had a considerate head, who allowed me to switch to part-time, which meant I could devote my wholehearted attention to the Degerfors job. To go from assistant to head coach was a huge step. All of a sudden everyone was looking to me. If things were to go wrong, I knew I would soon feel the wrath of the entire community.

Our team manager, Tore Karlsson, had been with the club since the dawn of man. One day I was sitting on the bus reading *Expressen*, the conservative tabloid, when Tore ripped the paper out of my hands and threw it out of the window. Degerfors, where most men were employed at the ironworks, was a working-class town. It was not a place where one read *Expressen*. Tore made that clear to me. He also did not like it when I complained that the players drank too many beers on the bus coming home from an important away win.

'Listen, young man,' he said. 'You just worry about the football.'

On a few occasions I sent Anki to scout opponents. She had become more interested in football. I guess she had no choice. We had set our wedding date for 7 July 1977 – that is, 7-7-77. There was just one problem. I had been accepted on the final course to get my coaching licence, and the class was ending on 7 July. Moving the date was not popular with Anki, but what else could we do?

For my thesis, I gave a presentation on 4-4-2. I talked about how you press your opponents high up on the pitch and how you close down space when defending. My mantra was 'understöd', the Swedish term for defenders providing support for each other. If a full back could not contain a quick winger, he obviously needed support from his team-mates. It was common sense. The attack also had to have a clear structure. The goalkeeper would throw the ball to the right back, who, in turn, would pass it to a forward. The forward could either come down to meet the ball or go long. Nothing else. Under no circumstances would the formation be changed. If I took off a forward with five minutes remaining and the team leading 1–0, I still had to put on another forward. This was revolutionary stuff at the time. My questioner for the thesis presentation, Hasse Karlsson, a seasoned football manager, was very impressed. I passed the test.

Anki and I got married on 9 July in the Swedish Church in Oslo. We had not planned a honeymoon and discovered that no hotel rooms were available. So we went to visit some friends whose parents had a summer cabin in Värmland. They were happy to see us. The weather was beautiful and we stayed for a few days before it was time to go home and get back to training.

● ● ●

My first season as head coach of Degerfors ended like the previous one. We won the league convincingly but fluffed the play-offs, too nervous to play our usual game. It was as if we had some kind of mental block. Something had to be done, so I contacted Norwegian sports psychologist Willi Railo, who had written a book entitled *Best When It Counts*. The message was simple – think positively and good things will come to you.

We met at the town hall in Degerfors one Sunday morning in December. It was the players' day off and calling them in for extra training was not appreciated. Things did not get better when I explained the purpose of the meeting and introduced Willi.

'A psychologist, what the hell for?' snorted our left back, 'Old Man' Johansson.

The mood among the players was one of contempt, but Willi didn't let it bother him. He started his presentation and, to my surprise, in just a few minutes he had everyone's attention. Willi described how little details could affect a player's focus before the match, such as when one player took another player's place in the dressing room. The players nodded in approval. After the talk, Willi conducted a relaxation exercise. He asked the players to close their eyes. I was to keep mine open and watch. In a soothing voice, he began to talk and, one by one, the players fell asleep. I suppose it was some kind of hypnosis. Willi kept talking about the benefits of thinking positively. After a while, he clapped his hands and the players jerked awake, except Old Man Johansson. He was completely gone. Willi clapped his hands again, but there was no response. Willi almost panicked. He went over and shook him. That finally woke him up.

'Is it over?' said Old Man Johansson. Everyone laughed.

The next season we were using Willi's methods from the outset. Before a match, I would talk to him about what I wanted the players to concentrate on and he recorded those instructions on tape. Before away games, we would stop the bus a couple of hours before arriving at the stadium. The players would recline their seats or lay down in the aisle of the bus. Then I would play the tape of Willi calmly reiterating the importance of pressing and covering in defence.

I also used Willi's methods on myself. By using something called autogenous training, I could make myself fall asleep within ten seconds. It took a couple of months to learn how to do it. The trick required a trigger that would tell the brain to shut down the body. My trigger was the clenching of my right fist. I did that, breathed in deeply and then breathed out – and I was asleep.

We reached the play-offs again and this time, with Willi's help, we won all three games. I had brought Degerfors back to the second division. I don't know if Willi's methods were crucial, but I used them for the rest of my coaching career.

● ● ●

One autumn evening I was called in for a meeting with the club's board to talk about players ahead of next season. My contract was about to expire and I assumed they would be willing to extend it but nothing was said. I did not bring it up. When the meeting was over, I just left, thinking, 'Stingy bastards.'

When I got home, Anki was at the door, waiting for me and ready to burst from excitement.

'Guess what's happened?' she exclaimed. 'IFK Gothenburg have called. They're looking for a new manager and they were wondering if you've signed a new contract with Degerfors. Did you?'

IFK Gothenburg? The Angels? One of Sweden's biggest teams, with stars including Ralf Edström, Björn Nordqvist and Olle Nordin? It must be some kind of mistake. Clearly they would not be interested in me for manager. Maybe they were looking for a coach for one of the youth teams. In that case, I was not interested. Then I would rather stay with Degerfors.

'You must have got that wrong,' I told Anki.

The next day I took a call from Bosse Johansson from IFK Gothenburg. The senior team's head coach, Hasse Karlsson, would be leaving the post after two years and the club were looking for a new manager. Would I be interested in the job?

And that is how a 30-year-old Torsby lad who had never coached a team placed higher than the Swedish third division got the offer to take over at one of Sweden's biggest football clubs. Accepting the job was never an issue. I did not call anyone for advice. I just said yes.

Soon after that, Gothenburg's chairman, Bertil Westblad, called. He told me that the manager of Glasgow Rangers had been approached about the job but could not come for another six months. Westblad had asked if there were no up-and-coming Swedish coaches with new ideas about how to play football, and Hasse Karlsson mentioned my name. He remembered me and my thesis project from the coaching course. If they were looking for an ambitious coach with fresh ideas, I fitted the profile. Westblad had nodded. I was their man.

I told the Degerfors board that I had got an offer from IFK Gothenburg and accepted it.

'I'll be damned,' said the chairman. 'We would have liked to keep you here.'

A couple of weeks later I got on the train to Gothenburg and signed the contract.

THE ANGELS 4

THEY called it 'champagne football', the happy-go-lucky style of play popularised by IFK Gothenburg in the 1970s. It was attacking football, with lots of trickery and turns. A play for the gallery. It drew big crowds, but hardly big results. After Gothenburg was relegated to the second division in 1970, it took seven long years before the team got back to the top flight.

When I came to the club in 1979, IFK Gothenburg had finished third in the league the year before, but with an old team. Champagne football was still ingrained in the club. Would I really be able to change that? It was one thing to create a strong collective among a group of unknown Degerfors players; quite another to do it with a motley crew of stars such as Ralf Edström and Torbjörn Nilsson.

My signing for Gothenburg was the biggest football-related thing that had happened in northern Värmland and it generated a lot of headlines. In Torsby, it was huge news.

'Gothenburg? Well, I'll be damned,' my father said when I told him that I had got the job.

My dad was very interested in football. He came to all the matches I played in Torsby, and also to Karlskoga and Degerfors when I played and coached there. He was the equipment manager for the Torsby senior team and brought all the socks, shorts and shirts home to be washed. He probably got a hundred kronor, that's about ten quid, at Christmas for the trouble. Or maybe some flowers.

But if my appointment as Gothenburg manager was the big talking point in Torsby, it was met by complete confusion in the rest of footballing Sweden. No one knew who Sven-Göran Eriksson was. I was 30 years old, six years younger than Björn Nordqvist, Gothenburg's star international, and had two years' experience as a head coach for a division-three team. How was this going to turn out? I can only imagine that my mother and my father were very nervous when I moved to Gothenburg.

It may have been during the winter off-season, before I started my new job, that I travelled to England to watch a match between Ipswich and Aston Villa. For the past ten years Ipswich had been coached by Bobby Robson and the day before the game I went to the Ipswich training ground to study his coaching methods. I asked if he would meet me for five minutes after training. That five-minute meeting turned into an hour. Bobby asked me about my seat for the game the next day.

'I'll be in the stands,' I said.

'No, no, you can sit next to me,' he said. 'On the bench.'

The match was broadcast live on Swedish television, and my father saw me sitting on the Ipswich bench, next to Bobby Robson.

• • •

It was cold and windy and the footballs would not stay in one place the first time I stepped into Valhalla, the artificial turf pitch where IFK Gothenburg trained during the winter season. I don't know if people could tell, but I was very nervous. I had never been nervous. Come to think about it, I have never really been nervous since, at least not in a footballing context. In Degerfors, I had felt at home. Maybe it was because I was among my Värmland peers. Here I was the outsider, a country bumpkin in Sweden's second-largest city. But as I watched the players – the stars – standing there on the pitch, it hit me that many of them were country bumpkins, too. Tommy and Tord Holmgren were from the far north. Veteran and captain Olle Nordin came from a village in Småland. Ruben Svensson was a Värmland native. There was nothing to fear.

I would succeed. It was not something I just told myself. I felt it. No, I knew it. There was no reason why the system that I had implemented at Degerfors would not work here. There were probably those who doubted me, but I didn't. Self-confidence has never been a problem for me.

A complete brainwash would be required if the players were to adopt my philosophy, however. Pressing and covering were Greek terms to them. The fact that I used a football in 95 per cent of training exercises probably came as a positive surprise, but they must have been shocked at how strict and regimented the exercises were. On the pitch, I would go between players and manoeuvre them into place, like pieces on a chess board. If the goalkeeper threw the ball to Ruben, the right back, Ruben had two alternatives. He could play it to Ralf, who met the pass, or Torbjörn, who went long. Nothing else. If we lost the ball, the midfielders had to win the second ball. If the ball ended up on the left flank, the team had to move as a unit from right to left. The defence was based on zonal marking. This was also something completely new to the players. Instead of marking an opposing player, man-to-man, they had to mark a zone. It was a more advanced system, but also more effective. When it worked.

• • •

Anki and I bought a nice house in Skintebo, a new housing development south of Gothenburg. It was a cross between a townhouse and a villa. Anki was taken on as maternity cover at a local middle school. What the school didn't know was that Anki herself was six months pregnant. She felt bad for not informing the school in her application and tried to hide her pregnancy by wearing loose clothes and sucking in her stomach, but that did not work for long. She worked until the day our son, Johan, was born, on 27 May 1979.

At this time, big Swedish clubs such as IFK Gothenburg were only semi-professional. The players got paid, but not enough to give up their ordinary jobs. They were plumbers and chefs. As the manager of one of Sweden's biggest teams, I got an annual salary of 90,000 kronor, that's about £9,000. It was less than what I made as the coach of Degerfors plus working part-time as a PT teacher. When we moved to Gothenburg, we could not afford to buy new furniture but had to bring the furniture we had built ourselves out of plywood and painted in the apartment in Karlskoga. We had nothing to complain about, though. On the contrary, we were the luckiest people in the world.

Today, IFK Gothenburg of that time is viewed as a working-class team with deep roots in Social Democratic politics. It is true that Gothenburg was a blue-collar town and it would be surprising if the majority of Gothenburg supporters did not lean towards the left. Several men on the club's board even had ties to the Social Democratic party. Some of the players, including Ruben Svensson, also known as 'Red Ruben', probably saw parallels between the team ideology based on collectivism and their own political ideology.

On my father's side, I was a distant relative of Tage Erlander, a Social Democrat who served as prime minister of Sweden for more than twenty years, but politics was not discussed very much at home and I was never politically active. I understood that some people saw a connection between football and politics, but to me they were separate fields. There was no political ideology behind my footballing philosophy. I wanted to build the best possible team. If you played as a team – one for all and all for one – you achieved better results. It was not more complicated than that.

● ● ●

We were achieving good results but had to endure a lot of criticism from the newspapers. Some journalists believed our football was excruciatingly dull. The mistake I made as a young coach was to read the garbage that they wrote about us. What did they know about my job anyway?

I never felt a need to deliver entertaining football. How did you define that anyway? To me, our style of play was good football. Results mattered, not backheels and trickery. In any case, we were not as extreme as Houghton's Malmö or Hodgson's Halmstad. When they played each other, you could hardly watch. It was only long balls and offside traps.

Anki came to watch all our home games. Away games were trickier with Johan, so she listened to the radio instead. She was so nervous that she could not sit still and often did the ironing at the same time, just to have something to do. When there were no more clothes to iron, she would start all over again. My shirts have never been as well ironed.

When Johan was six months old, Anki got a new teaching job. I was completely absorbed by my work, even during the off-season. In the winter, I would sometimes travel to England to watch matches while Anki stayed at home with Johan. He was a nightmare as a baby, because he never slept. When I was home, Anki and I would sleep in different rooms, so that only one of us would have to try to sleep with Johan. After a while, Anki had to reduce her work hours to part-time. She was completely exhausted. Johan did not sleep through the night until he was two years old.

In my first season, we won the Swedish Cup, and my second started very well with five victories and four draws before we lost to Öster in the tenth round. We finished third in the league and I felt it was only a matter of time before we won it. During this 1980 season I made the great discovery that football could also be played in the middle of the pitch. Before then I had mainly regarded the midfield as a cog in the defensive machinery. Our team manager used to joke that you could rent out the midfield at our stadium, Nya Ullevi, during games. No football was ever played there anyway.

The importance of the midfield offensively was not something that dawned on me overnight. The realisation grew out of a lot of thinking and a lot of conversations with Tord Grip. I was thinking about football around the clock and tried to be open to new ideas. That is why I had been willing to give Willi Railo a chance. But not everyone in Swedish football was as open-minded at that time.

● ● ●

'Send the bastard back to the woods!' the crowd shouted. We had just lost 1–0 at home to Djurgården. The 1981 season had therefore started with three straight losses. The insults reverberated among the spectators at Nya Ullevi. There could be no doubt at whom they were directed. It was me the supporters wanted to send back to the Värmland forest. The next day I went to the board and said, 'If you want to sack me, I understand.'

'No,' said Bertil Westblad. 'We want you to stay.'

Before the next training session I gathered the players together. I told them about my disappointment at losing the first three games with the best football players in Sweden.

'Because you are, and the problem is you know it,' I said. I told them I would resign, if that is what they wanted. After that, we started to win and my job was safe. We did have Sweden's best team.

Anki and I put our house in Skintebo up for sale at the beginning of 1982. I had in all earnestness begun to think about what it would be like to coach a big team in Europe. Gothenburg hardly needed a coach any more. The players knew exactly what to do on the pitch. Anki was open to trying something new. If an offer came up, we did not want anything to hold us back. We wanted to be able to up and leave. Not that I had received any concrete offers or that there were even any indications that a team from outside of Sweden had any kind of interest in a young Swede who had still not won the Swedish league or made any kind of impression in the European club tournaments.

We assumed that it would take at least a few months to sell the house, but it sold immediately. Suddenly, we were homeless. Eventually, we found a large farm to rent in Stenungsund, 31 miles north of the city. There was still snow on the ground when we moved in there.

I don't remember exactly when I first heard that Benfica, the Portuguese club, were interested in offering me the job of head coach. But I know from whom I first heard the news – Börje Lantz. Börje was probably Sweden's first football agent. His nicknames were 'Mister Ten Percent' and 'The Man With the Cigar,' since he was always sucking on a fat Cuban cigar.

As a young man, Börje worked as a newspaper reporter. He was 26 years old when, according to his own version of events, he walked straight into the Brazilian dressing room after the World Cup final in Sweden in 1958 and talked his way on to the aeroplane carrying the team back to Brazil. He stayed in Brazil for twelve years, arranging friendly matches for the national team and doing other business. There was nothing that Börje could not sell. It was said that during the Soviet era he acquired the rights to sell advertising at Moscow airport.

Börje also sold advertising to Swedish television, and was an adviser to Hans Cavalli-Björkman, a prominent banker in Sweden and director at Malmö FF. It was Börje who had brought Bob Houghton to Sweden. I had met Börje in connection with some kind of anniversary match in Malmö. It could have been when I was with Degerfors. Börje came into our dressing room with a cigar in his mouth to wish us good luck.

'You can't smoke that in here,' I told him.

'I'm a professional,' he said with a smile. 'I never light it.'

I believe Börje ran into some tax trouble shortly after that and moved to Portugal. Sometime in the spring of 1982, he contacted me via Bo Rudenmark, a club supporter who was also a banker. That season, Gothenburg's fortunes in international competition had changed. We had qualified for the UEFA Cup and beaten Valencia and Kaiserslautern to reach the final against Hamburg. Our exploits in Europe had echoed around the Continent. Börje explained that Benfica might be looking for a new manager and that they were intrigued by the young Swedish coach who had done so well with Gothenburg. I think it was probably the other way around – it was Börje who had tipped off Benfica about me. Börje asked if it would be possible for me to leave Gothenburg in the summer, if Benfica made a move. I had a clause in my contract that stipulated I could leave if an offer came in from abroad. After that, Börje got in touch every now and then regarding Benfica, but nothing was settled yet.

'Just make sure you win the UEFA Cup first,' he said.

● ● ●

The rain was crashing down when we walked onto the pitch at Nya Ullevi on 5 May 1982 for the first leg of the UEFA Cup final against Hamburger Sport-Verein. To say that we were the underdogs would have been an understatement of epic proportions. Hamburg's team contained superstars including Felix Magath, Manfred Kaltz and Horst Hrubesch. They were on their way to winning the German league that year. Our league had only just got started – we had played two games. The only people who believed that a group of semi-amateurs had any chance of upsetting these German giants were us.

It did not turn out to be a beautiful contest. With the rain pouring down, the pitch was like a mud bath. After twenty minutes, Torbjörn Nilsson was brutally scythed down and had to be substituted. We would have to play most of the final without our biggest star. Despite that, we dominated the game, but we could not penetrate the German defence. Tord Holmgren, who ran and fought harder than anyone in our team, missed three good opportunities. It looked as though it was going to end goalless.

But with two minutes of regular time left, the ball was hoofed up the field towards Glenn Hysén, who was staying well forward. Glenn won a header and the ball sailed over two German defenders and fell at the feet of Tord Holmgren, who was breaking into the German penalty area. Tord let the ball bounce and then shot past the German goalkeeper, Stein. On that terrible pitch, the ball barely had enough speed to cross the goal line, but in it went and we won 1–0.

After the game, my parents, soaking wet after seeing the match from the open seats, came to congratulate me.

'Well done,' said my dad. 'But you know there's another game to come.'

My father was not one to get overly excited.

We had achieved the perfect result ahead of the return leg in Hamburg two weeks later. Despite that, the Germans did not seem worried. They were confident that they would turn things around. When we arrived in Hamburg, pennants were being sold outside the stadium proclaiming Hamburg '1982 UEFA Cup champions'. Hamburg's manager, Ernst Happel, was dead certain that the Germans would emerge victorious.

'It's pleasing that all the Swedish players are healthy,' he told the media. 'So that they can't make any excuses about injuries afterwards.'

Before the game, I asked someone from the club to go out and buy one of those pennants, and I hung it on the wall of our dressing room. I did not have to say anything more. Many people asked me afterwards what I told the players before the match, what instructions I gave them. I said practically nothing. Nothing needed to be said. In a way, our work was already done. We had eleven coaches on the pitch. They knew exactly what to do. When I warned them about the crosses coming in from Manfred Kaltz, aimed at Horst Hrubesch, Hysén just said, 'Yeah, yeah, we'll buy you dinner every time Hrubesch wins a header.'

Of course, it was not going to be that easy, at least not to begin with. When we stepped out in front of the 61,000 people at Volkparkstadion, it was like walking into a boiling cauldron. Once the game started, Hamburg immediately went on the offensive. In the nineteenth minute, Glenn Hysén had to come off with a groin injury. I had to move Ruben to centre back and bring on Glenn Schiller as right back. But for some reason, Schiller was nowhere to be found.

'Where the hell is Schiller?' I shouted.

At that moment, Schiller came running from the dressing room. It turned out he had got locked in the toilet. Typical Schiller. Anything was possible with him. Except he never got nervous. To run into a packed Volkparkstadion in a UEFA Cup final without having warmed up was nothing that fazed Schiller.

Hamburg kept pressing. Then in the twenty-fifth minute Torbjörn got the ball in our half. He turned one of the German players and hit a long, sweeping cross that landed on the foot of Tommy Holmgren. Tommy sped down the left flank and hit a ball into the penalty area that the German goalkeeper misjudged. At the far post, Dan Corneliusson popped up and banged the goal into the roof of the net. We were leading 1–0. Hamburg would have to score three times to win the tie.

Hamburg went forward, but we held on until half-time. The second half was Torbjörn Nilsson's show. He proved what I already knew – he was the best forward in Europe. In the sixty-second minute he got the ball in midfield and ran 40 metres, expertly keeping the German defenders at bay, before calmly rolling the ball into the far corner of the net. Three minutes later, he danced around the German left back, who proceeded to pull him down in the penalty area. It was a stone-cold penalty, which Stig Fredriksson duly converted. Game, set and match! After that, the Germans more or less gave up. From the stands I could hear 5,000 Gothenburg supporters singing.

● ● ●

I don't think there is a photo of me with the UEFA Cup on the pitch after the game. I did not want to be photographed with the trophy together with Gunnar Larsson. He was the new club chairman, who had arrived shortly before the final. Larsson was a big man on the political scene in Gothenburg but he had barely said hello to me or, as far as I know, the players. Now he stood there on the pitch, posing with the trophy. But it was Bertil Westblad and the other board members, who had made it all possible. Some of them had mortgaged their own houses in order to bring in new players. I felt very bad for them. They deserved to share the honour.

Four days later, we played another final, in the Swedish Cup, against Öster. Hysén was injured and Schiller played from the start. This time he was not locked in the toilet when the game began. We were down 1–2 at half-time, but turned things around in the second half and won 3–2. That was my last title with IFK Gothenburg. After the UEFA Cup victory,

I had been offered the job with Benfica and immediately accepted. Gothenburg went on to win the 1982 Swedish league.

My last match with The Angels was against Danish side Naestved in the Intertoto Cup on 26 June 1982. We won 5–0. It was a home game, but it was not played at Nya Ullevi or even in Gothenburg.

It was played in Torsby, at Björnevi.

BENFICA

WE landed at Lisbon's Portela airport on a hot day in June. The plane came to a standstill away from the terminal amid a great commotion. Hundreds of people were gathering by the plane. I thought maybe they had come to welcome a prime minister or some other dignitary but they had come to welcome me, the new manager of Benfica, one of the world's biggest football clubs.

Börje and Fernando Martins, the Benfica owner and president, had come to meet me and we drove to the Benfica stadium, Estádio da Luz, 'The Stadium of Light'. At the time, it was Europe's biggest football stadium with a capacity of more than 100,000 people. When we arrived, I was immediately taken to the club's trophy room. Benfica had won the Portuguese league 24 times, the Portuguese Cup 17 times and the European Cup twice. The room was packed with trophies. I had never seen anything as impressive. That's when I realised what was expected of me at Benfica. I suppose that was the reason they showed me that room.

Martins had taken a big risk in picking me for the head-coach position. I succeeded Lajos Baróti, an old Hungarian coach who had just retired after leaving the club. With Baróti at the helm, Benfica had finished second in the league the season before, a completely unacceptable result for a club of Benfica's stature. Only titles were good enough. At the same time, Benfica were a very conservative club. Martins' choice of a 34-year-old Swede as manager was not something that had overly impressed the board. During a big meeting, what the Portuguese called an *assembléia*, many of the board members had apparently been up in arms over my appointment. Finally, Martins had faked a heart attack to get away from the increasingly hostile atmosphere and been taken away in an ambulance. Apparently, eighteen club directors resigned in protest after the meeting.

After that initial visit, I went back to Sweden to get Anki and Johan. Lots of people and hordes of journalists greeted us at the airport again. Anki made a bit of a faux pas by wearing a green-and-white striped shirt – the colours of Sporting Lisbon, Benfica's fierce rivals. Martins suggested that perhaps the next time Mrs Eriksson was seen in public she could dress differently.

● ● ●

Benfica were at a whole different level from IFK Gothenburg. It was said that no football club in the world had as many fans globally as Benfica, and certainly the team was followed intensely in Brazil. But football was football, the game was the same. In my mind, I had taken the biggest step going from Degerfors to Gothenburg. I had already proved that my football philosophy worked and I never thought about the possibility of failure. People worried too much about that, I thought.

However, at the Benfica training ground, which was situated next to the stadium, I had a shock. The squad was huge, way too bloated. They had forty-five in the senior squad and I would have to get rid of a substantial number of them. The club had grown stagnant. It required new ideas, a revolution. For that I needed help.

I was offered Fernando Caiado, a 57-year-old former Benfica midfielder and Portuguese national team player, as assistant manager. I felt immediately that my chemistry with him was not right. Caiado had old ideas. The person I clicked with, on the other hand, was Toni Oliveira. Toni was my age and also a former midfielder at Benfica. After 13 years and almost 400 games he had retired as a player the season before. Toni was a thinker. He had studied at the renowned university in Coimbra, he lived for football and he was curious. Plus he spoke English. I chose Toni as my assistant instead.

In pre-season, Benfica had always travelled up to the mountains for two weeks of tough physical training. It was not something that the players appreciated. When I informed them that, this year, we would be staying at the Estádio de Luz, everyone was happy. It meant they could stay at home with their families. We ran one session in the morning and another one in the afternoon. In the beginning, we played a lot of eleven against eleven to give Toni and me the chance to evaulate the players and decide which ones we could dispense with. Every now and then I would ask Toni about some player who did not look up to snuff, 'Is he as bad as he looks?'

It went on like that for a week. In the end, we got rid of fringe players, mostly, and kept all the big stars – Manuel Bento, the goalkeeper, defender

Humberto Coelho and midfielder Fernando Chalana. Naturally, we also kept the star striker, Nené, who during his 14 years with the club had scored more than 200 goals.

With the squad cut down to size, it was time to organise the team. Just like at Gothenburg, I had to start from the beginning. The Benfica players were not used to 4-4-2. They had no idea about zonal marking, press and support. We worked one-on-one, two-on-two and three-on-three. The key was the defence. I grabbed a player and moved him a yard this way, another one a yard that way. How did you shrink space using zonal marking? If the left back had the ball when we attacked, what should Chalana, the winger, do? We practised the same movement patterns over and over. I can understand if the players hated those first training sessions.

But I loved it. The only problem for me was the language. The whole team was Portuguese-speaking, and my Portuguese was practically non-existent. I had taken four or five lessons and I had an interpreter, a Swedish guy whose dad worked as an executive in Portugal. The guy's Portuguese was perfect, but he was not a football person. The translations were always a little off. I preferred to speak English with Toni, who had picked up on my ideas. He knew what I was talking about. We both spoke football.

● ● ●

There were three big teams in Portugal at the time – Benfica, Sporting and Porto. They were known as the *Os Três Grandes*, 'The Big Three'. A team outside the big three had not won the Portuguese league for thirty-six years; that was Belenenses.

I had been impressed with Estádio da Luz when we trained there, and that was when the stadium was empty. Walking into a packed stadium for the first home game of the season against Boavista was something else again. I had never experienced anything like it. The roar was deafening. It was like walking into a wall. Egged on by the fans, we played some brilliant football and won 3–0 with two goals by Nené. We won our first eleven games. It was almost too good to be true.

The family loved life in Portugal. When we first arrived we rented a villa outside the coastal town of Cascais, but we soon moved into a house next to Börje and his wife Bodil, even closer to Cascais. To Anki, the Portugal move was a big adventure. She had it easier with the language than I did. Johan went to a Swedish pre-school where Anki helped teaching.

Moneywise, we were doing much better. I am not sure exactly how much I was making but it was probably four, five times more than in Sweden. The club paid for the house and my childhood friend 'Nenne' Sahlström, who worked for Volvo, arranged a car for me. The money lasted longer in Portugal, too. The country was not as developed as it is today. It was only a few years since the dictatorship had ended and the country had a Wild West feel to it.

One person who enjoyed that feeling was Börje. Early every morning I heard a big splash from next door – Börje jumping in the pool. After that, he went to play some tennis. Around six o'clock, when I had come home from work, he would knock on my door asking if I wanted to come over for a glass of whiskey. Bodil was from northern Sweden and a former air hostess. Börje said she fell into his lap during a turbulent flight. Anki and I spent a lot of time with Börje and Bodil. They had two children, Ulrika and Gustav. Bodil was tall, blonde and sophisticated. She spoke several languages, while Börje was a hell of a storyteller. He loved his wife, and it was easy to see why. She was able to stand his peculiarities. Sometimes we'd drink a glass or two of whiskey at my place. At midnight, he would stand up and say, 'God be with you. As for myself, I don't have the time.' Then he'd just go.

I also had a very good relationship with Fernando Martins, who, as well as the club, owned several hotels. He was loved by supporters and players, and came to every game, home and away. Before the big matches, against Porto and Sporting, he would come into the dressing room. 'Today, you get triple bonuses if you win,' he might say.

One person at Benfica was a bigger legend than everyone else – Eusébio. Eusébio had come to Benfica as an 18-year-old from Mozambique. During his fifteen years at the club he had scored more goals, 473, than he had played matches. He had won the league eleven times and was the star of the team that won the European Cup back to back in the early 1960s. As a teenager, I had watched those games with my dad at home in Torsby. The big question then was who was the greatest footballer – Eusébio or Pelé? People talked about those two like they talk about Messi and Ronaldo today.

Toni had played with Eusébio for seven seasons. He always said that Eusébio struck the ball harder than anyone he had ever seen. It almost didn't matter if Benfica were awarded a penalty or a free kick in a good location. Eusébio would score both.

After retiring, Eusébio had served as an ambassador for the club. But Martins wanted to let him go. I was shocked. Getting rid of Eusébio? Impossible! Instead, I suggested that we bring him on to the coaching staff as a goalkeeping coach. So that's what happened. Eusébio worked very well with our goalkeeper, Bento. After training was officially over, they would stay and bet on how many shots out of ten Eusébio would put past Bento. I don't remember who the winner usually was, but I would not be surprised if it was Eusébio. Despite his dodgy knees, he still had a canon of a shot on him.

● ● ●

Benfica had become my team. During the spring of 1983 I could have told the players that the sun was green and they would have believed me. We were well on our way to winning the league. We also wanted to win the UEFA Cup, having advanced to the quarter-finals. Six weeks before the match, I travelled to Rome to spy on our opponents, Roma. They'd had a fantastic season up to that point, losing just two league games, and I was going to watch them in action against Cagliari. No Italian matches were televised in Portugal at that time.

I had never been to Rome, and while I was there, I met Nisse Liedholm, who had enjoyed a wonderful career in Italy as a player and now as a manager. I felt privileged to talk football and have dinner with him. I don't know if he had something to do with it, but Italy made a very strong impression on me. The first thing I said to Anki when I got home was, 'We are going to live in Rome.'

We beat Roma 3–2 over the two legs, and a Romanian team, Craiova, 1–1 in the semis, going through on the away-goals rule. For the second year in a row I had taken a team to the UEFA Cup final. With Gothenburg we had been the giant killers. With Benfica it was different. We were one of the giants, and we would be facing another one, Anderlecht of Belgium.

At the Heysel Stadium in Brussels, we did not play well. Anderlecht took the lead in the first half and in the second half we had a man sent off. Our aim was to not concede any more goals, and in that we succeeded. The match ended 1–0 to Anderlecht. Despite not scoring an away goal, we still felt that we had a good chance to turn things around at home.

Expectations were sky high at Estádio da Luz two weeks later. Benfica had not won a European trophy since Eusébio and his team's exploits twenty-one years earlier. We started strongly and soon took the lead, but suffered a huge setback when the Spaniard Lozano equalised for Anderlecht on a counterattack. Now we needed to score two goals to win it. We had to go forward but at the same time make sure we did not concede another goal. It was a race against the clock. Early in the second half I made two substitutions, bringing on forwards, but they did not pay off. It was too late. The game ended 1–1. Anderlecht had won the UEFA Cup.

It was my first big defeat. Still, I was not overly disappointed. We'd had a terrific season. We had won the league easily, losing just a single game, and reached the Cup final, which was due to be played in August. And we had gone all the way to the UEFA Cup final. I did not read the papers any more, but Börje said that the Portuguese media wrote about me in god-like terms.

The family and I went home to Sweden. We had bought a summer house outside Åmål, where Anki grew up, and came to spend large parts of the summer there. We also spent some time in Torsby. I used to visit my grandparents in Stöpafors. My grandmother would always give me a couple of hundred crowns, something like £20. I needed the money, she said, since I didn't have a real job. That summer only my grandmother was there. My grandfather had passed away a couple of years earlier. Later that year, my grandmother passed away, too.

Like all Swedish people, I thought the Swedish summers were fantastic, but I was never going to be able to enjoy them fully. As a football manager, I was constantly working, even in the off-season. This was the time when you bought and sold players. I was constantly on the phone.

● ● ●

My second season at the club started as well as my first. We won the Cup final against Porto 1–0, even though the game was played in Porto, and didn't lose a league match until the spring. With the league championship practically already won, the focus during spring 1984 was on the European Cup. We had advanced to the quarter-finals by beating Irish minnows Linfield and the Greek team Olympiakos. But in the quarters we were facing much tougher opposition – Liverpool, the English champions and winners of three European Cups in the previous seven years. Like so many Swedish football fans, I had been a Liverpool supporter as a young man. Now I would get the chance to lead out a team at the legendary Anfield.

I felt we had a team that could challenge Liverpool. The most important thing was not to concede a bunch of goals in the first leg away. I selected a somewhat defensive formation, and we played well. But in the second half we could not withstand the Liverpool attack and Ian Rush scored. I was fairly happy with a 1–0 result. We still had a very good chance of advancing. Things would be different in Lisbon.

At home, I chose a much more attacking line-up with two up front, Nené and Maniche. We started positively, but ten minutes into the game, it all came crashing down. Liverpool hit a cross into our penalty area and although Ronnie Whelan's header was weak and directed straight at the goalkeeper, somehow the ball rolled between Bento's legs. Things got worse. We lost the ball in our own half and Kenny Dalglish and Ian Rush pounced on it. The ball was played out to an unmarked Craig Johnston, who scored for 2–0. After that, it was all over. We got a goal back in the second half, but Liverpool scored two more and won 4–1. We were out of the European Cup.

The supporters took the loss very hard. Everyone had had high hopes of reaching the final and it was as if the air had gone out of the club. Out of me. I started wondering if I'd reached as far as I could go with Benfica.

• • •

One day when I was driving home from training, a taxi pulled up next to me, honking and flashing its lights. A man sitting in the back was waving at me to pull over. It turned out he was from the Italian embassy and he had a message – Dino Viola would like to speak with me.

Dino Viola was the president of Roma. The man from the embassy said our meeting was highly *confidenziale*. He gave me a phone number for Viola and instructed me to call as soon as possible. I went home and made the call right away. Riccardo Viola, one of Dino's two sons, answered. Riccardo explained that his father had been very impressed with Benfica's play against Roma in the UEFA Cup the previous season. They were looking for a new manager and were wondering if the Swedish coach who had obviously done a great job with Benfica would be interested in the job.

This time I did not say yes right away. But I could have. I knew immediately that this was a chance I could not pass up. I had told Anki that we should live in Italy. The world's greatest football league was there. Now I had an offer to manage the current Italian champions.

Börje was my agent, even if we did not have anything signed to make that official. I sent him to Rome to negotiate with the Italians and he came back with a contract for me to sign. Everything looked in order. There was only one problem. In Italy, special rules applied to non-Italian managers. They were not allowed to have any contact with the team during a game. They could not sit on the bench. Nisse Liedholm had got around those rules by becoming an Italian citizen. I was assured, however, that the rules would be changed in time for the next season. It just had not happened yet.

Around the same time, I was contacted by Tottenham Hostpur. The chairman, Irving Scholar, was interested in bringing me to the club, but I was never offered anything concrete. I probably would not have accepted it anyway. Tottenham and England did not interest me then. A more interesting option arose when Helenio Herrera, the great Argentinian manager, called from Barcelona. He warned me about signing for Roma, because I would not be able to sit on the bench.

'Come to Barcelona instead,' he said.

Barcelona had not won the Spanish league for ten years. They had an exciting team with Argentinian wizard Diego Maradona. I definitely did not want to get entangled in any Italian bureaucracy, but at the same time I had been assured that the rules governing foreign managers would be changed in time for the new season. Italy was my preferred destination. I wanted to go to Roma. I had made my mind up.

There was one person I dreaded disappointing – Fernando Martins. After my first year at Benfica, my contract had been extended and, as at Gothenburg, I had asked for a clause to be included that stipulated I could accept an offer from another big European team. That did not mean that Martins would just let me go. He wanted me to stay. Börje and I met him for lunch at the Altis Hotel. When I told him about the Roma job and that I had decided to take it, he became very upset.

'No, Mister, you can't do that,' he said.

He tried hard to convince me to stay, promising to buy new players and to make Benfica bigger than it had ever been. I felt bad, as if I was betraying Martins, the players and the supporters. It was a good thing that Börje was with me. He loved this kind of stuff, the discussions and negotiations. He reminded Martins of the excellent job that I had done for Benfica. Even if I still loved it there, it was time for me hand the job over to someone else, he said.

After we had won the league, I travelled to Rome to watch Roma play Liverpool in the European Cup final. I kept a low profile as I sat in the stands and watched my new team lose a dramatic penalty shootout.

AMONG ROME'S
EMPERORS

DINO Viola began his career as an engineer. After World War Two he opened a factory that built mechanical parts for the military. Apparently there was a lot of money to be made in that sector, even after the war, and Dino Viola became one of Italy's richest men. When he took over Roma in 1979, the club had finished twelfth in the league and had major financial problems. But with Viola's financial firepower, things soon began to change. In 1983, the same year that Viola was elected Senator in the Italian parliament, the club won the Italian scudetto.

One year later I arrived to replace Nisse Liedholm as Roma's new manager. Rome was even more beautiful than I remembered it. Anki was as enthusiastic as I was about coming to Italy. We moved into a residential complex on Via Aurelia, the road along which Julius Caesar once rode out of Rome on his way to the battlefield.

Riccardo Viola and his wife Anna lived in another big apartment in the complex, and our two families immediately got on well together. We made pizza in a wood stove and had dinner underneath the palm trees in the garden. Riccardo and Anna had three children. Their youngest son, Giacomo, was five years old, the same age as Johan. The two became instant friends. A large wall surrounded the residence so they could play and do whatever they wanted inside. There was a tennis court and later a swimming pool. We loved it there from the start. The only problem for me was the football team.

● ● ●

On paper, I had inherited one of the world's strongest clubs, packed with superstars, including Falcão, Cerezo, Pruzzo, Conti and Graziani. One month before I got there, Roma had played the European Cup final. They had finished second in the league after winning it the season before. But in reality, Roma were a tired and unmotivated team. I would soon find out how bad things were.

We travelled to the Alps for pre-season training. Everything was perfectly arranged, but it was impossible to get my players going. Roberto Pruzzo, who had been top scorer in the league in 1981 and 1982, had become grumpy. Conti, the artist, had lost his mojo. Graziani, the old star, had lost his pace. Things did not get better when we returned to Rome. The players would arrive half an hour late for training and blame the traffic. Apparently, things had been a little lax under Liedholm's regime. Training started when the players got there. But that was not my style. I required focus and organisation in training. Liedholm had almost let the players take care of practice themselves.

As time went on, I also realised how superstitious Liedholm had been. He had kept a *mago*, the Italian word for fortune teller, at his side. In his coat pockets he carried some little horns that were supposed to give him magic powers. Before the games, special water from Fregene had been sprinkled on the players' shirts. He had also got rid of players whom he considered brought bad luck. I was told that during one training session, Herbert Prohaska, the Austrian midfielder, had hit Liedholm on the head with a ball. After that, Liedholm went to Viola demanding that Prohaska be sold.

Then there was Falcão, *ottavo re di Roma*, or the 'eighth king of Rome'. Falcão was among the best and highest-paid players in the world. He was a calm and agreeable man. Everyone on the team listened to him. You could tell right away that Falcão was someone who knew football. The problem was he had begun to struggle with injuries. His stature in the club had also taken a knock when he refused to take a penalty against Liverpool in the European Cup final. Falcão claimed his leg had been cramping, but it was not an explanation that had gone over too well.

The biggest problem was that the rules governing foreign managers had still not been changed. The first week I was not even allowed to coach the team in training. I was restricted to standing on the sidelines watching. When the season started, I was forced to accept the job as technical director. Roberto Clagluna was officially made head coach, and the chemistry between us was never right. He wanted the same status as I had. I was supposed to be the man in charge yet he was the one who got to sit on the bench during the matches, while I had to sit in the stands with Dino Viola.

There was no flair in the team and the players were tactically poor, so it was not too surprising that we got off to a bad start. Liedholm had used zonal marking but had not organised the team very well. Falcão's injuries were a big blow. Out of the first eight games we did not win a single one. I started questioning myself. What was I doing wrong? How come I could not get the team to fire? I started doubting my move to Roma. I thought about how I had spurned the opportunity to go to Barcelona. The Catalans started the season with fifteen games without a loss and went on to win the league that year.

● ● ●

I took Johan to school on his first day. We had decided that he would go to an English-speaking school, St George's British International School in Rome. Johan had not spoken English before then and in the days leading up to the school start he was getting increasingly nervous about speaking a language he did not know. What would he say if he had to go to the bathroom? When we got to the school, I held his hand. A teacher came up to us. She recognised Mister Eriksson, Roma's new manager, from all the pictures in the papers. She explained that parents were not allowed to bring their kids into the school. They had to say goodbye outside. After that, she took Johan by the hand and led him inside. There were never any problems with him and school after that.

Thanks to his friend Giacomo, Johan learned Italian quickly. It was more difficult for Anki and me. After two years in Portugal, I had learned to speak decent Portuguese. Now I had to start all over with a new language. I took lessons at home. But with the team, I needed an interpreter, Vincenzo Morabito. He had worked at Volvo in Sweden and knew Swedish well, but he had the same problem as my interpreter at Benfica – he knew nothing about football. Mostly, he read books. But he was a fan of Lazio, the rival team in Rome. When Viola heard that, he immediately told me that Morabito could not stay much longer as my interpreter. Maybe he would divulge secrets about our tactics to Lazio? I protested and said that Morabito did not know anything about football anyway. But Viola had made up his mind.

'You have to hurry up with your Italian,' he told me.

Dino Viola always had a mischievous sparkle in his eye, but he was a complicated man. He spoke in riddles. People said he spoke Violese and that he was *furbo*, 'sly'. To Italians, that was a compliment. Viola saw conspiracies in everything and when it came to football, he did not trust anyone. Dino often visited Roma's training ground, Trigoria. He was always dressed in a suit and tie, but he never put his arms through the sleeves of his jacket. The jacket just hung from his shoulders. While the players warmed up, Dino and I walked a lap around the pitch and talked about the team. No one else was allowed to join us, except one time when Dino brought Giulio Andreotti, a round-shouldered former prime minister, who, after World War Two, was said to have got his hands on a lot of secret documents from the Mussolini era. Andreotti was a man to keep at your side, said Viola. He was very powerful.

After six months, my Italian was good enough for me to communicate with the team, and Morabito was promptly fired. But Morabito had developed an appreciation for football. Fifteen years later he became one of the leading football agents in the world.

● ● ●

It took me six months to get the team into any kind of shape. I worked a lot on the tactical side of things. We did the defensive drills over and over, just as I had done at Gothenburg and Benfica. In time, it started to pay off. Near Christmas, we went on a winning streak. But it was still an uphill battle. The players didn't like my training sessions. They were too tactical.

Maybe things would have been different had Falcão not been injured. The season before he had signed a new contract making him the highest-paid player in the Italian league, but his knee injuries meant he could play just the odd game. Finally, he travelled to New York for a knee operation. Viola wanted to terminate his contract, or at least renegotiate it, but Falcão refused. Matters got worse and after a while it was practically open war between Viola and Falcão. The case ended up in court. At one time, Viola showed me the stack of documents his lawyers had compiled for the case. It was over a metre high.

With Falcão injured, I made Carlo Ancelotti, the 25-year-old midfielder, captain of the team. Ancelotti was quiet but a great guy. He was the best team player we had – plus he was very keen on my new ideas and training methods. He was the kind of player who went home after training and thought about what we had practised.

But the wins we had put together before Christmas soon turned to losses again. It didn't help that I was still unable to give instructions to the players during the game. At half-time I could talk to them – except one time, during an away game. We had played poorly and I had plenty to say to the team. I was heading down the stairs to the dressing room when a man blocked my way. He pulled open his jacket and I could see that he was wearing a holster with a gun in it. There was nothing I could do but turn around and go back to my seat in the stands.

We had reached the quarter-finals of the Cup Winner's Cup, but were easily beaten by Bayern Munich. During the spring of 1985 we again played eight league games without winning a single match and when the season was over we had finished seventh in the table. Verona caused a huge upset that year by winning the scudetto. It was by far the worst season I had ever experienced as a football manager. But I told myself that next season would be different.

● ● ●

Finally, the rules about foreign managers were changed. I was going to be allowed to sit on the bench during games from now on. Despite the poor result during my first year I still had Viola's trust. He realised that the team needed reinforcements. Falcão left the club and moved back to Brazil. Viola had to find the right replacement for him.

The owners of the major Italian clubs were all big men who competed with each other over the top players. The biggest club in Italy was Juventus, from Turin. They were the reigning European Cup champions. The club was owned by the Agnelli family, who also owned Fiat. One of the big Juventus stars was Zbigniew 'Zibi' Boniek from Poland. He was loved by the Juventus president, Gianni Agnelli, who called Boniek '*Il Bello di Notte*', 'the beauty of the night', because of his brilliant performances during evening games.

Viola wanted to steal Boniek from Agnelli, and somehow made contact with him. Boniek appeared to be open to a move, so Viola, Riccardo and I went to see him and his agent somewhere in northern Italy. Boniek arrived at the meeting in a Ferrari that he had borrowed from his team-mate, Michel Platini. Viola pointed at the Ferrari and said to me, 'If we win the league, I will get you one of those.'

With Boniek on the team I was convinced that we could do it. He was exactly the kind of attacking midfielder that we needed – quick, technically brilliant and a single-minded winner. He also had an ego the size of which I had never seen. Some time later, the team were invited to a private audience with the Pope. It was a huge occasion for the players, who were almost all Catholic. The Pope, John Paul the Second, walked around and greeted the players one by one as they stood in a half circle. All but one bowed deeply. Boniek did not bow. Instead, he looked the Pope in the eye and said, '*Allora*, who is the most famous Polack in this country? You or me?' The Pope did not answer.

When the manager rules changed, I let Clagluna go. It was now going to be my team. I wanted clear directives about who was going to do what. As my assistant manager, I brought in Angelo Sormani, an Italian-Brazilian former striker who had played with Pelé at Santos in Brazil. He turned out to be a loyal and capable coach. We got along very well.

After an uneasy start to the 1985/86 season suddenly everything clicked. The newspapers feted us. We played the best football in Italy, they wrote. Everyone was talking about *grande Roma*. Nothing and no one could stop us. Börje Lantz came to visit. Then he disappeared for a couple of days. When he came back, he had a new contract for me. I thought he meant he had extended my contract with Roma. But it was a contract to manage Juventus. Incredible! In less than a year, I had gone from close to being fired from Roma to being offered the biggest coaching job in Italy. I was very flattered. At the same time I knew that I could not leave Roma. We were the best team in the country. So I said thanks, but no thanks. Soon after that we played Juventus at home, won 3–0, and I met Gianni Agnelli again.

'I knew that Mister Eriksson was a very good football coach,' he said in his rasping Turin accent. 'But that he was an unintelligent man, that I didn't know.'

My turning down the Juventus job was probably the first time Agnelli had heard the word no.

When we beat Pisa away 4–2 while Juventus only managed a draw against Sampdoria, we were suddenly top of the table with two matches to play. I was on my way to winning the biggest league title in world football.

• • •

Riccardo Viola and I became close friends. Riccardo was intelligent and funny. He resembled his father, although it could not have been easy to live up to the Viola name. Riccardo and I often played tennis on the clay court at home. They were epic matches. Riccardo saw himself as a much better player than I was, but I always beat him. I could run and somehow I managed to get the ball back over the net. It was not pretty, but it was effective. Riccardo was furious. He ordered the gardener to water the court more, because he thought that would favour his game. In the end, we had the wettest tennis court in Italy. But still I kept winning.

Sometimes Anki and I went out for dinner with Riccardo and Anna. Everyone recognised Mister Eriksson. I was constantly asked to sign autographs and pose for pictures. I did not mind but it irritated Anki. She became known as 'Eriksson's wife' and she did not appreciate that, but she still wanted us to go out and see friends at night. With Riccardo and Anna, we sometimes went to a restaurant near to where we lived and where we were generally left alone.

• • •

Italian football had long been plagued by corruption and match fixing. The worst scandal, which was known as Totonero, had been exposed in 1980 and involved at least twenty players and several teams in both Serie

A, the top division, and Serie B. It resulted in Milan and Lazio being relegated to the second division. Other teams had points deducted at the beginning of the following season, and players received bans ranging from three months to six years. One of those players was Paolo Rossi, who, after a two-year ban, came back to football and went on to become the top scorer at the 1982 World Cup, which Italy won.

Roma had not been involved in the Totonero mess. The club had, however, been accused of bribing the referee in the second leg of the European Cup semi-final in 1984. Their opponents Dundee United had won the first leg in Scotland by 2–0. Roma were alleged to have paid French referee Michel Vautrot 100 million Italian lire to ensure that the home team won the return game, which they did, 3–0. The deciding goal came as a result of a dubiously awarded penalty.

I knew of the allegations when I came to Roma, but had no idea if they were true. It was not something that concerned me. But the allegations would not go away. One day, I am not sure exactly when, I asked Riccardo if it was true that the club had bribed the referee. Riccardo nodded slowly. Unfortunately, it was true, he said. Many years later he acknowledged it publicly.

Ahead of the second to last game we were leading the league table, with the same number of points but better goal difference than Juventus. On paper we had two easy games left. If we won them, we would in all likelihood win the scudetto. The first game was at home against minnows Lecce. It was already settled that they would be relegated, so in theory they did not have anything to play for. Juventus, on the other hand, had a difficult home game against Milan. When we entered the packed Olympic Stadium on 20 April 1986, we were met by a deafening roar and a sea of red and yellow Roma flags. Before the game, Dino

Viola and the mayor of Rome walked around the pitch and waved at the crowd. They were acting as if we had already won the title. I did not like that.

The match started well. Graziani scored with a header in the seventh minute and the crowd went crazy. We controlled the game and created a lot of chances but suddenly the play turned. The ball was lofted into our penalty area and, for some reason, our two centre backs switched off while a Lecce player ran between them and headed the ball into the goal from just a few yards out. Ten minutes later, Lecce successfully converted a penalty. At half-time we were trailing 1–2. In Turin, the score between Juventus and Milan was still 0–0.

In the dressing room, I was angry. We were so close to winning the scudetto. We had started well, scored and controlled the game, and then just switched off.

'What the hell is going on?' I demanded.

One of the star players just looked at me and said, 'Relax, Mister, we will get them in the second half.'

I did not understand what he meant. Relax? We were about to lose the title!

In the second half, we started well again. But after ten minutes, we suffered a catastrophic setback when Lecce scored to make it 3–1. After that, we practically laid siege to the Lecce goal, but their goalkeeper played the match of his life. He saved everything. Time ticked away. Finally, Pruzzo managed to get one goal back with a header from close range. The game ended 2–3. In Turin, Juventus had beaten Milan 1–0 after a goal by Michael Laudrup. In the dressing room, the players were shocked. In a television interview, I congratulated Lecce on the win but inside I wondered how in hell we could have lost that game.

That night, Riccardo Viola came by my place. He had something important to discuss. Riccardo explained that there were suspicions that some
of our players, as many as five, had bet money on the half-time result in
the game against Lecce. What was he saying? That the players had thrown
the game?

'Never,' I said.

Maybe it was the Torsby boy in me who reacted like that. The idea that
the players would have thrown the game was completely alien to me. My
players! It was not until later that I thought back to what that player had
said at half-time – 'Relax, Mister, we will get them in the second half.'
What did he mean by that? We had taken an early lead, but then thrown
it away by letting in two cheap goals. Lecce were about to be relegated.
The odds on them leading against us at half-time would have been pretty
high. Anyone who bet on such a result could have potentially made a lot
of money. Maybe the idea was to allow Lecce the lead, and for us to come
back in the second half and win the game. Had the plan gone awry? We
had conceded another goal early in the second half and never managed
to get back after that. My mind was spinning. In Sweden, something like
that could never have happened. But this was Italy. There was a lot of
money at stake. Was this how things worked here?

The next day, Dino Viola came to talk to me. He was convinced that
the players had bet illegally on the match. As it turned out, big bets had
been made on the half-time result. The odds on a Lecce lead at half-time
had fallen dramatically right before kick-off. Viola was determined to prove
the guilt of the five players. For days I was stuck in meetings with the
club's lawyers. They wanted to know what I knew. But I did not know
anything. I just had a dirty feeling.

In the end, no conclusive proof emerged. No charges were filed. The following weekend we played our last league match, away to Como, and lost. Dan Corneliusson, my former Gothenburg striker who now played for Como, scored the game's only goal. Juventus beat Lecce away. They won the league four points ahead of us.

The whole affair had left a bitter taste in my mouth. I wanted to leave Roma. At the same time, we had reached the Cup final, where we were going to face Sampdoria. It was not played until a month after the league was over. Serie A ended early that year because of the impending World Cup in Mexico. Many of our internationals, among them Boniek and Conti, had already joined their national teams when the Cup final was played. I had to field a young team, filled with promising new players. We lost the first match away 2–1, but a week later we won the return leg at home 2–0 and so secured the Cup.

That was when I changed my mind. I felt I had a promising team for the future, filled with young talent. After that, I never thought about what had happened in the Lecce game again. Maybe my romanticised view of Italian football had been knocked but I had to make a decision. Either I had to leave Italian football, or I had to accept it, warts and all. If I stayed, I had to trust my players. I could not walk around and suspect them of match fixing. It was time to turn the page.

● ● ●

My third season with Roma was a catastrophe. The young players never developed as I hoped, and we lost Cerezo. During the previous season he had fallen out with Dino Viola, just as his compatriot Falcão had done.

It happened on the one day I was sick and stayed home during my time at Roma. I was in bed when Sormani, my assistant, called me.

Something serious had happened, he said. Dino Viola had, as he often did, come into the dressing room after training. He wanted to inspect every-thing. Cerezo had confronted him about some money that he thought Viola owed him. Viola's answer had apparently not satisfied Cerezo, who proceeded to attack Viola, grabbing his shirt and lifting him off the ground in front of the rest of the shocked team.

It could only end one way. The next day Viola told me that I could use Cerezo as I saw fit for the rest of the season, but before the next season, he had to go. To Viola, Cerezo was a dead man. I understood that there was nothing to argue about. Cerezo was lost. When I asked him what had happened, he said he lost his head. He knew the second he put his hands on Viola that it was over for him at Roma. We sold Cerezo to Sampdoria where he played for another five years before ending his career with a European Cup final against Barcelona.

In Cerezo's place, we brought in Klaus Berggren, a Danish midfielder from Pisa. Klaus worked very hard, but he was no Cerezo. I was interested in English players at the time and was offered John Barnes from Liverpool. But we were allowed just two foreign players in Italy at that time and I already had Boniek.

The air had gone out of Boniek, however. He was unmotivated and lethargic. After a while, he said he wanted to play libero. Since my time at Benfica I had started to experiment with formations other than 4-4-2. I was not as rigid in my thinking any more. I had realised that you needed to adapt the system to the players you had at your disposal. So I decided to let Boniek try out as libero. But that did not work. In a game against Milan, with the score 1–1, the ball came to Boniek in his own penalty area. For some reason, he just stepped over it, a Milan player latched on to it and scored. Milan won. After the game, Boniek said he thought the referee had blown the whistle.

Pruzzo also returned to his old, unmotivated self. Conti, meanwhile, had problems with his Achilles' tendon. I sent him to Richard Smith, a physiotherapist in Holland, renowned for his toughness, but that did not work out. Being woken up at seven in the morning and forced to train three times a day was not something that Conti liked very much.

● ● ●

We were stuck in the middle of the table when I travelled to Sweden for Christmas. Anki, who was eight months pregnant, had gone ahead with Johan. We celebrated Christmas with her and my parents in Torsby and in Åmål, and then Anki suddenly fell ill. The doctors found that her blood pressure was way too high, and she had to stay in hospital in Karlstad. They did not want her to give birth prematurely, so they gave her medicine to keep the blood pressure down. I had to go back to Italy, because the league was starting up again after the Christmas break and we were going to play Sampdoria away.

It was minus 27 degrees Celsius on the morning of 2 January 1987 when Anki, still in hospital, gave birth to Lina. Three days later, after we had drawn 0–0 against Sampdoria, I flew back to Sweden. It snowed when I got there and the plane had to land in Jönköping. From there, I had to drive the 155 miles to Karlstad. When I arrived, Lina had been put in an incubator. She weighed 2.2 kilos, just under 5lb.

Back at Roma, despite a ten-match unbeaten streak against bottom half of the table teams, it was obvious something drastic had to be done. I told Dino Viola the only way I would stay at the club was if we got rid of Pruzzo, Conti and Boniek. His reaction was predictable. How could he get rid of our three biggest stars – especially Boniek? Viola had snatched him from Agnelli. If he sold Boniek now, it would seem like Viola had made a mistake in buying him.

'It's impossible,' he said.

But I knew there was no way back with the old players. Ancelotti was on his way out, too. Viola thought that he was finished because of his knee problems. For years, Ancelotti had taken a hell of a beating and he had trouble getting out of bed in the mornings. I still rated him very highly and tried to convince Viola to keep him, but come the end of the season Viola sold him to Milan. Ancelotti stayed there for five years and won everything there was to win.

I resigned the day after we lost a game against Milan. Dino Viola was probably relieved that I had chosen to do that, but it was the first and only time in my career that I left a job without having anything new lined up. What would I do now? I had no time to think about that, however, because for the first time in my life something happened that made me put football to one side.

● ● ●

Lina was a dream baby. She almost always slept. After a while, Anki started to suspect that something was wrong. Lina was not growing and it was not hard to see why. She hardly ate anything. We had to drip-feed her.

Anna Viola arranged for a paediatrician to come to our house to examine Lina. There was no danger, he said, but to be safe, he would refer her to a children's hospital for some tests. The doctors ran an ECG test and when the results came back, they realised immediately that something was wrong with her heart. They just didn't know what. To find out, they had to put some kind of a camera inside her body to take pictures of her heart. However, the doctor who was able to perform such a procedure was away for another two days.

Those two days were rough. We were sitting at home in bed with Lina. The television was on and suddenly Dino Viola was being interviewed. At one point he turned to the camera to offer a special greeting to the Eriksson family. 'They know what it's about,' he said.

It turned out Lina had a very serious heart defect and needed an operation immediately. Anki and I were completely dumbstruck. Lina was a baby. How could she have her heart operated on? And where? Which was the best hospital in Rome? The doctor said, 'You are Swedish. I advise you to get on the first flight to Sweden with your daughter.'

The next morning we flew to Sweden and took Lina to Sahlgrenska Hospital in Gothenburg. Bengt Eriksson, who worked with the Swedish national swim team at the time, made the diagnosis. Lina had total anomolous lung venous return, or TAPVR. Only half of her heart was working properly. All the blood went to one side. The condition was extremely rare. In Sweden, on average, just two children were born with the disease each year. Usually it was discovered during the first week or two after the child's birth. The doctors had never seen a child live for five months without an operation. Lina had survived because of another problem with her heart – a hole between the two chambers allowed blood to get through. But the operation had to be done immediately. Her chance of survival was 70 per cent.

Doctor Eriksson contacted Göran Sydow, who worked for a private hospital in Gothenburg. Sydow was regarded as one of the best heart surgeons in Sweden. After receiving Eriksson's call, he got on his bicycle and cycled to Sahlgrenska Hospital. He had agreed to operate first thing in the morning.

At 7 a.m. on 19 May 1987, we handed Lina over to the medical team. The operation would not be over until after lunch. We were advised to leave the hospital and return at two o'clock; otherwise we would go crazy. We did as the doctors said and got into our car and drove around Gothenburg. It felt like time stood still. We went to visit some former neighbours who had bought a new house outside the city.

We returned to the hospital around one o'clock and sat and waited – two o'clock, a quarter past two, two-thirty. Anki started to panic. Even I was jittery. Suddenly we heard rapid footsteps on the stairs and I knew right at that moment that the operation had been a success. No doctor would run to deliver bad news.

Lina's veins had been so thin that the doctors had had to fix the drip to her temple. During the operation she had been lying on an ice bed to prevent bleeding, hooked up to a lung and heart machine. Her heart had apparently had two veins on one side and none on the other. Sydow had cut off one of the veins and attached to it to the side that did not have one. Incredible! When we finally got to see her, Lina was anaesthetised and had myriad pumps and hoses coming in and out of her body. It was very hard to look at her in that condition. But she was alive.

Since then we have celebrated two birthdays with Lina – 2 January, the day she was born, and 19 May, the day she survived.

LA VIOLA

AFTER Lina's operation, I travelled back to Italy and reached an agreement with Fiorentina to become their new manager. Fiorentina, or 'La Viola' as the Florence-based club was known, had been bought in 1980 by Flavio Pontello, who came from a family of Tuscan noblemen. Pontello changed the club emblem and traditional hymn and the fans got very upset, but when he brought in big players, such as the Argentinians Daniel Passarella and Daniel Bertoni, the protests quietened down. The second season after Pontello bought the club, Fiorentina battled with Juvenus for the title, but finished as runners-up.

After that, things went downhill. The club did not get near the league summit again. The Pontellos hired new managers only to get rid of them less than a year later. The big star and midfield maestro Antognoni was constantly injured and finally left Fiorentina in 1987, the same year I arrived. By that time, Pontello had almost given up hope of ever winning the league. He wanted the team to play good football and, if possible, qualify for European competition. That was enough.

I was far from certain that managing Fiorentina was the right job for me. Since my time at Degerfors, my career had gone in an upwards direction. Now it felt as if I had traded down, as if I had gone against my own ambitions. It was unlike me. At the same time, I had no other offers. I had been to visit Real Madrid to talk about a possible job there, but they had not come up with a concrete offer. I preferred to stay in Italy. Italy still had the best football league in Europe.

After the tumultuous time in Roma, my family needed some stability. Lina had gained weight after the operation and was suddenly a happy baby. But she had almost died. Anki needed some peace and quiet. She had stayed in the hospital with Lina while I returned to Italy, and she had taken care of Johan, too. It had been a very tough summer for her. In Florence, we could live a quiet family life. Anki loved the city. And it was a football city, even if you could not compare it with Rome.

● ● ●

I had managed many great players in my career up to that point – Torbjörn Nilsson at Gothenburg; Chalana at Benfica; Falcão, Boniek and Pruzzo at Roma. Special talents. But I had never managed – and would possibly never manage again – a greater talent than Roberto Baggio.

Baggio was 15 years old when he made his debut as a senior player for Vicenza. When he arrived at Fiorentina in 1985, he was 18. His first season at the club was ruined by a serious knee injury. The second season he played just five games. Now, in his third season with the club, he was ready to blossom. Baggio was an individualist. He played as a *rifinitore*, a second striker, in a free role behind the advanced striker. He was hard to fit into a system, but you had to give some players free rein to do what they did best – win matches for you.

He still struggled with injuries and I had to take it very easy with him. We wanted to make him stronger, and the club brought in sprinting coach Carlo Vittorio as Baggio's personal fitness trainer. Vittorio had been coaching Pietro Mennea, the Italian sprinting legend. He was a highly respected man in Italian athletics, but he knew nothing about football. However, after he trained with Baggio for a while, Vittorio started seeing himself in a new light. He wanted to help coach the senior team. That was obviously out of the question but I suggested that he could help with the youth team. Soon the training regime in the youth team changed dramatically. All the players did was run intervals. The regular youth-team coach was despairing. Vittorio stayed for a year only, but he and Baggio became good friends.

In front of Baggio, Argentinian striker Ramón Díaz had a glint in his eye and a nose for goal. He was not a player who would overly exert himself. Some people would probably call him lazy. I have never liked describing a player as lazy. To me, that means not being interested. Díaz was not a hard-working player, but he had his own theories about that.

'Mister,' he used to say. 'I can't run around chasing the ball in defence. I will have no energy left to score when I get the ball.'

Maybe my contempt for the word laziness had something to do with how I viewed my own training. As a player I probably trained harder than anyone else. I knew my talents were limited. I got nothing for free. I therefore had a hard time respecting players who had talent in abundance but did not show enough desire or ambition to use that talent and work hard.

• • •

The second game of the season was away to Milan, which in February of 1986 had been bought by media mogul Silvio Berlusconi. Milan dominated the match completely, but we defended heroically and with fifteen minutes left Díaz scored on a counterattack. A couple of minutes later Baggio extended the lead to 2–0. I think those were the only two times we had crossed the halfway line during the whole match. Afterwards, Pontello, the pompous nobleman, walked up to Berlusconi and said, '*Amministrazione normale.*'

But the truth was it was far from normal administration. AC Milan were on their way to replacing Juventus as the kings of Italian football. Berlusconi had invested huge amounts of money and resources in the club. They had big players, including Donadoni, Evani, Baresi and Maldini. Ahead of the season, he had bought Dutch superstars Ruud Gullit and Marco van Basten. And Carlo Ancelotti, of course. The team had a new manager, too – Arrigo Sacchi. It was a job that was supposed to be mine.

In the spring of 1986, right after Berlusconi had bought Milan and we played our best football at Roma, Berlusconi contacted me and we met in secret in Rome. In the middle of the night, I left my house to drive to a rendezvous spot, the parking lot of a local grocery store, where a car waited to take me to Berlusconi's apartment. It was a grand place. Berlusconi welcomed me. Adriano Galliani and Ariedo Braida were there, too. We sat down and started to talk football.

Berlusconi explained that he wanted to turn Milan into the greatest football club ever, not just in Italy but in the world. He was building an ultra-modern sports laboratory and creating an exclusive television channel for the club. The venture required some forward thinking, he said, and a forward-thinking manager, unlike Milan's current manager, Nisse Liedholm. Berlusconi was tired of magic; he wanted science. These were modern times in football. I represented the future, Liedholm the past.

'We're changing managers,' Berlusconi said, 'and we want you. Are you interested?'

Of course I was interested.

'Good, then you can talk money with these men,' he said and pointed at Galliani and Braida.

Galliani asked me how much I was making at Roma. I don't remember how much it was, but I remember that it seemed like nothing to Galliani. There was, however, a problem, he said to Berlusconi. Mister Eriksson had one year left on his contract with Roma. Apparently that was something Berlusconi was unaware of, because he flipped.

'I can't steal Senator Viola's manager,' he said.

Berlusconi was a media tycoon but he also had political ambitions. The last thing he wanted was to make an enemy of a powerful man like Dino Viola. The deal was off. I stayed in Rome, while Liedholm ended up staying another year in Milan before he was finally sacked. A former Milan player by the name of Fabio Capello took over temporarily as Milan manager for two months before Sacchi got the job. Under Sacchi, Milan would win the European Cup twice. But he won the league just once. If I had got the chance to manage Milan then, I think I would have won it all.

At Fiorentina we were good going forward with Baggio and Díaz. The problem lay in defence. Fiorentina had not been able to replace Passarella, the old libero, after he left for Inter the year before I came to the club. I decided to bring Glenn Hysén to Fiorentina. Hysén was in his prime and would be able to do a very good job for us. But the supporters had not forgotten Passarella and Glenn would forever be compared with the Argentinian legend. He was unlucky that way.

Some reorganisation was required. Fiorentina, like most Italian clubs, had been using a three-man defence with a libero and two man-marking centre backs. I was going to introduce zonal marking. In a straight four-man defence, players would be responsible for a particular zone and mark whichever opposing player came into that area. It was no more complicated than that.

But the simple can sometimes be the most difficult. Zonal marking was ingrained in Glenn Hysén's brain, but his defensive partner, Celeste Pin, had never played anything but man-to-man marking. Pin was a big, strong, no-nonsense defender. If you told him to mark a particular player, that's what he did. But when he was asked to mark zonally, he was lost. He didn't know where to go.

One player in the league was impossible to neutralise, no matter if you played zonally or man-to-man. He was undisputedly the greatest player in the world at the time – Diego Maradona. The diminutive Argentinian had become like a god in Napoli, where he had gone from Barcelona in 1984. In 1986, he had almost single-handedly won the World Cup for Argentina. In 1987, he led Napoli to its first scudetto ever. If Baggio was the best player I had coached, Maradona was the best player I had seen. To describe his strengths is pointless. He had no weaknesses.

One time we played Maradona's Napoli twice in four days, both times away. The first game, an Italian Cup game, was played on a Wednesday. Maradona was listless. It was, after all, just a Cup game. Napoli was more interested in the league. The game turned into an entertaining affair nonetheless, and we ended up winning it 3–2. Afterwards, Maradona came up to me and put his hand on my shoulder. Sunday's league game, he said, would be '*musica differente*'.

And so it was. In front of a packed Stadio San Paolo, a boiling cauldron like Benfica's Estadio da Luz, Maradona put on a master show. He completely toyed with us. Halfway through the first half – after Maradona had turned our left back, Stefano Carobbi, inside out with his tricks – Carobbi ran over to the bench and yelled, 'What the hell do you want me to do with Maradona?'

'I don't know,' I yelled back. 'Kick him in the legs.'

I don't think that Carobbi or anyone else on our team got close enough even to do that. Maradona was unstoppable. On one occasion, he received a short corner and started to juggle the ball with his back towards our goal before hitting a perfect cross with a bicycle kick. Napoli won 4–0. They beat us in the return leg in the Cup, too.

● ● ●

Flavio Pontello had two brothers and one sister. They lived in different houses in the direction of Pisa, and occasionally wanted me to come over and talk football – but always individually, never together. I had breakfast with one brother and lunch with another. They would ask me how Baggio was doing or what players I might want them to buy. If I said something of interest to one sibling, I had to promise not to tell the others. They were a polite and generous family, if a little curious.

The managing director of the club, Pier Cesare Baretti, from Turin, was a former renowned journalist for Tutto Sport, and very well known in Italian football. We did not share the same ideas about how exactly football should be played, but I respected him a lot. He was very passionate about the club. Every day he was at the office, from seven in the morning to seven at night. After that, he would go to meetings with supporters' clubs. He was a very good speaker. Most players and managers did not like to go to those kinds of meetings, but Baretti did. He must have been to hundreds of them and he was always at the games.

Baretti was also an amateur pilot. One day in Turin he was going flying together with an instructor. The weather was poor and before taking off, Baretti talked to the club secretary on the phone. The secretary told Baretti that if the weather was bad, it was probably better if he did not fly that day. But Baretti said he needed the flying hours to keep his certificate valid. When else would he have time for it?

It was the last time that anyone at the club talked to Baretti. His plane left Turin in poor visibility and never returned. The whole night passed without any word of what had happened. I sat by the telephone, waiting to hear something. At one point, word came through that they had landed safely, but it was not true. In the morning, confirmation arrived that the plane had slammed into a mountain and both Baretti and his instructor had been killed.

The funeral took place the next day in Turin. The Pontello family were there, as well as the players and the coaching staff. It was the first time I had been at a funeral with an open casket. Baretti was wearing the pilot's jacket he had worn when his plane had crashed. It felt unreal. I had spoken with Baretti just a few days earlier. He was a workaholic, full of energy. I felt very uncomfortable watching him in that casket, lifeless.

A shadow fell over the remainder of the season. We lost our first home game after his death, to Inter 2–1. In the next thirteen games, we won just one, 1–0 at home against my old team, Roma. Baggio had been good, but he scored just six goals that season. We finished eighth in the league and missed qualifying for the UEFA Cup. No one was terribly upset about the results. We had done as well as had been expected of us.

● ● ●

The move to Florence had not been easy on Johan. He was nine years old and had been forced to leave his best friend Giacomo in Rome. Johan was a bit of a rogue. He was also incredibly stubborn. He refused to learn the multiplication tables. Anki nagged me about practising it with him.

He also refused to play football. In Rome, I had put him in Roma's youth programme when he was around six or seven years old. One day the kids were going to learn how to use their left foot. But Johan wanted to use his right. The coach said that if he didn't try to kick with his left foot, Johan would have to run a lap around the football pitch. So Johan ran. When he returned, the coach asked if he was ready to practise his left foot. He was not. So he had to run another lap. It went on like that. When I came to pick him up after practice, Johan had decided not to play football any more. And that is what he did. He stopped playing football.

As soon as the school year finished, Anki took him and Lina to Sweden. I followed once the season was over. We spent most of our summer at the house in Åmål. Anki's parents were there a lot, too. I had a good relationship with her whole family. Her father, Karl-Erik, was a sports man. He thought he knew everything about football. The players at that time could not shoot, he argued, because they always leaned back when they struck the ball. It was futile to argue against him. He was a school principal and used to being right. At night, we played five-card poker. Anki's grandfather was there, too. He was the one who taught Johan how to play cards. My parents would also come to visit, and my brother, Lasse.

Back in Florence, I had an unexpected visitor – Roberto Pruzzo. Viola had let him go. Pruzzo was thinner than when I last saw him. He was 33 years old and thought he had at least one more season in him. There was never any doubt that Pruzzo was a good football player, and a phenomenal finisher. He had been top scorer in the Italian league three times. Now he came to us on a possible free transfer and offered to play for a low salary. So I took him. It would prove to be a good decision, even if Pruzzo started just one league game in the whole season.

Our best signing, however, was the Brazilian, Dunga, a defensive midfielder who had played at Pisa. I had been impressed with Dunga when we played Pisa the previous season. He played as a forward then and kept pressing our defenders the whole game. They beat us 2–1. Dunga was not fast, but he ran and ran and never gave the ball away. He was also a leader, someone who did not talk too much but all the players respected.

I thought we had a much better team for 1988/89 than we had the season before, but it was soon clear that we would not be involved in the fight for the top places in the league. Perhaps we had a chance to nab a UEFA-Cup spot.

● ● ●

My parents came to Florence to live with us for six months. My dad, who was getting close to retirement, had taken leave of absence from his caretaker job at Volvo in Torsby, and my mother had stopped working.

They were starting to become lonely. I think that is why I wanted them to come to stay with us. They stayed in an apartment in the same building as us. It was perfect. My mother ironed shirts and cooked dinner. Anki no longer had to drive the kids to school. My dad did that.

Kurt 'Kurre' Hamrin, the legendary Swedish football player, at that time lived in Florence with his family. We spent quite a bit of time with them. Kurre and I played a lot of tennis. They had some kind of trading business in Italy. His wife and kids worked for the company. Kurre mostly played tennis. Each person should do what he is best at, Kurre said, and what he was best at was tennis. My dad liked him. They were the same generation. But after a while I think my dad tired of Florence. He did not understand the language and he missed Sweden. At six o'clock in the morning, he wanted a Swedish cup of coffee and the Värmland newspaper. After six months, my parents returned to Sweden.

I don't know what happened, but it was something about my parents visiting that stirred up emotions in me. I felt like I had been close to my parents, but maybe not as close as Anki was to hers. She always called them several times a week. I decided that I would start calling my parents more often. In fact, I would call them every day from then on. Maybe I felt guilty for leaving my parents alone in Sweden, but I don't think so. I think I called them simply to be nice. A son should call his parents.

● ● ●

Even if we were out of the title race at an early stage in the season, we played better football my second year at Fiorentina, especially at home, where we beat both Juventus and Inter. Baggio got his real breakthrough and formed a brilliant partnership with Borgonovo. Dunga was a great enforcer in midfield. Towards the end of the season we were locked in battle with Roma for the last UEFA Cup spot.

Ahead of one of the last games of the season, I don't remember which one, Nardino Previdi, our sporting director, came to see me in my office. I liked Previdi. We had worked together at Roma where he had been the sporting director in my first year at the club. He had a lot of contacts in Italy. Previdi wanted to talk about the game we were about to play. It would be a tough game, he said. Perhaps a draw would be sufficient? Yes, I said, a draw would be good, but a win would be better. Previdi looked at me. Then he said, 'If we are happy with a draw, perhaps it can be arranged.'

Suddenly, I realised what he was getting at and I shook my head.

'No, no, no,' I said.

It was the only time in my career that I had been asked if I wanted a match fixed. I did not give it a second's thought. I knew from my time at Roma that kind of cheating existed in Italy, but I never wanted to get involved in it.

● ● ●

With three games left we were four points ahead of Roma. In our next game we would play them at the Olympic Stadium in Rome. If we could get one point there, we would most likely secure the UEFA Cup spot. The match was played late, on 11 June. The league season had been delayed because of the European Championship the year before.

The game was tied at 1–1 deep into the second half, despite Roma's dominance. We were on our way to securing our valuable point. Close to the end our forward Pellegrini got the ball in Roma's half. Dunga screamed at him to play the ball back so that we would not lose possession, but Pellegrini did not listen. He went for goal and unleashed a wild shot that did not hit the target. Roma's goalkeeper quickly put the ball back in play and it found its way to the Brazilian Renato, who hit a shot that our goalkeeper saved. But up popped Rudi Völler, the German striker whom I had helped sign for Roma, and headed in the rebound for Roma. We lost the match 2–1.

In the dressing room afterwards, Dunga was furious. When Pellegrini came in, Dunga walked up to him and, without any warning, socked Pellegrini with one punch on the jaw. Pellegrini fell to the floor. The dressing room went very quiet. Although the players were shocked, no one felt sorry for Pellegrini. If he had held on to the ball, we would have managed a draw and secured a place in Europe. As it was, we managed just one point from the last two games, while Roma got three. We finished on the same number of points and since goal difference did not count at that time, we would have to play a one-off deciding match, a so-called *spareggio*.

Perugia was the neutral location, and the match was set for 30 June 1989. I had one problem. Borgonovo was injured. Together with Baggio, he had scored the majority of our goals that season. It meant I had to play Pruzzo. Pruzzo had started one league match all season, and had not scored a single goal. Yet he had been a positive influence on the team, and kept a very good attitude. He often stayed after training with the younger players to practise finishing.

Early in the game Baggio hit a cross from the left flank that sailed over the Roma defence and found Pruzzo at the far post. He headed in for 1–0. After that, Roma pressed and created a lot of chances, but could not score. We won and so qualified for the UEFA Cup thanks to Pruzzo's one and only goal that season.

Afterwards, Dino Viola shook my hand. He was grumpy. He said I had been right about the three players I had wanted to get rid of at Roma. But there was one thing for which he could never forgive me.

'What's that?' I asked.

'That Pruzzo scored,' he answered.

It may have been the last time I saw Dino Viola. Two years later he died from intestinal cancer. In the dressing room, I thanked my players. I knew it would be the last time I did that as manager of La Viola.

WAR IS WAR

IS it possible to move forward by taking a step back? That was the question I asked myself when Benfica contacted me during the spring of 1989 with an offer to go back to Portugal. I did not really want to leave Italy but I realised that if I stayed at Fiorentina, I would not move either forwards or backwards. I would stay exactly where I was, in the middle. Fiorentina was a mid-table team and without some serious investments, it would stay there. I had greater ambitions than to fight over UEFA Cup spots. I had already won the UEFA Cup. I had won the Portuguese league, too, twice. But Benfica were going to play in the European Cup. I wanted the job.

There was one problem. Toni had taken over as head coach of Benfica. After I received the offer, I called him. If my going there meant Toni would be fired, I would turn down the offer. But Toni said they would fire him regardless, so I decided to take the job on one condition – that Toni became my assistant manager. Toni did not want to leave Benfica. The name of the club was written on his forehead.

To Anki and me the move back to Portugal was literally a homecoming. We had bought a house in Portugal while we were living in Florence. During my first time in Benfica we had often driven out to Cabo da Roca, Europe's western-most point. On the way there, we had always admired a particular house when driving by. One day Börje Lantz called us in Florence and said that the house was for sale. We asked Börje to negotiate a price and bought it, sight unseen.

We remodelled practically everything inside the three-storey stone house, even doing some things twice. The basement, for example, eventually became a pool room. The living room had big windows with a fantastic view of the ocean. We wanted to build a gym and a sauna behind the house but there was not enough room for an excavator. So the builders removed all the earth by hand. They probably went back and forth over a thousand times with wheelbarrows full of soil.

Börje had bought the piece of land next to our house. A small shed stood on it and he planned to build a big house but could not obtain a building permit. Construction never actually got going, which was probably just as well because Börje was no longer the same person as before.

● ● ●

During the years I had been away, Portugal's *Os Três Grandes*, 'the big three', had turned into *Os Dois Grandes*, 'the big two'. It was now between Benfica and Porto. Sporting had fallen behind. Benfica had a good team, definitely good enough to win the league, but after five games, Porto were huge favourites. However, the league was not our main target that year.

We had our eyes on the European Cup. This was the most prestigious of the European club tournaments. Only teams that had won their respective leagues got to participate and so far fewer teams played in the European Cup than play in the Champions League today. And with no group stages, only knockout rounds, fewer games were played.

Benfica had won the European Cup in 1961 and 1962, when Eusébio was playing. After that, the club had reached the final four times and lost each one, three times during the 1960s and once in 1988, when Toni had taken over the coaching job in mid-season. Toni's Benfica met PSV Eindhoven, which was then managed by Guus Hiddink. PSV took the title on penalties. Maybe the club thought that things would have turned out differently with me as manager. The reason they had brought me back to Benfica was to win the European Cup. Toni had taken the team to its first European Cup final in twenty years and under his leadership Benfica had easily won the league the following year. But it was not enough. It was up to me to make Benfica champions of Europe.

After the Heysel Stadium disaster during the European Cup final between Juventus and Liverpool in 1985, when thirty-nine Juventus fans died, all English teams had been banned from European football. In the first and second round we easily dispatched some smaller teams. Real Madrid, one of the favourites, were knocked out by Milan in the second round. In the quarter-final we played FC Dnipro Dnipropetrovsk from Ukraine, which was still part of the Soviet Union at the time. We won 1–0 at home and 3–0 away. So we were in the European Cup semi-finals together with Milan, Bayern Munich and the team we were going to face, Olympique Marseille.

The first game was played in Marseille. I remember that we loaded crates of wine into the team bus, which was going to be driven from

Portugal to meet us at Marseille airport. To the Portuguese, food and wine are very important. Most players drank a glass of wine at lunch or dinner. There was nothing strange about that. It was the same in Italy. But to drink French wine was unthinkable to the Portuguese. The wine had to be Portuguese.

Marseille at that time were a top team with world class-stars, including Jean Tigana and Didier Deschamps in the midfield and Jean-Pierre Papin in attack. Marseille won the French league five times in a row, from 1989 to 1993. They had fanatical fans and the stadium, Stade Vélodrome, was known as one of the most intimidating in Europe for away teams. But not to us. We had Estádio da Luz, the most intimidating arena of all.

We knew that Marseille would attack and it was important that we defended well, but in the interests of scoring an away goal, I lined up with two forwards. It turned out to be a good move because, although we lost 2–1, we had our all-important away goal.

For the return leg, the atmosphere at the Estádio da Luz was electric as usual. We pressed hard, but it felt more and more desperate. Then, in the eighty-second minute, we got a corner that was lofted into Marseille's crowded penalty area. From the bench, we could not see anything – just that the ball came off our player, Vata, and went into the goal. Everything went so fast. A few of the Marseille players protested wildly but the goal was allowed and I remember our forward, Mats, running down the pitch with his arms up in the air. We withstood Marseille's final push and won 1–0. We had reached the European Cup final.

It was only after the game that I heard what the commotion surrounding our goal had been about. The Marseille players claimed that Vata had handled the ball. In the dressing room afterwards, I went up to him and asked him how he scored the goal. Vata did not answer. He just looked down on the floor. I told him that I was not angry. Quite the opposite. We had won and we were in the final. Vata stood up and showed how he had knocked the ball into the net with his arm. Okay, I said. I think I even patted his shoulder.

Later at the press conference, Marseille manager Gérard Gili and I were answering the journalists' questions when the Marseille president, Bernard Tapie, suddenly stormed into the room. Tapie was a business tycoon. He had just bought adidas. He was outraged. Marseille had been cheated, he screamed. The team would file a protest. But he knew as well as everyone else that nothing was going to change the outcome of the match. The referee had not seen the hand ball. The goal had been allowed. Marseille were out of the European Cup.

Three years later, they reached the final of the first Champions League tournament, winning 1–0 against Milan. But the same year it was revealed that Tapie had bribed some referees in the French league. Marseille had their 1993 French title revoked, but got to keep the Champions League title. Tapie, who at the press conference had scolded us for our dishonesty, was put in prison.

● ● ●

The European Cup final was going to be played at the Prater Stadium in Vienna on 23 May 1990. Anki came to watch, of course. Tord Grip came, too. Our opponents were Milan, current holders of the European Cup. The year before they had crushed Steaua Bucharest 4–0 in the final. Milan had the world's best defence – Mauro Tassotti, Alessandro Costacurta, Franco Baresi and Paolo Maldini. In midfield they had Frank Rijkaard and

Carlo Ancelotti; in attack Ruud Gullit and Marco van Basten. On paper they looked unbeatable.

But I was sure we could beat them. Towards the end of the season, Milan had slumped in the league. After losses to Juventus and Inter, Milan had been passed by Napoli in the table. In the end, Napoli had won the title. The Italian league had ended early because of the World Cup that summer. Milan had had a month to rest up before the final, but without competitive games I thought they might lack match fitness. I also knew the manager, Sacchi, well. He was predictable with his offensive play.

Tactically, we played a brilliant game. We did not give Milan any space to exploit. The defence was in perfect control of Gullit and van Basten. Milan did not create any real chances. The problem was, we didn't either. We lacked bite going forward. Mats had scored forty goals for us during the season, but against world-class defenders, such as Baresi and Costacurta, he was powerless. The first half ended 0–0.

The mood in the dressing room at half-time was positive. Although we had not been able to penetrate the Milan defence, the players were pleased with how they had performed. Milan had been huge favourites before the game, but so far it was an even affair. We felt that we had a real chance of winning the game, if only we could find a way to get past the Milan defenders. Mats got nowhere. I talked to Valdo, our quick midfielder, about making runs from deep in midfield. It was something we had practised.

The second half started like the first. We kept our shape well, but then our centre back Aldair stepped up a little too far. Rijkaard went past him, received the ball from a little flick-on, and suddenly had only our goal-keeper to beat. He made no mistake, scoring for Milan with the same kind of play that I had talked to Valdo about making. After that, Milan closed up shop. I threw on a forward, Vata, but we were absolutely powerless in attack. Milan won and Benfica had lost its fifth straight European Cup final.

We were terribly disappointed. After the match, we received a lot of criticism for not being attacking enough. But Toni and I were convinced that we had done everything possible to win the game. Magnusson and Vata were good enough in Portugal, but they were no Gullit and van Basten. What irked me was that we had been so close. Not many players or managers got the chance to win the European Cup. When the chance came, you had to take it. At the same time, I was a young manager, 42 years old. I was convinced that I would one day get the chance to lift the trophy.

● ● ●

After the final, the whole family went back to Sweden. Benfica had lost just two league games in the whole season, but we still finished second in the league, four points behind Porto. I had gone through a season with Benfica without winning anything.

Later that summer I found myself back in Italy where the World Cup was going to be played. For the first time in my career I worked as a commentator for Swedish television. I did not have anything else to do. Staffan Lindeborg, a Swedish television announcer, and I travelled around the country, watching games. He and I had a great time. Everywhere we went, we were well received. Everyone knew Mister Eriksson in Italy. But the television work itself was not something I enjoyed. I was not the kind of person who liked talking too much. I found it difficult to criticise players or coaches. Maybe it was because I knew there was more to the game than could be seen on the television screen.

The expectations of Sweden in the 1990 World Cup were very high. Sweden had won their qualifying group ahead of England. Olle Nordin, my old captain from IFK Gothenburg, had been the Sweden manager for several years. Before the World Cup, he and his girlfriend had visited us at our summer house in Sweden. Olle had told me about his World Cup plans and I thought they sounded very good. He had put a lot of thought and energy into the preparations and he was sure that Sweden would do very well in the tournament. They did not. Sweden lost all three games at the group stage by 1–2 and Olle resigned as national team manager. I felt for him. He planned everything in the most minute detail. But sometimes that planning could become too much.

● ● ●

Benfica went on a summer tour to Angola and Mozambique. The two African countries were former Portuguese colonies and Benfica had many fans there. We had two players from Angola, Vata and Abel Campos, and of course, Eusébio came from Mozambique.

Anki and I spent quite a bit of time with Eusébio and his wife. Eusébio liked spicy food and he always carried a bottle of Tabasco in his jacket pocket. He told amazing stories about growing up dirt poor in Mozambique and how he played football barefoot using a ball made out of bunched-up newspapers. His wife was also from Mozambique and herself a famous athlete. She was incredibly beautiful. Plenty of stories were floating around about Eusébio and various women, but if someone asked him about it, he laughed it off.

I will always remember one incident during our visit to Mozambique. We were going to play a friendly in Maputo. When we arrived at the stadium, we were greeted by a sea of young men, mostly shirtless. Eusébio and I were sitting in the front of the bus, and there was a lot of noise outside. But when the bus stopped and the doors opened and Eusébio stepped out, everything went quiet. Standing on the steps of the bus, Eusébio raised his hand as if to greet the crowd. A boy stepped forward. He was probably around 12 years old. Slowly, he reached out to Eusébio and touched his hand. Suddenly, the crowd erupted. It was as if no one had truly believed that the great Eusébio was actually there until the young boy confirmed that he was indeed real. I have never seen anything like it. I had never thought about how big Eusébio was in Africa.

● ● ●

During the five years I had been away from Portugal, the football there had become dirtier, more corrupt. There were a lot of scandals and always talk about referees. Porto had grown much more powerful. After losing the European Cup final, it was as if the air had gone out of us in Benfica. Since we had not won the league, we had not qualified for the European Cup in my second season back, but had to make do with the UEFA Cup. We were knocked out in the first round by Roma.

The league was between Porto and ourselves, as usual. When we met for the second time, towards the end of the season, we were leading the table by one point. Whoever won this match would most likely win the league.

When we arrived at Porto's stadium one and a half hours before the match, so many people were gathered outside that the bus got stuck. A stone was thrown at one of the windows, which fortunately did not break. The players sank down in their seats and pulled the curtains, but everyone knew the Benfica team were in the bus. Despite the crowd seeming to expand, there was nothing else to do but get out of the bus, unload our equipment and walk the last bit to the dressing rooms. So we did, surrounded by screaming Porto supporters. It was a very tense and scary scene.

When we got to our dressing room, it was locked. I asked the security guards to unlock it, but they completely ignored me. Pinto da Costa, the Porto president and the most powerful man in Portuguese football at the time, appeared, saying that according to the rules, the away dressing room had to be made available just one hour before the game.

'I respect Mister Eriksson very much as a person,' he said. 'But war is war.'

When the dressing room was finally opened, we discovered it had been sprayed with some kind of chemical that made it impossible to breathe. Our players had to change in the hallway outside. I asked a Porto official if we could at least have access to the pitch, but the orders from da Costa were that the away team could go out on the pitch half an hour before kick-off and not before. When we did get out on the field, the surface was so wet that you could hardly hit a pass on it, and the touchlines had been redrawn to make the field smaller. Our coaching bench had been placed almost in line with the penalty area, and secured so that it was impossible to move.

The game, unsurprisingly, turned quite hostile, and there was a slew of yellow cards, but no goals. In the eightieth minute, I sent on striker César Brito and a minute later, he headed in. Four minutes later, he added a second goal. Soon after that, the referee blew the whistle and we had won 2–0. Enraged Porto fans started a riot that lasted well into the night. But in Benfica, Brito, a peripheral player who would never be heard from again, had written himself into the history books. That night, Brito was king. Benfica went on to win their twenty-ninth league title, my third with the club, and qualify for the European Cup. I should have left then, when I was on top.

● ● ●

It was around this time that the football agent business started to take off. Börje Lantz's career, however, had taken a dive. He was having more and more problems with both his finances and his drinking. Börje had become mean when he drank. Bodil, his wife, never wanted to go out for dinner with him. It was the same with Anki. In the end, we stopped seeing them.

One agent who was making a name for himself was Pini Zahavi, an Israeli. Pini visited me at Benfica. He had a lot of contacts in the former Soviet Union, which had just then opened up. Pini was best friends with the legendary Russian coach Valerij Lobanovskij, and he represented Vasilij Kulkov from Spartak Moscow and Sergej Yuran from Dynamo Kiev, both of whom he sold to me.

But my third season at Benfica was a nightmare. We had two young midfielders, Rui Costa and Paolo Sousa, who broke into the first team, but we were weak going forward, and I don't understand how I was able to put together a defence. The Russian signings never settled in. Yuran longed to go back to Kiev, where he was king. He liked the good life, but he was not used to the money. He did not trust the bank, and kept his money in his mattress.

We were doomed in the league from the start after we lost the opening game against Boavista. In the European Cup, we did better and were drawn against Arsenal in the second round. English teams had been allowed back into European competition after a five-year absence. In the second leg at Highbury, Arsenal took an early lead but we equalised through Isaías, a Brazilian player I fought with a lot because he was both overweight and lazy. At full-time, the score was 1–1, the same score as in the first leg, and the game went into extra time. First Kulkov scored and then Isaías added his second goal for the evening. We won 3–1 and advanced to a group stage, which was being used in the European Cup that year.

Things did not go well there for us. We were drawn in a group with Barcelona, Sparta Prague and Dynamo Kiev. I think Águas broke his leg in the first match. We lost to Dynamo Kiev away and drew the next three games. We still had a chance to go through by beating Barcelona in the last game, but Barcelona – who had Hristo Stoichkov, Michael Laudrup, Ronald Koeman and Pep Guardiola, and were managed by Johan Cruyff – were too good. They beat us 2–1. We were out of the European Cup. Barcelona ended up winning the final against Sampdoria.

● ● ●

It was obvious that Benfica's time had passed. I was open to trying something new. Despite the poor season with Benfica, my name was still strong in the footballing world, even outside Europe. At one point I met Sunil Gulati, president of the US Football Association. We ate lunch at a restaurant in Paris. Gulati was a lively man, full of energy. He wanted to know if I would be interested in managing the United States ahead of the 1994 World Cup, which was to be played in America. I was not. The United States was the most powerful country in the world, but not in football terms. They did not even offer me a salary commensurate with what a decent manager would get paid in Europe. It was as if the job was an honorary assignment.

A far more interesting possibility was Bayern Munich. The German giants had had a lousy season. The coach, Jupp Heynckes, had been sacked two months into it and the team had finished tenth in the Bundesliga. They were looking for a new coach. The great Karl-Heinz Rummenigge, who now worked as a director of the club, came to see me in Portugal. Anki made us lunch. Rummenigge offered me the job. It was interesting, no doubt about it. The Bundesliga had lost a bit of its shine in recent years, but Germany had won the 1990 World Cup, and Bayern Munich were always Bayern Munich. I was given a few days to think about it.

But the truth is I wanted to return to Italy. Ahead of my third season with Benfica, Inter had contacted me to see if I wanted to go there. Benfica's sporting director, Gaspar Ramos, had convinced me to stay for at least another year. It had been a mistake to do that, and I was not prepared to make the same mistake again. I was drawn to Italy. I had unfinished business there. I wanted to win Serie A. So when another offer came, this time from Sampdoria, I knew immediately that I had to take it. Sampdoria was a team with big ambitions.

I met the owner Paolo Mantovani at the Loews Hotel in Monaco. He had sent a private plane to fetch me. Sampdoria's two big stars – Roberto Mancini and Gianluca Vialli – were with him. Mantovani said that these two had got it into their heads that I was the right man for the coaching job. So I might as well just talk to them. I had never experienced player power like that, but I immediately got along with Mancini and Vialli. They were winners. Sampdoria had won the league a year before and wanted to continue winning. That was the aim.

I told Mantovani that I would take the job. Now we just had to agree on the salary. Mantovani said that he would pay me the same as he had paid Boskov, the previous coach. He took out a napkin and wrote down a number. I looked at the napkin and thought, 'That's pretty good.' But Mantovani snatched back the napkin and crumpled it up.

'I can see that you're not happy,' he said.

Then he took a new napkin and wrote down a new number, which was considerably higher than the previous one. He gave me the napkin. I nodded. We had a deal. I was going back to Italy.

THE OLIVE TREES

ANKI was still a die-hard football fan. She came to most of my games. Her life, like mine, revolved around football. She loved the game. What she despised was the constant moving. She understood it was part of the job and very few football managers stayed in one place. But that did not mean she accepted it. When I got the offer to return to Italy, there was never any discussion whether or not I would take it. It was my career that decided where we should go. Anki wanted to stay in Portugal. We had found our dream house there. But it was once again time to pack our toothbrushes and move.

In Genoa, where Sampdoria played, we lived at first in a house that we did not like. Soon we moved into an apartment with an ocean view, but that was no good either. So we moved again, this time into a house on the outskirts of town. Anki's friend in Florence, who was an estate agent, arranged it. The house was old and large, with a big garden, and it was located just five minutes by car from the Sampdoria training ground, Bogliasco. Anki never really settled in Genoa, though. It was one move too many. When we were young, all the moving had been part of the adventure, but after ten years abroad, Anki no longer saw the adventure in it. I felt at home everywhere, as long as I had football. Anki needed more.

After a while it was no longer fun to come home from work. I knew there would be a lot of nagging. Sure, I understood Anki's frustrations. She was tired of sitting down for dinner only for the phone to ring and the food to get cold while I talked to the club president for an hour. Sometimes she screamed at me. I just walked away. I did not like fighting. I was never home at weekends. After training on Saturdays, the team and I always checked into a hotel before the Sunday game.

One day Anki had had enough. She wanted me to leave coaching. She asked me straight out. I did not have to leave football, she said. Perhaps there was another job within football that I could take. As long as I was not coaching. As long as I did not have to sleep with the team. This came as a complete shock to me. To stop coaching was unthinkable. What would I do if I didn't coach football? I was 45 years old. I had twenty years left of my career. Later, Anki maintained that we had struck a deal when we left Portugal that we would stay in Italy for two years and then return to Portugal to live a new life. I don't remember such an agreement. I don't think I would have ever agreed to leave football coaching.

● ● ●

From the time I first met Mantovani in Monaco, we struck up a special bond. He was an oil magnate, one of the few people who had been able to transport oil to Europe during the oil crisis in the late 1970s. That is how he made his money. At the end of the 1970s, he bought Sampdoria. The team was then stuck in Serie B, but with Mantovani's money, the club's fortunes soon changed. Sampdoria were promoted to Serie A and in 1991 won the scudetto. The following season, Sampdoria even made the European Cup final, losing to Barcelona. Mantovani had promised that he would invest more money in the club. It was my mission to win the league and after that bring home the European Cup.

After I signed the contract with Sampdoria and left Benfica, I went back to Värmland. A week or so before pre-season, Mantovani called me. Things had changed at the club, he explained. He could no longer compete financially with Milan, Juventus and Inter. He had to sell Vialli and bring the team to a lower level.

'I know that's not what I promised you, so if you want to get out of the contract, it's okay with me,' he said. 'But we would be very happy if you stayed.'

I said I would think about it. I was disappointed, of course. I had looked forward to taking over a potential championship team. Without Vialli and Mantovani's investments, it would be very difficult. At the same time, Sampdoria had a lot of young and promising players. Perhaps it was an opportunity to build something new. We were also getting close to pre-season and I did not have any other offers. I appreciated that Mantovani had been straight with me. So I called him back an hour later and said I had decided to stick with the job. Mantovani thanked me. It was much later that I learned other factors were at play, not just financial. I did not know it then, but Mantovani was sick.

● ● ●

One of the best words in the Italian language must be *rompipalle*. It literally means 'ballbreaker'. A *rompipalle* is an extremely demanding person. But it is an affectionate term. At least, I saw it that way. At Sampdoria, we had the biggest *rompipalle* I had ever met – Roberto Mancini, *rompipalle grandissimo*. I say that with utmost affection.

During my time at Roma, Falcão had talked to me about a young player they called 'Mancio'. He thought I should buy him. Mancio had moved from Bologna to Sampdoria when he was 17 years old. That was in 1982. During the following ten years, Mancini had developed into one of Serie A's biggest stars. When I came to Sampdoria, he was the club's undisputed king, especially after Mantovani sold Vialli. Mancini was a playmaker like Baggio. He was an incredibly intelligent player who saw things on the pitch that others did not see. In training, he was a leader but also someone who was open to new ideas. He wanted to be involved with everything. Before games he would call the kit man to make sure that the socks were put in their proper place. He infuriated me sometimes. But if I got angry, he just apologised, saying, 'Sorry, Mister.' It was impossible to stay angry with Mancini. Everyone loved him. But the person who loved him most was Mantovani.

Mantovani owned an enormous house on a hill in an exclusive area southeast of Genoa. From his house you could see the ocean below. We often ate lunch on his terrace. In the entrance of the house hung a gigantic painting depicting the Mantovani family tree. It was full of names. In the middle of the family tree, between himself and his wife, Mantovani had stuck a picture of Mancini. I don't think either his wife or children appreciated that very much. Before each away game, Mantovani would call me to ask if Mancini was playing. If not, Mantovani would not bother coming to the game. Mantovani had never had the same feelings for Vialli, not even when he was top scorer in Serie A. It was said that Mantovani thought Vialli 'just ran around scoring goals' whereas Mancini was an artist.

Vialli was not the only big-name player to leave Sampdoria before I took over. Toninho Cerezo, the Brazilian whom I had managed at Roma before he fell out with Dino Viola, had also moved on. As his replacement, we signed Vladimir Jugovic, who had won the European Cup with Red Star Belgrade. We tried to fill the Vialli vacancy with several young strikers, among them Enrico Chiesa. We also brought in an established English defender, Des Walker. Des had a lot of pace and I thought he would fit in well with our tough centre back, Pietro Vierchowod.

After racking up several wins, we were taught a lesson by Fiorentina, whose team included the Argentinian striking sensation Gabriel Batistuta. We lost 4–0 and Batistuta scored two goals. It soon became clear that Des Walker would struggle in Italy. In England, he had got away on pace alone. He could simply run down players. But that did not work in Italy. He was also too timid.

'You are playing as a centre back in Serie A and you practically don't have a single yellow card,' Vierchowod reprimanded Des Walker after half the season had gone.

We fell behind in the league relatively early. None of the young forwards really blossomed. Mancini was our leading scorer on fifteen goals and we finished seventh in the league. After the season's end, Des Walker returned to England. He would need to be replaced, but more than that, we needed top-class attacking players. During the summer I was constantly pushing Mantovani to make some signings. One day, just as the transfer window was about to close, he called to tell me that he had bought three players – Ruud Gullit, David Platt and Alberigo Evani. Three world-class players.

'I hope Mister Eriksson is satisfied now,' Mantovani said.

● ● ●

During my first season with Sampdoria, Johan had gone to an American school near us. Lina started there, too. But the following school year, Johan, who was then 14 years old, decided he wanted to go to a boarding school in Rome. It was his own decision. At home, Anki's and my relationship had deteriorated and I had discovered that there were other women in this world, and that some of them even seemed interested in Mister Eriksson.

One such woman was Graziella Mancinelli, a dark, curvy Italian beauty. Her son was a year or two older than Johan and went to the same school as he did. I had seen her there. We had said hello to each other, but nothing more. No flirting. But it was obvious that she had an interest in me. It was her way of smiling at me. She was divorced and single.

One autumn day in 1993, when I took Lina to school, Graziella and I got talking. I don't think I had thought things through, but I asked her if she wanted to meet me for dinner. I was pretty sure she would say yes. I did not have a mobile phone at that time, so I could not give her my number. Instead, we decided that we would meet at a restaurant outside Genoa, where we could keep things discreet. Anki was going to be away with the kids. I knew I was doing something I was not supposed to do. Lust and curiosity took over.

After that first date, Graziella and I started meeting more or less regularly, maybe once a week, sometimes at her place. She worked as a scientist at a laboratory that belonged to the Genoa hospital. To be with a new woman was exciting. I liked her and she liked me. It was not that I wanted to leave Anki and move in with Graziella. I don't think I thought too much about how the future would play out.

● ● ●

That autumn, Mantovani was hospitalised. We knew his health was poor. He chainsmoked and I think he had respiratory problems. Mantovani always talked about how good the climate was in Arizona, where he had a ranch. He spent a lot of time there. Sometimes he was in Switzerland, where his wife lived. They had two daughters and two sons, Enrico and Filippo. One day I visited Mantovani at the hospital. He had been there for a few weeks and knew he was dying. He wanted to ask me for a favour.

'Make sure my sons do not take over the club,' he said.

He did not think they could handle the job of running Sampdoria.

Paolo Mantovani died on 14 October 1993. The funeral was held at a church in Genoa and presided over by Mario, the Sampdoria priest. Mantovani had not wanted people to grieve at his funeral, but rather for it to be a celebration of his life, so when we came out of the church, a jazz band from New Orleans was waiting. As the coffin was carried in a procession around town, the band played and it was as if the entire city of Genoa came out into the streets to celebrate Mantovani. He was a man with a big heart and very much appreciated by everybody. At one point, one of the people along the road asked if a president had died. 'Yes,' I replied. 'The best president I ever had.'

I kept my promise to Mantovani and talked to his sons after his death about the future of the club. I explained to them what their father had told me, but it was futile. Football was in the Mantovani sons' blood. Soon after, Enrico took over as president of Sampdoria. Filippo and one of the sisters began working for the club, too. Enrico was smart and serious and he knew business. But he did not fit in to the antiquated business world of Italian football, run by old men and tradition. Enrico and I maintained a professional relationship, but things were never the same as during his father's time. Mancini's relationship with the Mantovani sons deteriorated as time went on. Perhaps there was some jealousy involved. It was, after all, not Enrico's photo that had been sitting in the middle of the family tree.

● ● ●

Despite tumultous times, the team were playing well. We won six of our first nine games, four of them away. The new signings were all a hit. The midfielder Evani, who had come from Milan, did not talk much, but instilled respect. Platt, whom we had bought from Juventus, was a happy-go-lucky guy who fitted right in to the team. The best buy of them all was Gullit, the brilliant Dutchman who had made a big name for himself at Milan during his six-year spell there. He scored goals from the outset. In Milan, Gullit had had a rocky relationship with his coach, Fabio Capello. Two weeks after Mantovani's death we were playing Milan at home. Gullit wanted nothing more than to show his old coach that he had made a mistake letting him leave Milan.

I wanted to beat Capello, too. He was clearly a good football coach, but at the same time, he'd had Europe's best team served up to him on a silver platter. Berlusconi had made Milan what it was. Capello had been groomed to take over from Sacchi. Berlusconi had sent Capello around the world to study football. He had even come to see me at Benfica to analyse my training methods.

We suffered a nightmare start to the game when Albertini scored for Milan. Soon after that, Brian Laudrup extended the lead to 2–0. It felt hopeless, but in the second half we came out as a new team. We got a goal back relatively early. Then Mancini converted a penalty, and, as the game was coming to its end, a long ball found Gullit. He received it on his chest and struck it on the half volley just inside the penalty area. It was a sweet strike. The Milan keeper got his fingers to the ball, but the shot was too hard and the ball went into the net. Gullit celebrated like a madman. It was as if all of his frustration with Milan had been unleashed with that one shot. We won 3–2.

After the game, I went to thank Capello for a good match. Usually we would just say thank you and that was that. This time, the first thing Capello said to me was not thank you. He said Milan should have had a free kick twenty seconds before Gullit scored the winner. A free kick? 'I don't think so,' I said and smiled.

● ● ●

As soon as the kids' Christmas holiday started, Anki travelled with them to Sweden. I followed a few days later and then returned on my own to Italy. We were playing Lazio on 2 January. One night, at a time when I was usually home, Anki called me. But I did not answer. I was with Graziella. Anki continued calling the whole night. When she finally got hold of me in the morning, she wondered where I had been. I did not answer. So she asked me straight out.

'Have you been with another woman?'

'Yes,' I replied.

There was a moment's pause.

'You can go to hell,' she said and hung up.

A few days later, Anki came back to Italy. There were heated discussions. Anki was angry and hurt, and understandably so. She said I had been gutless not to tell her about the other woman. Later, Anki claimed that I had promised her I would not see Graziella again, but I am not sure if that is so. In any case, I continued seeing Graziella. I think Anki suspected it. She invited both my brother and Tord to come to Italy to talk to me. Neither of them had much to say. There was not much to say. It was just the way it was. Anki and I continued sleeping in the same bedroom, but things were not good between us.

• • •

Football was football, and my private life was something else. My marital problems never affected how I did my job. Despite Mantovani's death and the rocky times, the club was having a great season. We had a very good balance in the team between older and younger players. We beat Roma away and Inter at home. The more we won, the more our self-confidence grew. Gullit said later that if the players had known from the start how good they really were, we would have won the league. Instead, we finished third, six points behind Milan and three points behind Juventus, having scored sixty-four goals, the most in Serie A that season. We also made it to the Cup final, beating Ancona 6–1. It was the perfect end to the season, which ended early because of the World Cup that summer.

We travelled with the team to China and Japan, and on 25 May 1994, played the Chinese national team in a packed stadium in Beijing. We were invited for dinner in the Forbidden City. Mancini did not want to eat Chinese food. He was a typical Italian – only Italian food was good enough for him.

Anki called me in China. She had found out that I had continued seeing Graziella. It turned out that Mario, the club priest, had told her. Mario's brother was our gardener. Mario would often come to visit his brother at our house. He played football with the kids. One day when I was away, he had suggested to Anki that he knew of our marital difficulties, but in order to talk to her candidly about it, Anki would have to come to confession. So she did. Mario had told her that he knew I was seeing another woman. When Anki asked if he knew who the woman was, Mario replied that she lived nearby. Anki knew immediately that he was talking about Graziella.

It was over between Anki and me. Anki would take the kids to Sweden. We had already separated, but Johan, who lived in Rome, did not know that. Anki said I had to go to Rome to fetch him and tell him the truth. I had to tell him that we were getting divorced. It was not an easy conversation. Johan was 15 years old and, unlike Lina, who was seven, he took the news very hard. I explained that I was still going to be his dad and that I was always going to be there for him.

It was time for me to move again. Out.

● ● ●

In the summer of 1994, I went to the United States to provide commentary for Swedish television from the World Cup and I took Graziella with me. I still did not like the media job that much, but it was a great way of experiencing a big football tournament. Everything was arranged for you – transport and tickets. All I had to do was show up. I travelled across the country with the seasoned Swedish presenters and realised how huge the United States is. When we had a few days off, Graziella and I went to Cape Cod and rented a cabin. Our relationship had not come out in Italy. Not that it would have caused a stir if it had.

Italy got to the final, losing to Brazil on penalties. Baggio, who made his international breakthrough while at Fiorentina with me, was the big star. He'd had a great tournament but he was the one who missed the deciding penalty. I really felt for him. He was a great guy.

Sweden also had a great tournament, finishing third after beating Bulgaria 4–0 in the match for third place. Tommy Svensson had taken over from Olle Nordin as manager, with Tord Grip as his assistant coach. I was invited to the celebratory dinner after the game in Los Angeles. Tommy Svensson gave a speech and said a few words about me and what I had meant for Swedish football. I liked Tommy. He was very good at creating a good atmosphere in a team. I also think he benefitted a lot from having Tord at his side. Tord did a lot of the tactical work. I think Tord was at least as important as Tommy in getting Sweden to third place in the World Cup. I flew back with the team to Sweden. It was an amazing journey. When we entered Swedish air space, two fighter jets came up on each side to escort the plane into Arlanda airport.

• • •

Back in Italy, we approached the new season with some confidence, having probably played the best football in Italy the previous term. But we suffered a huge setback before the season even started when Gullit decided he wanted to return to Milan. He had been our top goalscorer. More importantly, he had been a hugely positive influence on the team. It took me by surprise that he wanted to go back to Milan and Capello. We brought in a few new players, among them goalkeeper Walter Zenga, who was a very confident guy. He fitted in right away. The most important signing we made was Siniša Mihajlović, a Serb whom we brought in on loan from Roma.

Mihajlović had up until then played as a left winger. He was not fast enough for that position and I made him play left back instead, which he reluctantly agreed to do. Mihajlović was a tough guy who had opinions about almost everything, but I liked him from the beginning. He had the best left foot I had ever seen and will probably ever see. When Mancini went deep, Mihajlović could hit a sixty-yard cross that would land on Mancini's foot every time. It was more than just talent that made that possible. Mihajlović's sweet left foot was the product of hundreds, maybe thousands, of hours on the training pitch, hitting free kicks and crosses. Mihajlović would be out there before and after every training session, practising free kick after free kick. There were those who thought he should have spent more time practising with his right foot. My theory was that it was more important for a player to practise what he was already good at. Then he would possess a weapon that few opponents would be able to guard against.

Ahead of one match, we had trouble with injuries and suspensions in central defence. I told Mihajlović that I wanted him to play centre back.

'Me? Centre back? Never,' he said.

But I had made up my mind. Mihajlović played centre back and he did it so brilliantly that I kept him there. He played for me for many years to come. When he came to the club, he was on a pretty mediocre wage and he became one of the highest-paid players. I made him a very rich man.

After every goal he scored, he would run over to the bench and give me a big hug.

We started the season decently, but then lost 1–0 away to both Juventus and Roma. It was clear that the sting had been taken out of our attack with the loss of Gullit. After a couple of months I got a phone call. It was Gullit. Things had not worked out for him in Milan. He wanted to come back to us on loan. I was thrilled. I knew Gullit could make the difference in our attack, and in the beginning he scored some goals. But then he went on a dry spell that lasted a couple of months. Gullit was not as hungry as he used to be. His whole demeanour was different. He had become a player among others.

● ● ●

I moved into a house by the sea on my own. It belonged to an older lady. I rented the downstairs. From the living room and bedroom you walked into a big garden where there was a grill and a dining area. At the end of the garden, a gate opened on to the shore. You could practically dive straight into the sea. The garden was full of tall olive trees, which blocked the sun and needed trimming. The lady did not want to pay for that, so I offered to pay for it. The gardener who came to do it pruned the trees dramatically. They ended up about chest-high. The lady was shocked when she saw it. She said the garden looked like something out of Dante's *Inferno*.

Anki moved with the kids back to Florence, the city she had fallen in love with. The divorce took a year to finalise. I had never counted any of my money but it suddenly became a central issue when Anki and I got divorced. She got herself a lawyer, which meant I had to get one, too. We had some money deposited in banks in Italy and Switzerland, which we split 50–50. I got the house in Portugal; she got the summer house in Åmål and additional cash.

Her father got involved with the financial dealings. He and I had had an argument over the summer in Sweden. Anki's parents were sad and disappointed about how things had turned out between Anki and me. Her mum, Mait, yelled at me. I could understand that. But when Karl-Erik started lecturing me about money and how I had better take care of Anki financially, I got really mad. He brought up a bunch of trivial stuff and wanted me to sign some papers saying I would not lay claim to a summer house that Anki and her brother had inherited. What did I care about an old summer house of theirs? I was insulted that he thought I would not care about Anki and the kids.

'I'm not as finicky as you about money,' I told him.

That made him quiet. We were not on speaking terms for a while after that, but with time things got better. Her parents were able to see things from my perspective, too. Mait had always criticised Anki for taking the kids to Sweden the first chance she got.

'You are married, but you are away from your husband for months,' she told Anki. 'He is only doing his job.'

After Anki moved, it was tough. Sometimes the kids came to visit in Genoa and watched our home games on Sundays. Every Monday, when we had a day off, I would drive the two hours to Florence to see them. I was not welcome at Anki's house, however. Most of the time I took the kids to dinner at a restaurant. It was all very awkward. Lina was too small to understand what had happened. Johan, on the other hand, knew exactly what was going on. In the beginning, he took his mother's side. He was probably pretty mad with me. When I dropped off the kids after dinner, Anki would yell at me.

There were times when I regretted how things had turned out. I felt guilty. I remember one time coming back to Genoa after a particularly emotional visit and Johan calling me. He wanted me to make things right. Everything. But with time, matters got better. After a while, Anki would let me into her house. We could even have dinner, all of us together.

● ● ●

Victory in the previous season's Cup gave us entry to the 1995 Cup Winner's Cup. It was the first time one of my teams had participated in that tournament since Gothenburg in 1980. Then we had been completely outplayed by Arsenal in the quarter-final. This time in the quarter-finals, Sampdoria were going to play Porto, who were managed by Bobby Robson. There has never been a nicer man than Bobby Robson. I will forever remember how he invited me, an unknown Swedish football coach, to sit next to him on the bench during an Ipswich match.

We lost the first leg at home 1–0. In Porto for the return leg, I ran into Pinto da Costa, Porto's president, and reminded him of the match with Benfica a few years earlier, when the Porto officials refused to let us into our dressing room. He just laughed. I would have the last laugh this time. We won 1–0 and the tie went to penalties. We scored all five of ours and went through to the semi-final, where Arsenal waited. In the first game at Highbury, Steve Bould, the Arsenal defender, scored two goals, one of them after a big mistake by Zenga, our keeper. We came back with a couple of crucial away goals and, although Arsenal won 3–2, we were still in with a good chance.

At Sampdoria we had some of the most rabid supporters in Italy. At our stadium, Stadio Luigi Ferrari, the stands were close to the pitch, creating

an intimate and intense atmosphere. The supporters had whipped themselves into a near frenzy by the time the game against Arsenal kicked off.
When Mancini scored early on, the fans were euphoric. At that point, we
were through on away goals. But in the second half, Arsenal's Ian Wright
equalised. Now, Arsenal were through. Time ticked away. With ten minutes
left, I threw on a 19-year-old striker, Claudio Bellucci, who until then had
not played many games. After a couple of minutes on the pitch he scored,
and soon after that we scored again for 3–1. It looked as if we had secured
our place in the final.

But with two minutes left of regular time, Arsenal got a free kick outside
our penalty area. The Arsenal player who lined up to hit it with his left
foot was Stefan Schwarz, a former Benfica player of mine. Stefan had a
ferocious left-foot shot and he struck the ball perfectly. The ball went in
at the bottom right corner. Arsenal had their important second away goal
and the game went to extra time and then penalties. Against Porto in the
quarters, we had scored all five penalties – not this time. Arsenal's goalkeeper David Seaman was one of the world's foremost penalty stoppers.
He saved Mihajlović's first penalty, and the next one, which Jugovic took.
Maspero and Mancini scored for us, but Seaman saved our fifth strike,
from Lombardo, and Arsenal were through to the Cup Winner's Cup final.
We had come so close. But I did not feel I had made any mistakes. As a
manager, I was not able to exert much influence on the outcome of a
penalty shootout. At least, that's how I felt then.

● ● ●

After Paolo Mantovani's death, Sampdoria became a selling club. Before
my fourth season there, David Platt went to Arsenal. We lost Vierchowod

and Lombardo to Juventus. Gullit went to Chelsea. Established players were replaced by some who were up-and-coming, including Clarence Seedorf and Christian Karembeu. Filippo Mantovani found them. He had an impressive network of contacts. Later on, he became an agent.

Seedorf, a 19-year-old Dutchman with his roots in Suriname, came from Ajax, where he had been educated in that club's famous football academy. He had marvellous technique, but could play only short, quick passes, which is what he had done at Ajax. He thought we played too defensively. I had many discussions with him about it. When I benched him a few times, he was distraught. In time he learned that there were actually ways to play football other than the all-out attacking game he had been taught at Ajax, and he became a better player. When we beat Juventus 3–0 away in the spring, Seedorf scored one of the goals and was the man of the match.

Midfielder Karembeu was a Frenchman who grew up in New Caledonia, a small island in the South Pacific. I had never seen anyone with a greater work capacity than Karembeu. When he ran intervals in training, no one was able to keep up. I asked him how on earth he could run so much and never get tired. He explained that he grew up in a large family and each child had been given a job to do. His was to fetch bread from a shop located several miles away. Each morning he had run there and back, faster and faster.

One player who truly blossomed was Enrico Chiesa. He scored twenty-two goals that season and formed a formidable partnership with Mancini. Mancini became a father figure to Chiesa. Not that Mancini always set a perfect example. After being denied a penalty at home to Inter, Mancini began shouting at the referee. It ended with him ripping off the captain's armband and storming off the field, vowing never to play again. I convinced him to return to the match, only for him to be sent off for a wild tackle on Paul Ince. Mancini was suspended for six games. We finished eighth that season, twenty-one points behind the champions, Milan.

● ● ●

I had been at Sampdoria for four seasons, longer than I would stay with any club in my career. I knew things would not get much better at the club but even though we could not compete with the best teams in Italy, I still enjoyed myself there. I had found a nice rhythm to life. Graziella and I often went out for dinner. I did not really have any obligations, except to my children. So when the club, ahead of my fifth season there, once again sold some of our best players – Chiesa to Parma, Seedorf to Real Madrid – I received the news with relative calm.

We brought in a fantastic young player who would go on to be one of my absolute favourites – Juan Sebastián Verón, a 21-year-old Argentinian midfielder from Boca Juniors. Verón was a more offensive-minded player than the other South American midfielders I had managed, Falcão and Dunga, and he had incredible vision, like Mancini. I had some trouble with him off the pitch, however. Verón had a reputation as a party guy and he liked going to nightclubs. After a while, I tired of hearing about his nightly escapades.

'If you want to party, do it at home,' I told him.

We had a better season than the one before, finishing sixth in the league, twelve points ahead of Juventus, which meant we had qualified for the UEFA Cup the following year.

But my ambitions were, after all, higher than to fight for UEFA Cup places. After five years at Sampdoria, it was time to move on. It had been a time of great change for me personally. I had left my family. Strangely enough, though, I felt that those years at Sampdoria had been the happiest of my life. When I moved out of the house, the old lady whom I had rented the downstairs apartment from told me she was sad to see me go. I had been right about the olive trees, she said. They had needed to be cut and had grown back perfectly.

We always spent Christmas at home with the family in Värmland. The Christmas goat has been with us since I was born. I still have it somewhere in Björkefors.

I graduated from primary school – ninth grade – in 1964. We are standing outside the house my parents built in Torsby. To my mother, there was nothing more important than my education. She was not given the opportunity to further her own education. My father was less concerned with school matters. But he looks pretty proud of me here.

It seems like I have perfect control of the ball. I would not be surprised, though, if I lost it the second after the picture was taken. As a football player, my technique was never my strong suit.

The big derby between Sifhälla and Säffle in 1971. I was a hard worker in midfield. What I lacked in sophistication, I made up for with sheer determination.

The 1967 Torsby line-up. Standing to the far left is "Åsen", baker and football coach. Third from the left is Arne West. He could have made it to the top, but he didn't want to leave Torsby. Sitting front row far left is Leif Gunnarsson, who had the prettiest girlfriend in town. I am sitting in the front row second from the right.

KB Karlskoga 1973. I am in the front row, third from the left. I must have just broken into the team then. Tord is in the back row, fifth from the left. It was his last season at Karlskoga. He was still player-manager then.

At Degerfors, I was given a car sponsored by Opel. It had the club logo and my name on the side. The players also got cars. Football was serious business in Degerfors, even though we played in the third division.

This photo is actually taken before Anki and I got married. We stopped on our way to Norway, where the wedding took place, to snap photos. There was a heat wave in Sweden at the time and we were both sweating. The photographer took way too long and I got irritated. We came close to getting divorced before the wedding!

Going for a walk near my parents' house in Torsby. I am not sure exactly how old Johan is in the picture. He was three when we moved to Portugal. Johan was a bundle of energy as a child. He barely slept during the first two years of his life.

At IFK Gothenburg, I was coaching the best team in Sweden. But my third season with the club started with three straight losses. I offered to resign. But the players wanted me to stay. Good thing I did.

I am sitting in a hotel room in Enschede, Holland in 1980. We were going to play against Twente. People often tell me how glamorous my life of travelling is. It is true that I have travelled more than most. But as a football manager, almost all you see is airplanes, hotel rooms and stadiums. It is not a life for everyone, but I love it.

Roy Hodgson was one of my main role models as a young football coach. Roy and Bob Houghton were enormously successful in Sweden before they returned to England in 1980 to co-manage Bristol City. This picture is taken in 1982.

Left: Dan Corneliusson opens the scoring in the 1982 UEFA Cup final. You would have heard a pin drop at the Volkparkstadion in Hamburg, if it were not for the 5,000 Gothenburg supporters going wild.

Right: Conny Karlsson raises the UEFA Cup trophy. We were the first Swedish football team to ever win a European club tournament. The team was so well-drilled, it no longer needed a coach. In Torbjörn Nilsson, we had the best forward in European football at the time. He proved that in the final.

On my first day at Benfica, I was taken to the club's trophy room. It was among the most impressive places I have ever seen. I suppose that was the point of bringing me there. From then on, I knew what was expected of me.

Standing with one of the greatest legends in the history of football: Eusébio. Before I came to Benfica, Eusébio had worked as an ambassador for the club. I made him the goalkeeping coach.

Glenn Strömberg was 23 years old when I brought him to Benfica. He was not as cocky then as he had been as a teenager in Gothenburg, but he was a brilliant footballer with an unwavering winner's mentality.

Left: Nisse Liedholm and I shake hands at a match between Roma and Milan in 1986. "Il Barone", as Liedholm was called, was nearing the end of his long and glorious footballing career. I was still on my way up.

Below: Having a chat with Cerezo and Conti in Roma in 1984. It was the worst year of my coaching career. I took over a tired and unmotivated team. But Cerezo was a player who always worked hard. When I got into my car to go home from training, I would see Cerezo still out on the pitch, training on his own.

Left: Posing for a picture in Florence with Glenn Hysén and one of the biggest legends in Swedish football history, "Kurre" Hamrin. "Kurre" was my tennis partner during the years we lived there. We played epic games that lasted for hours.

IL MITICO

10

TOWARDS the end of my final season at Sampdoria I had been contacted by Athole Still, an agent I had met for the first time ten years earlier at Roma when he tried to sell me John Barnes. No deal was made and Barnes went to Liverpool instead. During the following years I met Still here and there. We had never done business together, but now he called me about a job offer – Blackburn, who were a Premier League team, wanted me as manager.

Blackburn were owned by steel magnate Jack Walker, who had pumped enormous sums of money into the club since taking it over in 1991. His investments had yielded results. In 1995, Blackburn won their first league title in over eighty years. However, the following year, the team finished seventh and the year after that lower still. Now Jack Walker wanted to get back to the top. When men like him win, they always want to win again. I went to meet him at his daughter's house outside Blackburn. He had left England for tax reasons many years earlier and moved to Jersey in the Channel Islands, where he owned an airline, Jersey European Airways. He told me about his future plans for the club and that he was going to strengthen the squad with new players. It sounded good and after Athole negotiated the deal, I signed the contract. After that, I travelled with Walker in his private plane to Jersey. On the plane, Walker, who spoke with a lisp, said, 'Now that we're friends, you can call me Johnny.' Then he pulled out a bottle of Johnny Walker.

From Jersey the plane brought me back to Italy. I told Mancini that I had accepted the job at Blackburn and asked if he wanted to come with me. Mancio was very curious about English football, but problems arose when I told Walker that I wanted to bring Mancini with me to Blackburn. How much would he cost? 'Nothing in the transfer fee,' I said. Mancini's wage demands were high, but I told Walker that Mancio was worth it. Walker was not convinced. He was unwilling to pay so much for Mancini and blocked any deal. I was very disappointed. Things had not got off to a good start with Blackburn. It was then that I got another phone call.

Sergio Cragnotti was the enormously wealthy owner of food conglomerate Cirio – and Lazio football club. He was calling with an offer for me to manage Lazio. Cragnotti had poured money into his club in the beginning of the 1990s. Now he wanted to win the league – the Italian league, which I had tried for ten years to win. It was a chance of a lifetime. I had to take it. After Jack Walker had said no to Mancini, I had had second thoughts about Blackburn but how could I get out of a signed contract? I decided to call Jack Walker and ask to meet him.

In a room at Milan airport, I explained to Walker that I wanted to pull out of the Blackburn job. Walker was stunned. That would leave Blackburn in a big jam, he said. He tried to convince me to stay. Maybe he would be willing to bring in Mancini after all.

Maybe it was an irony of fate, but at that very moment it came out that Roy Hodgson had been fired from his job at Inter. Roy was an Englishman. He would be perfect for Blackburn. I had no reservations in recommending Roy for the job. Jack thought about it. He understood that I no longer wanted the Blackburn job. 'Okay,' he said, tore up the contract and wished me good luck.

● ● ●

Historically, Lazio had never been one of the big teams in Italy, or even in Rome. Lazio had won the league just once, in 1974, but Cragnotti was determined to make Lazio the best team in Italy and he was not willing to tolerate anything less. Halfway into the previous season, the manager, Zdeněk Zeman, had been sacked after two straight home losses. Legendary goalkeeper Dino Zoff had taken over for the rest of the season. Now I had arrived and expectations were sky high.

A negative mood prevailed in the team. Many of Lazio's big players had been there for years without winning anything. The club now had the financial firepower, but Lazio were still seen as losers. After my years at Fiorentina and Sampdoria, some people had started calling me *Il Perdente Successo*, 'the successful loser'. There were whispers among journalists that Eriksson would never win the league. I hated that. I had to make Lazio my team and instil a winning attitude in the club.

Lazio's big star was forward Giuseppe Signori. In five years he had scored over a hundred goals for the club and won the title of top scorer in Serie A a couple of times. Signori was known for his penalty kicks, which he took without a run-up to the ball. The fans loved him. But I never got on with Signori, and he did not fit in with my way of thinking about football. He had a negative attitude. Lazio would never win anything, he maintained. He was exactly what we did not need. We needed winners.

We had one winner in Alessandro Nesta. As an 18-year-old, Nesta had broken into the Lazio senior team. Now he was 21 and on his way to becoming one of the world's best central defenders. We also had Czech midfielder Pavel Nedved. He had come to Lazio the season before and scored seven goals. But we needed more winners. I went to Cragnotti and told him that if we bought three players – Mancini, Mihajlović and Verón – we would win the league. It was a pretty arrogant statement, and not really typical of me. Cragnotti was not convinced. Of the three, he got me Mancini.

Instead, we bought Alen Bokšić, a Croatian forward who had played for Lazio before but then moved on to Juventus; Matías Almeyda, a tough-tackling Argentinian defensive midfielder; and Vladimir Jugović, whom I had managed at Sampdoria. I liked players with whom I had worked before and with whom I had a good rapport. We started the season in mediocre fashion, however, and suffered four losses in our first eleven games. On the way home from a cup game against Fiorentina, our team bus broke down on the freeway. Signori whined. He said things like that only happened at Lazio.

'Have you ever heard of Milan's team bus breaking down?' he asked.

In light of Signori's negative influence on the team, I went to Cragnotti and told him that Signori had to go. Impossible! Signori was 'Mister Lazio'. After a while, I benched Signori, which he did not like much. When I asked him to warm up during an away game in the UEFA Cup but then did not put him on, he completely lost his head, screaming at me. I think that was the final straw. Signori himself wanted to leave and a few days later we sold half of his ownership rights to Sampdoria where he played for the rest of the season.

What I did not know, and what Cragnotti had not told me, was that, a few years earlier, the club had tried to sell Signori to Parma. The fans had become enraged and stormed Formello, the Lazio training ground. The club had backed off and Signori had stayed.

I did not anticipate the negative reaction that my decision to sell Signori would generate. A few days later we played at home to Udinese. I started with Mancini and Casiraghi with Bokšić on the bench. None of the forwards scored and we lost 2–3. At the press conference afterwards, all the questions were about Signori. Things got a lot worse the next day at training at Formello. The fans were furious. They climbed over the fences and into the training ground to confront Mister Eriksson, the idiot who had sold the club's talismanic striker. The police advised us to abandon training, and told me to leave Formello through the back door. I refused. I was not going to slink out, tail between my legs. I had not done anything wrong. I got into my car, alone, and drove through the main gate. There must have been over a thousand Lazio supporters there, all screaming, 'Signori! Signori! Signori!'

Things got completely out of control. Several of the supporters jumped on to my car. They were lying on the bonnet, screaming at me. I tried to inch forward, but I did not get anywhere. It was nasty, of course, but somehow I was not scared. I did not think they would kill me. Who would manage their team then? Finally, I was able to make some headway. As I drove off, I could still hear the furious fans chanting, 'Signori! Signori! Signori!'

The next week we lost to Juventus away, 2–1. That was the last time we lost for several months. We went undefeated for sixteen league games. Soon, no one was asking about Signori any more.

• • •

When I returned to Rome I moved into one of the smaller apartments in the Viola residence, where we had lived before. I was single now. Graziella had wanted to move with me to Rome, but I think I had tired of her. Lina lived with Anki in Florence and sometimes came to visit on weekends. Johan had graduated from high school and moved to the United States, where he was going to study sports psychology.

In the autumn of 1997, I decided to invite a Swedish woman whom I knew to Rome. The team had the weekend off and she and I went to Saturnia Thermae, a spa near Rome that was known for its hot springs. One evening as we were having dinner, a woman and two men came walking towards us. The woman was a dark beauty, the kind whom other guests turned around to watch.

'Wow!'

The older of the two men introduced himself as Giancarlo, a major Romanista. How could Mister Eriksson sign on to manage Roma's arch rivals, Lazio, he asked, jokingly. He claimed that the football Roma had played during my second year at the club was the best football he had ever seen. Giancarlo was a pleasant man, short and stocky, but I could not take my eyes off the woman. It turned out she was his wife, Nancy Dell'Olio. We chatted for a while before they went to their table. The next day we met them again, this time at the swimming pool. Nancy wondered if I would like to come over for dinner sometime at her and her husband's place in Rome. Yes, I said, that would be very nice.

It did not take long before she called with an invitation for dinner. A handful of other people were there, too. Giancarlo was a lawyer and, judging from their luxurious apartment in Parioli in the northern part of Rome, a successful one. Nancy was also a lawyer, but she did not seem to work very much. At the dinner table, she put me next to her. I had a very nice evening. The other guests were politicians and attorneys. Someone was an artist. No one worked in football, but everyone wanted to talk football with me. Nancy soon invited me for dinner again and then again. She always wanted me to sit next to her at the dinner table.

On 5 February 1998 I turned 50 and celebrated with a party at a restaurant and nightclub in Rome called Bella Blu. I invited fifty or sixty people, among them Riccardo and Anna Viola, as well as Anki. Cragnotti came along with some other people from the club, but no players. I firmly believe managers should not socialise with their players. Nancy came, of course, together with Giancarlo and Silvio, the man who had been with them at the spa the first time we met. I did not bring a date. After the party, I went home with Riccardo and Anna and Anki, who was staying at their place. The four of us had a drink and the talk turned to Nancy. She had apparently made a big impression on everyone, not just on me. Anki said, 'I bet Nancy Dell'Olio will soon end up in Mister Eriksson's bed, if she hasn't already.'

Naturally, Anki's prediction would come true. During another dinner at Nancy's, she and I were left alone in the room at one point. She asked me when I was going to ask her out for lunch. I said, okay, when would she like to meet?

'Tomorrow,' she replied.

'Any ideas where?' I asked.

'How about at your place,' she responded.

There was no doubt where that was going to lead. I don't know if we ate much lunch, maybe some toast. She had not come over for the food.

● ● ●

Football is a team sport and generally requires players who can fit into a group. Alen Bokšić was, above all, an individualist. If I told him we needed to act as a team, he had no idea what I was talking about. In his youth in Yugoslavia, he said he never passed the ball. As an attacker, he did not see it that often, he said, so that when he got the ball he did not want to let go of it. Then he laughed his high-pitched laugh, hi-hi-hi!

I liked Bokšić. Although the collective and team spirit had always been fundamental building blocks for me in football, I also knew that you had to make room for individualists with special talents. Bokšić was definitely a special talent. He had everything – pace, vision and divine technical skills – but he also had some kind of mental block. In training, he would score for fun. In games, something happened to him. In our first eleven games, he scored one goal. I decided to call Willi Railo.

Willi flew to Rome and made a deal with Cragnotti to work with Alen. Willi would get paid for each goal that Alen scored above his goal tally from the previous season. I think it was about £10,000 a goal. Alen loved working with Willi. I think he scored ten goals that season. Cragnotti joked that he would go bankrupt if Alen continued scoring. Willi wanted to go on working with Alen. He claimed he could make him the greatest player in the world but Cragnotti was happy with Alen getting back to scoring and Willi flew back to Norway.

A few years later I wrote a book with Willi Railo. *Sven-Göran Eriksson On Soccer* it was called. The book was about how to develop a winning attitude, an important quality not just in football but in everyday life. It sold pretty well. Willi used it in his lectures and I think he made good money from it. I did not see any money, however. Willi blamed some Dutch publisher, but that is where our relationship ended. I know Willi developed a problem with alcohol and died a few years later. I did not find out about his death until a long time after his funeral.

• • •

With seven games left of my first season at Lazio, we were third in the league, one point behind Inter and two points behind Juventus. On 5 April 1998, when we played Juventus at home, we had a chance to go top of the league. Stadio Olimpico, which we shared with Roma, was sold out and fantastic tifosi created a magnificent atmosphere. Despite it being late in the season we had no injuries and could field our strongest team. Juventus also had a very strong team, with Zinedine Zidane and Edgar Davids in midfield, Pippo Inzaghi and Alessandro Del Piero up front. The team was managed by Marcelo Lippi, who had won Serie A in his first season with Juventus a few years earlier.

It was a tight game with few clear-cut opportunities. In the sixtieth minute, Zidane hit an outswinging corner that Pippo Inzaghi met with a perfect header: 1–0 Juventus. I took off Almeyda and threw on Casiraghi, an attacker, but then Nedved was red-carded and after that it was good-night. We lost five of our last six games and finished seventh in the league, eighteen points behind Juventus.

We did, however, reach the Cup final, where we faced Capello's Milan. The first leg was played three days after we had lost to Juventus in the league. Milan won 1–0 after African superstar George Weah scored in the ninetieth minute. Without an away goal, things looked bleak for the return leg in Rome, and after Albertini scored for Milan with a shot perfectly placed in the bottom corner of the net, we needed to score three to win the Cup. I could see the headlines: 'Eriksson, Il Perdente Successo, falling on the last hurdle'.

Hope was reignited when Gottardi, who never scored, first equalised for us and just a few minutes later was fouled by Maldini for a penalty, which Jugovic converted. Suddenly, we were playing like a team possessed. Casiraghi hit the post, and just a few minutes later Nesta scored when Milan failed to clear the ball after a corner. The match ended 3–1 and Lazio had won their first trophy in twenty-four years. The club had won the Cup just once before, in 1958. Cragnotti was thrown up in the air by the players, while Capello walked around the pitch sulking. In the papers the next day, Lazio were described as worthy winners. They wrote that Mister Eriksson, much maligned after getting rid of Signori, had shown everyone what a world-class coach he was.

One week later, we were due to play another final, the UEFA Cup. This year, for the first time, it would be decided with one game. We would face Inter at the Parc des Princes in Paris on 5 May 1998.

During the whole season I had worked on trying to instil a winning attitude in the team. A winning team was never satisfied, I told my players. Real winners had to keep on winning. However, it turned out my players were pretty satisfied with the Cup victory. In Paris, they did not have much more to give. We were outplayed. Zamorano scored early for Inter, and in the second half Zanetti and Ronaldo added a second and third. Inter won comfortably 3–0. It was clear that I still had a lot of work to do. Lazio were not yet a team of winners.

• • •

Nancy and Giancarlo had a boat called *Nancy One* on which they travelled around the Greek islands. I had joined them on one such weekend excursion before Nancy and I became intimate. One summer day, Nancy called and asked if I wanted to join her and some friends on the *Nancy One*. She had not told Giancarlo about the invitation. Her female friends were in the know about what was going on between Nancy and me, and so was Silvio. He was coming along on the trip as well.

Silvio was a good-looking playboy from a wealthy family. Silvio's days panned out pretty much the same. He would wake up around lunchtime and go to the tennis club. After playing a few games he would sit and smoke and play cards with friends. Around seven o'clock in the evening, he made his daily call to the family business to check on that day's receipts. Then it was time for dinner and partying after that.

On the boat, Silvio, who was a very good swimmer, had one job, probably the only job he had ever had. He was nominated to collect sea urchins that we could eat as hors d'oeuvres before lunch. He always brought back a bag full, which the crew cut up and served with champagne. It was a very pleasant holiday.

I also went with Nancy to France for the 1998 World Cup. We watched Brazil play in Marseille. We did not want to be seen so I arranged the tickets through a friend, not through FIFA, which I would have otherwise done. We sat far up in the stands, away from any attention.

After that, Nancy and Giancarlo came to Stockholm. I sent a limousine to collect them at Arlanda airport, and made sure there were roses and champagne in the car. Roger Palmgren, a football coach who had visited me at Sampdoria and was from Stockholm, arranged for balloon rides and excursions in the Stockholm archipelago. At one point I think Roger took Giancarlo back to the hotel so that I could spend some time alone with Nancy. I had feelings of guilt towards Giancarlo. He was a good man and he loved Nancy. He always carried her bags. She was expensive and impossible, but still the best thing that had happened to him, he said. I think he was trying to tell me not to take her away from him. I probably should have listened to him.

●　●　●

There had always been money to make, and lose, in football but towards the end of the 1990s, something happened that radically changed the financial playing field – the money paid for television rights to broadcast football skyrocketed. As a result, the salaries of players and coaches went through the roof. I never knew exactly how much money I had made at each club, but my salary at Sampdoria had probably been around two million kronor, or £200,000, a year. When I went to Lazio, I probably got twice that. When the television money came into play, my salary basically tripled overnight. Tom Egger, a Swiss banker whom I had known since my time at Roma, took care of my money. Every month, part of my salary was deposited in a bank account in Geneva and I never touched it.

With the boost in television money, Cragnotti had even bigger resources to spend to make Lazio one of Italy's great clubs and win the league. All the club owners I had worked with in Italy were genuine football fans, but there was no one who showed greater passion for the game than Cragnotti. He often came to Formello to talk football. One morning, after I had stayed there overnight, Cragnotti knocked on my door at seven o'clock in the morning. He had just returned from one of his business trips to Brazil and come straight from the airport to Formello. We were having breakfast alone in the restaurant when the TV news suddenly showed that Princess Diana had been killed in a car crash in Paris. It was probably the only time that Cragnotti and I did not talk football.

Cragnotti understood that Lazio needed to invest more to win more. It all boiled down to the players we had. A few players left, including Jugovic. In their place, we brought in midfielders Attilio Lombardo, Sérgio Conceição and Dejan Stanković, as well as another one of the three players I had wanted in the first season – Mihajlović.

Most of all we needed forwards, players who could win games for us. I have always said that if you have a great number ten, a playmaker, and a top number nine, a striker, you have come a long way. We had the number ten in Mancini, but we had not had a real goalscorer the previous season. Nedved, a midfielder, had been our top scorer with eleven goals. Casiraghi left the club and in his place we bought Chilean Marcelo Salas for 26 billion lire, a huge sum of money. Salas had been a big success at River Plate in Argentina and also scored four goals for Chile in the recent World Cup in France.

Cragnotti was not done. He thought we needed a real star striker. I had heard that Christian Vieri was unhappy at Atletico Madrid, despite being top scorer in Spain the previous season. We set up a meeting with Atletico in Milan. After coffee, negotiations began. How much would Vieri cost? Fifty billion lire, the Atletico director replied, about £30 million, which would make the deal one of the most expensive transfers of all time.

'That is a lot of money,' Cragnotti said.

'Yes, but he scores a lot of goals,' I reminded him.

Cragnotti asked if I would be interested in giving up one or two of our players in exchange. Atletico was especially interested in Nedved and Stankovic but there was no way I was going to let those two go.

'Okay,' said Cragnotti. 'I guess we have to do business the usual way.'

He did not try to bargain. The deal was made in five minutes.

Cragnotti was a cool man with great charisma. He never raised his voice and we had a fantastic relationship. Everyone knew that he was a big businessman. He always had a pack of advisers around him. It was unclear to me, however, exactly how he had made his money, unversed as I was in business. Probably I did not want to know, either. But I began to wonder if maybe Cragnotti had played a skillful game with me over the sale of Signori. It is possible that he too had felt it was time to get rid of Signori, but perhaps he did not want to be the one to face the wrath of the fans. Perhaps he had let me take the hit. He was clever that way, Cragnotti, and could play two hands at once.

● ● ●

The pieces were falling into place. Lazio was becoming my team. I still wanted to make one signing on the coaching side, though – Tord Grip. During all my years abroad, Tord and I had been in constant contact, often daily. His wife Siw had passed away some years earlier, but he had met another woman, Inga, with whom he was very happy. He often came to visit me and he was the first person I called with any football-related questions. He knew everything, and almost everything I knew about football I had learned from Tord. He knew that, too. Tord was a skilled instructor, both verbally and physically. Most of all, he was brilliant at handling players, especially those who had been left out of a team. The rules that had prevented me from taking a non-Italian as an assistant had just been changed, and so I immediately brought Tord to Lazio.

We trained twice a day. I would arrive at Formello at 8.30 a.m. to prepare for the first session, which would start at ten sharp. At eleven we stretched. At one it was time for lunch, and the chef would bring fresh pasta on the dot. The players ate together. No one could leave the table until everyone was done. And so it went. The whole day was scheduled to the last minute. If anyone was late for the team bus, he had to pay a fine. One time during a pre-season camp, we were all sitting in the bus with thirty seconds to departure. Tord had still not showed up. It was raining hard and suddenly Tord came running up in his socks, which were soaking wet. He had not been able to find his football shoes, but he did not want to be late for the bus. The players cheered.

The season began poorly and we won just three of our first eleven games. We were not creative enough in the middle of the pitch. One day Mancini came into my office to talk to me. He asked if I would be open to trying him as a central midfielder. It was the most idiotic thing I had ever heard. Mancio as a central midfielder? He was a second striker. He was incapable of defending. But I mulled over his idea in my head and, finally, I decided to give it a shot.

'But you have to start running,' I told him.

The thing is, Mancini did not have to run as much as other central midfielders did, because he always made the right runs. He could read the game and see when to intercept a pass instead of trying to tackle. We were surprised when we checked the statistics – Mancini won as many balls in midfield as Almeyda did. At the same time, Salas and Viera started to gel. From the end of November to early April, we did not lose a single match. During one stretch, we won nine in a row.

Football was easy that way. Every problem had a solution. Sometimes you had to act fast, sometimes you had to wait and think things over. It was important to be open to new ideas, such as bringing Mancini back to a deeper position. It was the world outside of football that was more complicated. To me, it was important to separate the two worlds, even if that was not always easy.

In Kosovo, a war was raging, and NATO was bombing Serbia. Our two Serbs, Stanković and Mihajlović, both had parents, siblings and relatives in Serbia. It was a hard time for them. I talked to the players and told them that I understood if they had different opinions about what was going on in the Balkans, but it was not our war. We were a football team and we had to stick together. We could not let anything affect our performance. Mihajlović later got into trouble when he travelled to Serbia and expressed support for the warlord Arkan. I don't know exactly what he said. Maybe I did not want to know, either.

I didn't believe that I should publicly express opinions about things I knew nothing about. At the same time, I had a moral responsibility to address public issues that were related to football. Italy had long had a racism problem among its football fans, and unfortunately the Lazio supporters were the worst offenders. A small but vocal minority would stand at Curva Nord, one of the sections of the stadium, and shout obscenities at black players. Before I arrived, the club had one black player, Dutch midfielder Aron Winter, but he had left by the time I got there. There were black players whom I wanted to sign, but Cragnotti was reluctant to do it. He did not want to risk any scandal. During my time at Lazio, racism was the only problem we had at the club and it bothered me a great deal. Lazio became a big club, but their reputation would be forever tarnished by the racist abuse that some of its fans directed at black players.

• • •

I have never liked confrontation but I had to face up to it regarding one matter that I had avoided for too long – Giancarlo. Nancy wanted to get out of her marriage. I called Giancarlo and wondered if I could stop by the following day. When I told my assistant manager, Luciano Spinosi, that I was planning to tell Nancy's husband about her and me, Spinosi hit the roof.

'Don't! You don't know Italian men – he can shoot you dead,' he said.

But I knew I had to. When I got there, Giancarlo was in a good mood and kind to me as usual. He called me his good friend and offered me some champagne. Nancy was there, too. I had talked to her about how to handle the situation. She was very nervous, running up and down the stairs, incapable of sitting still. Giancarlo and I chatted about nothing. Finally, I had to tell him there was something important I wanted to talk about.

'The thing is, Giancarlo . . .' I started.

I explained that I liked his wife. That I liked Nancy. And not just liked, maybe I was even in love with her. And she was in love with me. Giancarlo sat there, listening. I don't think he had suspected what I was telling him. But as usual, he kept calm. He told Nancy to sit down and asked her if what I was saying was true. She nodded. Giancarlo took the bottle of champagne and poured some more for Nancy. Then he turned to me and said, 'Sven, I think it is best if you leave us so that my wife and I can talk things through.'

I thought that was a good idea. We stood up and Giancarlo followed me to the door. He said he appreciated that I had been honest and had the courage to tell him the truth. Whatever happened, he hoped that we could stay friends. I had made Roma play the best football he had ever seen.

Two days later, Nancy moved out. I had bought a house in the coastal town of Fregene, outside Rome. The house was old and beautiful and right on the beach. After Nancy left Giancarlo, we stayed there for the most part. Those first few months were the best time we spent together. How could I describe it? It was romantic. We took long walks on the beach and had dinner out most of the time. A nearby restaurant, Mastino's, became our favourite eating place.

But it did not take long before I started to feel a little cramped by Nancy. She was very demanding. She always had to be the centre of attention. It was not something I was used to. After a while I began doubting if I had done the right thing taking her away from Giancarlo. One day, Giancarlo called me. He wanted to talk. I think we met in a car somewhere in Rome. Giancarlo wanted me to give him one more chance with Nancy. I was stunned. I had practically stolen his wife, and still he was asking for my permission to get her back. Different thoughts swirled around in my head. But there was nothing to think about.

'Absolutely,' I said.

Giancarlo told me that he and Nancy owned some properties and land in the West Indies. He suggested that, with my permission, he could call Nancy and ask her to come with him to the West Indies so that they could look at the properties together and decide what to do with them. His ulterior motive was to get some private time with her in an attempt to win her back. The fact that I agreed to his plan probably says a lot about how I looked at my long-term future with Nancy.

Giancarlo and Nancy were supposed to be away for a week. On the way to the West Indies, they stayed one night in New York. There, Giancarlo had made the mistake of booking a hotel room for them to share. Nancy real-ised what was going on, and that the whole trip had been a ruse planned by Giancarlo to get her back. She also found out that I had given my approval to the idea. Probably Giancarlo told her. She called and screamed at me over the phone. The following morning she was back at the airport in Rome.

Nancy and I were a couple. The next Christmas she came with me to Sweden. We stayed on the top floor of my parents' house. My mother was probably not overly fond of Nancy, but that was not just Nancy's fault. No woman was good enough for me, according to my mother. On Christmas Eve, the whiskey bottle came out. People drank in Värmland and soon it was empty. That made Nancy mad. She got it into her head that we all had to go for a walk, even though the roads were covered in ice. We had not gone far when we heard Nancy scream and saw her fur coat fly up in the air. She landed with a thonk on her back. She did not get any happier after that.

● ● ●

After Mancini started playing in the centre and we moved up the table, I was king of the town. I had put Lazio on the Italian football map. The supporters were euphoric. We had sixty- to seventy-thousand people at our home games. I was back where I wanted to be – on top.

With eight games to play, we led the league, seven points ahead of Milan. For the first time we felt that we had a very good chance of winning the championship but six games later the difference between us was just one point. Perhaps we still lacked that killer instinct.

The second to last league game was away to my former club, Fiorentina, where Giovanni Trappatoni was now the manager. The score was 1–1 at half-time. In the second half, we created a slew of chances, but were unable to penetrate the Fiorentina defence. We were throwing caution to the wind and moving forward but could not get the breakthrough. In Milan, the home team had beaten Empoli 4–0. Milan now led the league, one point ahead of us with only one match left to play. So much for our seven-point lead.

● ● ●

At the same time, we had reached the final of the Cup Winner's Cup. Mallorca were our opponents at Villa Park in Birmingham. Since it looked like we would not win the league, I felt we had, at least, to win the Cup Winner's Cup. It would be Lazio's first international title and mean a successful end to the season after all.

Ten minutes from the end of the game, with the score at 1–1, the ball landed at Nedved's feet on the edge of the Mallorca penalty box. He struck a volley so sweetly that it gave the keeper no chance as the ball flew by him and into the net. Some people think it is merely talent that enables a player such as Nedved to hit the ball like that. But it is the result of thousands of hours on the training pitch. Nedved was one of the hardest working players I have ever come across. In the summer, just a week after the end of the season when the players had gone on holiday, the equipment manager at Lazio called me from Formello. He said Nedved was there. He wanted to know if he could borrow some footballs to train with.

The final ended 2–1 and we had won the Cup Winner's Cup. This was the last time the tournament would be played, so the name of Lazio would forever be inscribed in the history books as the last winners of the trophy. After the game, the players danced and jumped around but the person who danced and jumped the most was Cragnotti. Four days later we played our last league game and beat Parma at home, 2–1. It did not matter, because Milan beat Perugia away and therefore claimed the championship. I had still not killed Il Perdente Successo.

• • •

Ferragosto was the name of the holiday weekend in August when the Italians flocked to the beach. Those with money and who liked the whole VIP thing went to Sardinia, preferably in a yacht. That was the place to be seen. Cragnotti was always there, mooring his yacht right smack in the middle of the whole scene. Then he raised the Lazio flag on his boat. When Nancy and I went there, we stayed at a hotel, but we spent one day each year on Cragnotti's boat. Nancy loved it. In February each year, the same people went to Cortina d'Ampezzo in the Dolomites, so that the women could show off their fur coats. Many of them had never stood on a pair of skis. I only went to Cortina once. Sardinia I could not escape.

Nancy and I rented an apartment in the centre of Rome by the Piazza del Popolo. It was posh and very expensive. I didn't want to live there. You could not park the car by the building, but instead had to park it five hundred metres away and then walk. It was hard to avoid the attention then. The apartment was, of course, completely decorated by Nancy. Lina thought it looked like a museum. From the terrace, we had a view of the Vatican and you could almost touch the church bell in the tower next to our building. Now and then, Nancy invited people over for dinner. They were lawyers, doctors and politicians. Most of them probably thought it was fun to talk football with Mister Eriksson. Everyone followed football. Nancy loved to show me off. I used to say that she would not have been as interested in me had I been a plumber. She did not like that.

• • •

The first time I met Sir Alex Ferguson was in Monaco in 1999 for the Super Cup – a game played between the European Cup holders, which was Manchester United, and the Cup Winner's Cup holders, which was us. By then, Ferguson had established himself as the king of English football. He had just been knighted. But he was known as a man who was down-to-earth. Ferguson and I spoke briefly before the game in Monaco. The Super Cup was not recognised as an important trophy but a title is a title, so I was pleased when we won the game 1–0. That was the beginning of a winning streak that few football managers would ever be able to match.

I had won three titles with Lazio but the most important one remained – the scudetto. It was now or never. But we would have to do it without out biggest star, Christian Vieri. After the season's end, Inter had expressed an interest in buying Vieri and he wanted to leave. He had a habit of changing clubs every year. He was a restless person. He also liked money. Cragnotti asked me if I thought he should sell Vieri. 'Yes,' I said, 'if he doesn't want to stay.' I have never believed in keeping a player at a club against his will. Cragnotti asked me how much money he should ask of Massimo Moratti, the Inter owner. We had bought Vieri for 50 billion lire.

'How about double?' I said. 'One hundred billion.'

Cragnotti thought I was crazy. But when he returned from negotiations with Moratti, he said he should have listened to me. He had not dared to ask for 100 billion, 'only' 90 billion. Moratti had immediately agreed.

It was still the highest transfer fee ever paid in the world of football. As part of the deal, we got Argentinian midfielder Diego Simeone, who would prove to be an invaluable addition.

The club had made a huge profit on the sale of Vieri, but we had also lost a world-class player. Normally, I would have insisted that we replace such a star with someone of equal calibre. This time we brought in young Simone Inzaghi. I felt that, even without Vieri, we had several potential goalscorers. I did, however, push for us to buy the last of the three players I had wanted to bring to Lazio when I started – Juan Sebastián Verón. This time Cragnotti gave his approval. My team was complete. We started the season very well this time. Out of the first nine games, we won six and drew three. Our goals were scored by eleven different players.

● ● ●

Every other weekend Lina would come to visit me in Rome. She used to take the train from Florence after school on Fridays. In the beginning, the nanny came with her but after a while she took the train by herself. On Friday nights, we would go out for dinner or stay home and eat and watch TV. During the day on Saturday, Lina came to the training sessions. She would stand on the sidelines and watch me work. Lina was 12 years old and her favourite player was Nesta. All young girls were in love with Nesta. I know that those visits to the training ground were the highlight of the weekend for Lina. Maybe it was because she got to be close to me. I hope so. The team and I would stay at a hotel on Saturday night before the game next day. Lina would come to the game. She sat in the family box, most of the time with Nancy. Sometimes my parents would come to visit, and Lasse came with his sons, too.

Nancy never spoke ill of my kids. There was never any suggestion that Lina should not come. I think they got along pretty well, even if Nancy was not the motherly type. She did not understand how Lina could get bored sitting at the dinner table and listening to grown-ups talk for hours. Lina thought some of Nancy's ideas were peculiar – her theory that you could lose weight by taking a bath in cold water, for one. Lina did not speak much. Instead, she observed. She saw that Nancy and I did not fit together. We sometimes fought. When we went out to restaurants, Nancy could complain about anything and everything – the service, the champagne, the lighting. She demanded constant attention. I got more and more irritated with her. Lina saw that, too.

What Nancy did not know was that I had rented a villa near Formello. I did that to get away from her. It happened that I invited other women there. One was Debora Caprioglio, an Italian actress. Our relationship was brief, but it came out in a newspaper, *Il Messaggero*, which wrote that Lazio's manager had been seen with the beautiful Miss Caprioglio. That was a blow below the belt. In Italy, at least at that time, newspapers generally did not publish gossip about football players or coaches. Lazio's press officer advised me never again to talk to *Il Messaggero*. I think the club banished the paper from Formello. When a reporter from *Il Messaggero* asked a question at the next press conference, I just ignored him and turned to the next reporter.

I don't remember if I got any grief from Nancy over the Debora affair. We had our difficulties as it was. Nancy wanted to get married, but I didn't. In the beginning, I had probably been in love with her, but now I felt differently. I should have ended things there and then, but I let it go on. Perhaps I felt a sense of responsibility towards Nancy. I could not leave her one year after taking her from Giancarlo, causing their divorce. Besides, it wasn't all bad with Nancy. She was full of life and fun to be around.

• • •

Our season continued on the right track. We had a very strong defence, in particular, and Nesta was a beast. In midfield, Verón and Simeone, both Argentinians, had formed an excellent partnership. It was a joy to watch a team filled with superstars playing for each other. Until the end of March, we lost just three games in the league. The problem was that Juventus also had a good – no, exceptional – season and had up to that point lost just one game. Zidane had been magnificent and Pippo Inzaghi, the brother of Simone, continued to score a lot of goals. Juventus had a new coach – Carlo Ancelotti, my old captain from Roma. From the day I first met Ancelotti, I knew he would make an excellent manager. He had done a fantastic job in his first year with Juventus and all signs pointed to them running away with the title. I refused to accept that. I told Cragnotti that we would win the league. He did not believe me. The players probably did not truly believe me, either, but I knew we had a championship team. With six games to play, three points separated us.

While our tussle with Juventus was going on, we had advanced to a second group stage in the Champions League. The format had changed from the time of the old European Cup when only the champions of each country qualified for the tournament. Now the top two teams in Italy automatically qualified for the Champions League the following season, while the third- and fourth-placed teams could reach it through a qualifying round. We had easily won our first group in the Champions League proper, but at the second stage, we were facing tougher opposition – Feyenoord,

Marseille and Chelsea, where Gianluca Vialli was the player-manager. In the last match of the group, we beat Chelsea away and advanced to the quarter-finals, where we faced Valencia. We lost 5–3 on aggregate. In the first game, Valencia had completely overrun us, winning 5–2. How was it possible? Later, allegations surfaced that the Valencia club doctor supplied performance enhancing drugs to players during this period.

Two years earlier, a doping scandal had rocked Italy. Zdeněk Zeman, the Roma manager, went public with allegations that doping was widespread in Italian football. He named several Juventus players, in particular, for using steroids. A major investigation followed and six years later Juventus's doctor, Riccardo Agricola, was convicted and given a prison sentence for supplying players with illegal drugs between 1994 and 1998. The verdict was appealed, however, and Agricola was later found not guilty in a higher court of law. Most people in Italy were still convinced that there was doping in Italian football. I don't know. I just know that no one could ever accuse me of being involved with doping of any kind.

In the league, by the second to last match, Juventus's lead had shrunk to two points. We were going to play Bologna away, while Juventus were playing Parma at home. If we could win the game and Juventus only managed a draw, we would overtake them. Signori, the former Lazio legend whom I had got rid of, played for Bologna then and he equalised for them in the first half. In the second half, we dominated and scored twice before Signori got another goal back. But Juventus had also taken the lead with a Del Piero header. It looked like they would keep their two-point lead.

Then, in injury time, Parma won a corner, from which Fabio Cannavaro, the Parma defender, scored with a header. Parma had equalised! We were top of the table! But no! The referee, Massimo De Santis, had blown for a foul against Parma, disallowing the goal. Cannavaro did not understand a thing. He and everyone else believed there was nothing wrong with the goal. But the referee had made up his mind. The goal was disallowed. Juventus won the match with the score 1–0.

The debate started right after the whistle had blown for full-time. Juventus were accused of having bought the referee and cheated their way to the league title. Cragnotti was beside himself. Outraged, he claimed that Lazio had suffered an 'unfathomable injustice'. De Santis maintained that he had seen a Juventus player pushed in the penalty area and that he had blown his whistle before Cannavaro headed the ball into the net. The replays, which were shown over and over again on Italian television over the next few days, showed that he had put his whistle to his mouth after the ball had gone in, and no Juventus player seemed to be fouled. Lazio supporters organised a mock funeral for Italian football. They marched through Rome with a coffin on which it was written '*calcio*'.

It was not the last time that De Santis was accused of favouring Juventus. He even earned the nickname 'Juve's Butler'. In 2006, he was banned from Italian football for several years after being named as one of the referees that Juventus's sporting director Luciano Moggi had bribed.

● ● ●

What was almost forgotten during that tumultuous week was that there was still one round of league matches to play. Juventus was going to meet Perugia, a mid-table team without anything to play for, away. We were playing Reggina, another mid-table team, at home. We were two points behind Juventus, but with better goal difference. So if Juventus drew and we won, we would win the championship. Juventus were, of course, huge favourites to win their twenty-sixth league title, but all week I told my players to focus on their own task at hand – winning our game.

The sun was shining in Rome when we entered the Olympic Stadium for what was not only our last game of the season, but also Mancini's last game as a player. He was almost 36 years old and had decided to retire. The next season he would become my assistant manager. He had already obtained his coaching licence. There was never any doubt that Mancini would be a coach once his career as a player was over.

We controlled our match from the start, scoring from two penalties in the first half, but at half-time something very odd happened. At kick-off, the weather had been perfectly clear in both Rome and Perugia. While the sun continued to shine in Rome, a violent storm suddenly swept in over Perugia, just 100 miles away. Within minutes, the pitch became water-logged. Referee Pierluigi Collina had no choice but to delay the second half until the rain stopped.

Our second half started as scheduled and when the referee blew the whistle for the end of the match, we had won 3–0. But in Perugia, where the score was 0–0, the second half had not even started. However, the rain had stopped and, after an eighty-two minute delay, the match restarted.

Although our game was over, hardly a single person left the Olympic Stadium. Everyone remained glued to their radios and telephones, following what was happening in the Juventus game. Four minutes into the second half, there was a goal. But it was not Juventus taking the lead, it was Perugia. The Olympic Stadium erupted with a deafening roar, followed by an almost eerie silence. There was still a long way to go and Juventus had a lot of time to recover. Many of the people in the crowd held their fingers crossed, which people in Italy did to lay a curse on somebody, in this case the Juventus players.

In the dressing room, the atmosphere was, if possible, even more tense. We listened to the radio, too. There was no television. None of our players had showered. No one said a word. There were those who could not bear even to listen. Simeone sat absolutely still in his place. To move could bring bad luck. Cragnotti had stayed in the director's box in the stands, but a couple of times he came down to the dressing room. He looked pale. As for myself, I was pacing back and forth. It seemed like I walked for miles. No rational thoughts floated around in my head. At some point I went out into the stadium. No one paid me any attention.

For a while I went to the coaches' room, where there was a television. You could see how waterlogged the pitch in Perugia was. Juventus wanted to suspend the match. Another referee would probably have yielded to their demands, but not Pierluigi Collina. He was considered the best referee in the world at that time – tough, but fair. He was not impressed by anyone. The match had to be played to its conclusion. And so it was. At the end of regular time, Collina added five minutes of injury time, but the match could probably have gone on for another hour without Juventus scoring.

When Collina blew his whistle, bedlam broke out in our dressing room. Everyone hugged everyone. Even me. Someone came in and asked me to go up to the VIP stand where Cragnotti was sitting. He was overjoyed. This was his life's work. His life was complete. But we did not receive the trophy that day. I guess it was kept in Perugia. No one suspected that we would be the ones to win it.

From the stadium, the team bus took us to Formello. From Formello, I took my own car to drive home before the victory party, which was to be held at a club in Rome. A couple of other people were in the car. I don't remember who they were. We had not thought about what it would look like in central Rome. Half the city had filled the streets, and thousands of people had invaded Piazza del Popolo. I had still a mile or so to drive when people suddenly spotted me in the car. They started screaming, 'Eriksson! Eriksson! Eriksson!'

The fans jumped up on to the car. This time they did not do it out of anger, but out of joy. I almost panicked. There were people everywhere. The police showed up and offered to help. I asked if they could drive me back to Formello. One of my passengers took over driving my car. When we reached Formello, everyone had gone. I took a shower and sat down. It was the first time I'd had a moment to think about what had happened. We had won. I had won. I don't remember what I did after that. Maybe I called my father. I just don't remember. Later that evening, at the victory party, I thanked Cragnotti for his support. I joked that he should have listened to me. If we had bought the three players I wanted at the start, we probably would have won the scudetto three times.

● ● ●

Four days after we won the league, we also won the Cup. In my first year at Lazio we had been satisfied with winning the Cup. It didn't really matter when we lost the UEFA Cup final. But that is not the mentality of a winner. A winner wants to win more. We had become winners now. I was no longer *Il Perdente Successo*. I was *Il Mitico*, 'the legend'. The man who took Lazio to the top. What I did not know was that the biggest coaching job in world football was waiting for me.

11

SVEN-SATION!

EUROPEAN club football was on an international break. Nancy and I were driving down to the Amalfi coast for a few days' holiday when my phone rang. It was Athole Still. I had not heard from Athole since he negotiated the deal with Blackburn a few years earlier. He was calling from Wembley Stadium in London and he sounded excited. England had just lost against Germany in a World Cup qualifier. After the game, Kevin Keegan, England manager, had abruptly resigned. In the VIP room at Wembley, where the top brass of the English Football Association were gathered, chaos reigned. What would happen now? Who was going to take over England? Athole was in the VIP room, listening to the chatter.

'How would you fancy the England job?' he asked.

Me? England manager? A Swede? Impossible!

'It's not April Fool's Day,' I said.

Athole explained that the FA guys had got stuck with the same old names for the job and that they were open to the possibility of someone with a continental perspective. Someone with solid international experience. Someone like me. It was a short conversation. When I hung up, I did not think too much about it. A few days later, when Nancy and I were heading back home, Athole called again. This time, he was serious. The FA wanted to talk to me. Would it be okay if Adam Crozier called me?

'Who's that?' I asked.

Adam Crozier was the 36-year-old Scotsman who had just taken over as Chief Executive of the English FA. He had previously worked in advertising and was regarded as both progressive and intelligent. I told Athole that there was no problem if Crozier called me. Soon after, Adam called. He did not beat around the bush.

'Are you interested in the England job?' he asked.

Yes, I was interested, but I explained that I had a contract with Lazio and did not want to leave the club. I was happy in Rome. I had made Mancini my assistant manager. We had kept our best players from the title-winning season and added two exciting new strikers – Hernán Crespo and Claudio López. The league had just started in Italy and I wanted to defend our title, and also have a crack at winning the Champions League.

Crozier wondered if he could at least come to Rome and talk to me about it. I could not say no to that. Despite my reservations, we were talking about the most prestigious managerial job in the world of football. I would be the first foreign manager of England, the country where the game was born. Of course I was interested in the job. I wanted at least to hear what they had to offer. Maybe I could take the England job and still keep my Lazio job until the end of the season? But first I had to talk to Cragnotti. I told him that I had an offer to manage a national team.

'Don't tell me it's Italy,' he said.

'No,' I replied. 'England.'

'Wow,' he said. 'What do you want to do?'

'If you were a football manager, would you turn this job down?' I asked him.

'No,' he replied. 'I probably wouldn't.'

Everything went very quickly after that. A couple of days after my conversation with Crozier on the phone, he came to Rome with Athole and the FA's Vice-Chairman David Dein, whom I knew. At Lazio we had negotiated with him about signing Nicolas Anelka from Arsenal, which Dein partly owned. I liked David Dein.

We met in highly secretive circumstances in an apartment in Rome that belonged to Dein's daughter, who studied there. I came directly to the apartment from training with Lazio. Later, I was told that Athole, who was a trained opera singer, had entertained Crozier and Dein by singing arias from *La Boheme* while they were waiting for me. We began to talk about the job and I explained that I was willing to take it only if I could stay at Lazio for the remainder of the season. They agreed to that request. Money was not a sticking point. I told them what I was making at Lazio and they agreed to pay about the same. We had a deal.

● ● ●

On Tuesday, 31 October 2000, it became official – the English national football team would have its first foreign manager. At the press conference,

Adam Crozier said that I had been their first choice. I had signed a contract that stretched over the 2006 World Cup. I was going to stay in Lazio for the season and take over England officially on 1 June 2001. Until then, Peter Taylor was going to be the caretaker manager with Steve McClaren as his assistant. We had agreed that I would come in to lead England for the World Cup qualifying games in the spring of 2001.

The next day Lazio played at home to Brescia. Right after the game, which we won 2–1, I was picked up by David Davies, one of the FA's directors, and taken to England where I would attend a press conference the following morning. Davies himself had worked for the BBC for many years before moving to the FA. On the private plane to England, we toasted the future with champagne. I don't think I had given too much thought to what I was getting myself into.

Before my appointment had been made official, the FA's technical director, Howard Wilkinson, had of his own accord come to see me in Rome. I think he wanted to be involved with the coaching set-up. When I asked him what the job of England manager was like, he replied that it was fantastic – as long as you did not live in England. He joked that I should move to Paris. At least, I think it was a joke.

Someone gave me a copy of *The Second Most Important Job in the Country*, a book by Niall Edworthy about the job of England manager. I skimmed through it enough to get the gist – basically, the job was impossible. I understood that ambitions for the England national team were incredibly high, but football was football. I was not worried that the assignment would be beyond me. I knew that there would be differences of opinion on my performance, but I was used to that.

Later, at Luton airport, I met Tony Blair, who was then prime minister, and Göran Persson, the Swedish prime minister.

'Sven, welcome to England!' Blair said.

Then he offered to make a bet.

'Who will keep his job longer, you or me?' he said. 'Because we both know they're two impossible jobs.'

I took the bet.

● ● ●

The press conference was held early in the morning at a hotel somewhere, I don't remember where. Half an hour before it was due to start, Paul Newman, who was the chief press officer for the FA, briefed me on the format of the press conference and what I was likely to be asked. I was mostly concerned about my English, a language I had spoken just now and then. I had never lived in an English-speaking country. But I think the people at the FA were more nervous than I was. I understood that it was important for me to make a good first impression with the press. That was in everyone's best interest.

The corridor leading to the room where the press conference was going to be held was packed with photographers. Security officers had to clear the way so that I could get through. Maybe that was the first time that I realised the magnitude of the job. The cameras flashed and fired as I sat down at the table before the horde of journalists. It did not bother me. As I began talking, that little tinge of nerves that I had felt disappeared. I gave mostly standard answers, which were all true. Yes, I had always been a big fan of English football and it had been impossible to turn down such an incredible opportunity. I also said that I was convinced that England would qualify for the 2002 World Cup, despite its lacklustre start to the qualifying campaign. Howard Wilkinson had said that England should forget about the 2002 World Cup and concentrate on the 2006 World Cup instead. That was the wrong thing to say.

I did have difficulties with the language, though. I didn't understand some questions and had to ask Paul for help. The journalists were trying to expose my lack of knowledge of English football. I said that I had worked in Italy, Portugal and Sweden, so naturally I did not know English football as well as someone who had worked in England all his years. But I promised it would not take me long to learn. One puckish reporter asked me who was the left back for Sunderland. I was honest with him.

'I have no idea,' I said. 'But by next time, I will have found out.'

I was glad when it was over. I thought I had done a pretty good job.

● ● ●

Training sessions with Lazio were a mess after that. People were climbing the walls at Formello – not supporters angry over my selling their favourite player, but the English press. They brought big cranes so that they could see and film over the walls. It was a major nuisance for everyone, especially the players. They had a hard time concentrating on practice and afterwards were bombarded with questions about me by the English journalists. They became increasingly frustrated by all the commotion.

On 15 November, England played Italy in a friendly in Turin and I went to see it as an observer. The match had been planned long before I was approached about the England job. Peter Taylor had picked a young team, which was to be captained, for the first time, by David Beckham. The game was a bit of a dud and England lost 1–0. Afterwards I went to say hello to the coaching staff. I did not meet the players.

I had agreed to take Taylor and McClaren as my assistant managers when I started the job but I was determined to bring Tord with me to England. The FA had no problem with that. At the beginning of November, right after my appointment, I sent Tord to England to start scouting players. Tord had enjoyed himself in Italy, but he loved English football. We talked daily and he told me about players he had watched. He said there was a midfielder at Liverpool who looked a little raw but could become a great player. He was talking about Steven Gerrard.

I did not think it would be a problem for me to do two different jobs at the same time. England did not have games during the winter months, so I would be able to concentrate on Lazio. However, everyone there knew that I was also keeping an eye on England. Possibly that affected the players. I did not have the same feeling with them after I had accepted the England job, and we struggled. We had advanced from the first group stage in the Champions League, but got off to a nightmare start in the next group round, with losses against Anderlecht and Leeds. Back-to-back meetings with Real Madrid were up next. It would be an almost impossible task to advance in the tournament.

In the league, things got increasingly worse. Right before Christmas we lost the Rome derby, and against Napoli at home on 7 January 2001, we lost 2–1, having conceded an own goal. Our home crowd booed us throughout the match. The fans were holding up banners that urged me to resign.

The next day, while driving to training, I decided I had to leave Lazio. It was obvious that I could no longer stay as manager. I called Cragnotti immediately and told him. He was disappointed, but understanding. We agreed to have a press conference arranged as soon as possible so that I could tender my resignation publicly. I think it was the only time that I did not lead the training session during my time at Lazio. Mancini took care of it. I told the players of my decision.

It would be difficult to leave Mancini. We had been together during my entire time at Sampdoria and Lazio and we were very close. Despite that, he would always call me Mister, even though I told him not to. Mancini had always said that he would move with me, wherever I went. But there was no job for him in England. I advised Cragnotti to make Mancini my replacement at Lazio, but Cragnotti thought Mancio was too inexperienced and he chose Dino Zoff, the goalkeeping legend, who had already managed Lazio once. Ten minutes before the press conference was about to start, and without telling me, Mancini walked into the room and announced that he, too, would resign. He was very disappointed about being snubbed for the head coaching job. The press conference was a low-key affair. I said I was sorry to leave Lazio, but that it was probably for the best.

The same day, Cragnotti turned 61 and Lazio turned 101. That night, the team played an anniversary game against the Chinese national team at the Olympic Stadium. Cragnotti insisted I go to the game, and although I did not want to do that, I relented. As I remember it, the stadium was full and the crowd gave me a standing ovation. It was a very emotional farewell for Il Mitico.

● ● ●

The English FA's offices were located in Soho Square in Central London. When I arrived on my first day, the street was filled with people. One man was dressed as John Bull, the personification of the patriotic Englishman. In his hand he held a placard that said something about how the English people should hang their heads in shame for having hired a foreigner to manage the English national football team. It did not bother me. He was just one person.

I think most of the press were on my side, at least in the beginning. I still did not read the newspapers but I knew some people wrote that it was wrong to hire a foreign manager. One idiotic journalist wrote that England had 'sold its birthright down the fjord to a nation of seven million skiers and hammer throwers'. There were a lot of errors in that sentence.

Some English managers were probably not happy that the biggest coaching job in English football had gone to a foreigner. I reminded people that an Englishman, George Raynor, had actually led the Swedish national team during the 1958 World Cup and that Sweden had reached the final of the tournament. The English–Swedish partnership had yielded positive results before, in other words. I don't know if anyone bought that argument. I probably did not appreciate the conservatism of English football, but times had changed. The English had a plan to build a team that could win the 2006 World Cup, and opted for a foreigner to help them realise that dream.

● ● ●

I first moved into an apartment near Hyde Park, which the FA paid for, but I was looking for a permanent place to live. After a while I found an apartment that I liked in the Battersea district of London. It was large and had windows from floor to ceiling. In the press, the story was that the new England manager was buying a luxury apartment for a ton of money. One paper published photos from inside the apartment, which the people who showed it to me must have given to the paper. That made me irritated, and I decided not to buy the apartment.

From the outset there was plenty of talk in the English press about how much money I was making. My salary was around £3 million a year before tax, I think. It was several times more than my predecessor, Kevin Keegan, had been paid. At the same time, it was not more than my salary at Lazio. Of course, it was a lot of money, but it reflected the market value of a football manager who had just won the biggest league in Europe. That argument did not really satisfy the English press, however, and they soon labelled me 'Greedy Sven', even though I had absolutely not taken the job for the money.

To this day, people have difficulty in believing that I never cared about the money. Some people would say that it's easy for me to say, because I was rich. I understand that. But I have never been interested in money, even when I did not have any. I didn't know how much a litre of milk cost, but I didn't know that when I was a student. I have never been interested in buying a lot of stuff, cars or boats. I spent money on things I thought were fun and exciting and maybe a little glamorous – nice holidays and fancy dinners – but in a way I had always done that, even when I was young and broke. Things had always worked out for me financially.

I was not interested in investments and I hated it when people asked me what I was planning to do with my money. When I came to England, Athole recommended that I open a bank account with Coutts, an old English bank. So I did. Once a month my salary was deposited directly into that account. I am sure the balance grew quite a bit, but I had no idea how much it was.

Finally, I found a beautiful three-storey house near Regent's Park, which I bought for a little over £2 million. The estate agent who brokered the deal was a Swedish woman, Suzanne Bolinder, and a Swedish interior designer helped me furnish the place. I was very happy with it. But there was one person who was not – Nancy. Of course, she wanted to design the place herself.

Nancy and I had been together for two and a half years when I got the England job. She wanted to move with me to London, but my hope was that I would be going there alone. I was over her. She was too demanding. The minute you woke up in the morning, you had to decide where you were going to eat dinner that night. It was exhausting. I don't know how many times I told her to go find another man, preferably someone with a lot of money.

But somehow she managed to come with me to London. Maybe I was afraid to say no. Maybe I still had some feelings for her. She was still fun to be around. In the beginning, she came to London to visit. For a while, she was commuting back and forth between England and Italy, but after a while, she spent most of her time in England. She liked it and she made a lot of friends. In the end, we were living together in the house in Regent's Park. I didn't really know how it happened. But that is the way my life was. Things just happened.

●　●　●

When we were children and played football, the weakest players were either made to play in goal or on the left side. Maybe it worked the same way in England as it did at home in Torsby, because when I came to England I discovered that there were very few good players in those two positions. The goalkeeping position and the left flank would come to be England's Achilles' heel during my entire time as England manager.

In all my years as a club coach I was used to being able to add to the team with new signings if a position required strengthening. Of course, it was different as the manager of a national team. I had to make do with the players at my disposal. That was not the only difference. As a club coach I was used to being out on the football pitch every day. Here, I would get to work with the players for just a few days before each game. Most of the time, I would sit in the stands, watching them play for their club teams.

My first major task was to select a squad for a friendly against Spain at home on 28 February 2001. I wanted to get to know as many players as possible, so I picked a big squad of thirty-one players. After watching every match I could, live, for the past month I felt I had a pretty good overview of the players who would be in contention. I knew that Sunderland's left back was Michael Gray. I also knew that he was not a contender. I was not convinced by Graeme LeSaux, the Chelsea left back who had played in the national team for several years before I arrived.

Instead, Tord found Chris Powell, a 31-year-old left back at Charlton, a mid-table team. We both liked him and I decided to include him in the squad for the Spain friendly. When the squad was announced, it was the English media's turn to have their knowledge of English left backs exposed. Many of them had never heard of Chris Powell.

Otherwise, the squad did not feature any major surprises. David Seaman, 37 years old, was still England's undisputed number-one goalkeeper. Rio Ferdinand from Leeds and Sol Campbell from Tottenham were established in central defence. In midfield I had three Manchester United players – Paul Scholes, David Beckham and Nicky Butt. I also selected a young trio from West Ham – Frank Lampard, Michael Carrick and Joe Cole. Among the forwards were Michael Owen, Robbie Fowler and Emile Heskey from

Liverpool, and Teddy Sheringham and Andy Cole from Manchester United.

The first time I met the players was at the hotel where we were staying in Birmingham ahead of the Spain game. People have asked me how it felt to meet all these big stars for the first time. I was a little excited, just as I had been in the past when I met new teams, but not nervous. It was not like being 30 years old and walking into the dressing room at IFK Gothenburg. I was 52 now, and had managed some of the best players in the world. This was nothing new.

I had also started to feel more comfortable with the English language, having taken lessons several times a week. My tutor and I had gone through my press conference and what mistakes I had made language-wise. Singular and plural were a problem, 'is' and 'are'. My vocabulary was also pretty limited. But I had started to speak English every day. The most important thing was not to be afraid of making mistakes.

'Hello, my name is Sven,' I said.

I introduced the coaching staff, Steve McClaren, Peter Taylor and Tord Grip. The goalkeeping coach, Ray Clemence, was there already when I arrived. Steve was well known to the Manchester United players since he was Alex Ferguson's assistant manager. I went through some basic rules. Nothing complicated – use common sense, be on time, show respect for everyone, enjoy yourselves but take your job seriously. There were no papers to be handed out or big speeches to be made. The goal was clear – qualification for the World Cup. Everyone was on the same page about that. I did not need to explain why people were there. They knew that perfectly well themselves.

This was the first time I did not need to explain my footballing philosophy to a new team. Four-four-two and zonal marking were terms well ingrained in English football's vocabulary. That was helpful, especially since

I would have such limited time to work with the players. As much as possible, I wanted players in the same positions as they were used to with their club teams.

My main job was to select the right squad and the right starting eleven. It was up to me to create a harmonious group who liked playing together. It was, of course, also my job to plan and lead training sessions. But a lot of the coaching responsibility would fall on the shoulders of McClaren and Taylor. I think they had been worried that they would be relegated to putting out the cones before training. So the first thing I did before the first training session was to put out those cones myself. I did not have to show anyone who was boss. Everyone already knew.

Out of McClaren and Taylor, McClaren was the leader. He was self-assured, bordering on arrogant, but a very good coach, especially defensively. He also knew the players from United. However, I do think the United players, in particular, liked me. Scholes, Beckham, Butt and the Neville brothers had never played for any manager other than Ferguson. It was perhaps a nice change to get away from him for a few days.

● ● ●

The Germany game was the last time England played at the old Wembley Stadium. During my time as England manager, we would come to play at different stadia around the country. I did not have anything against that, but I would like to have had the honour of leading England out at the old Wembley, perhaps the most renowned football stadium in the world.

My first match with England was played at Villa Park. I had fond memories of that stadium because that's where Lazio won the Cup Winner's Cup. It was a very cold night. The game kicked off at eight in the evening. This was the only friendly we were due to play before our important World Cup qualifying match against Finland the following month, so I wanted to try as many players as possible. I wanted to change the whole team at half-time and play a new starting eleven in the second half, but Spain would agree to seven substitutions only. Why, I don't know.

This was before Spain came to dominate world football, but they still had a very strong team on paper. In the opening stages, Spain kept most of the possession. We held our positions well, and it did not come as a huge surprise when Nick Barmby scored before the break. At half-time, I made my seven changes. Less than ten minutes into the second half, Emile Heskey scored. We were in complete control of the game and later Ugo Ehiogu headed in. Our goalkeeper Nigel Martyn saved a penalty and 3–0 was the final result. I had got off to the perfect start in my England career.

I knew better than to let one result go to my head, although the media had a hard time restraining themselves. 'Sven Is From Heaven' one headline trumpeted. I would soon come to understand that that is how the English press worked. If England won, nothing could stop us. If we lost, we might as well pack up and give up. I wonder what would have happened if I had not won my first game, or those that followed.

As it was, I did win the following games. In the World Cup qualifier at home to Finland, my first competitive match with England, we won 2–1. I played Steven Gerrard, the young Liverpool midfielder whom Tord had praised. He had been injured for the Spain friendly. After Finland, we played four days later against Albania and won again, this time 3–1. For that game, I selected 20-year-old Ashley Cole at left back, having first talked to Arsène Wenger, Cole's manager at Arsenal. He had assured me that the quiet and shy Cole was ready to step into the national team. Arsène was right, as usual. Cole was man of the match against Albania. He was fast like the wind and very strong in one-on-one situations. The left midfield would continue to be a problem position during my England days, but after the game against Albania there was never any debate about who would play left back for England.

The victories continued. In a friendly at home, we demolished Mexico, 4–0. On 6 June 2001, we played a tough World Cup qualifier away to Greece. Before the game, the big talking point in the papers was apparently that only one England manager before me, the legendary Walter Winterbottom, had won his first four matches. Winterbottom's England had drawn his fifth game. We put in a solid effort against Greece, especially in defence. In the second half, Scholes opened the scoring and later Beckham added a second goal with one of his patented free kicks. Five matches, five wins. I was historic, the press blared. It was not something to which I gave any thought. I preferred to look forward.

●　●　●

I don't think I have ever seen my father truly angry. From my mother I got a slap or two as a kid, but my dad never raised his hand against me. He never yelled at me or Lasse. I have tried to treat people, whether football children or my children, the same way – with respect. That is why no one has ever seen me stand and scream on the pitch in training. I don't think I have ever even used a whistle.

I could understand why the English media were bewildered. A football coach screamed, that's just how it was in England. It was 'fuck this' and 'fuck that'. How constructive is that? It hardly creates confidence or trust in the players, quite the opposite. I was probably viewed by many in the English press as a bit of a strange one. As long as we won, there was no problem. The question was could a quiet and dispassionate Swede really lead the English national team into battle against their greatest nemesis? Our next opponent in the World Cup qualifying campaign was Germany.

The game was to be played in Munich on 1 September 2001. England had always seen Germany as their biggest rival in football. It was a one-sided rivalry. The Germans saw the Dutch as their greatest rivals. To the English, a football match against Germany was like an extension of World War Two, at least it seemed that way if you read the papers leading up to the game. Everything that was written alluded to the war. I did not understand it. To me, it was a game like any other.

My winning streak had ended with a loss to Holland in a friendly two weeks earlier. The mood around the national team was still very positive. We had only lost a friendly. But everyone knew that the Germans were favourites. They were undefeated in the qualifying group. That was not unexpected, however. Germany had lost just one World Cup qualifying game – ever. That was an incredible record. They were three points ahead of us and only the winner of the group would automatically qualify for the World Cup. No one believed we could win the group. That required beating Germany in Munich.

'England can win,' I told the press before the game. 'If we play a perfect game and have some luck.'

I knew that I did not have to motivate the players in any particular way. They knew what was at stake. They did not need anyone to come in and tell them what a privilege it was to put on the England shirt, or that nonsense about how the nation was behind us. I never spoke in those terms. I suspect that my predecessor did. I believe the players preferred to focus on what they were supposed to do in the game. I did what I had always done. It did not matter whether I was the manager of England or any other team.

On match days, the routine was always the same. After breakfast at the hotel, we would go out for a jog or a walk. After lunch, the players rested. Later they ate a snack. A couple of hours before the game, we met to go through the line-up and how we would play that day. It was short and concise, five to ten minutes. Some managers would ramble on for an hour. My philosophy was that if you had not done the work in training, it was difficult to go through things verbally right before the game.

We would arrive at the stadium an hour and a half before kick-off. The first thing we did was go out and look at the pitch. In the dressing room, players kept to themselves. With less than an hour until kick-off, I would walk around and talk to each player individually. I might remind him of the pace of an opposing player or that an opponent liked to cut in and shoot with his left foot. Again, short and concise, never more than a minute. When the players went out to warm up, I often stayed in the dressing room and had a cup of tea. Time passed slowly. When the players returned, they made their final preparations. Maybe somebody needed re-taping. Then we all gathered in a huddle, and the captain said a few words. With England, Beckham would say something like, 'Come on, boys!' And that was that.

We had no injuries to deal with against Germany, and I had selected Heskey to play with Owen up front. They were used to playing together at Liverpool. It had rained in Munich and the pitch was very wet. We got off to a nightmare start when Carsten Jancker scored for Germany after five minutes, but Michael Owen soon equalised. Towards the end of the first half Germany had a golden opportunity to reclaim the lead, but Sebastian Deissler, alone with Seaman, missed the goal. Instead, the play turned. We won a free kick and the ball landed at Gerrard's feet just outside the German penalty area. With the last kick of the first half, he shot and scored a goal that was psychologically immensely important. We headed into the dressing room on a glorious high. That was the luck I had spoken about before the game.

In Italy, I was used to giving the players four to five minutes in the dressing room at half-time to calm down before I talked to them. With the English players, there was no need for that. They would come in, sit down and quietly wait for their instructions. It was amazing. I told them that the Germans would push forward, but that would open up space for us. Our best defence was attack.

'Don't sit back,' I told them.

The players listened. Three minutes into the second half we extended our lead after Heskey knocked down a Beckham cross and Owen pounced on it. Everything fell into place after that. Owen scored again for his hat-trick. After Heskey scored a fifth goal, thousands of German spectators began filing out of the stadium. When the referee, Pierluigi Collina, who had played such an important role in Lazio winning the scudetto, finally brought proceedings to end, I turned to the huge scoreboard. It read: Deutschland–England 1–5. Even I had a hard time believing that.

After the game, I was told that the father of Rudi Völler, the German manager, had suffered a heart problem during the match and been taken to hospital. Rudi had gone there right after the game ended. At the press conference, I expressed my hope that his father would recover, which he did. Rudi told me that when he called me a few days later. We talked briefly about the game and agreed that nothing had gone right for him and everything had gone right for me.

The English newspapers were over the moon. 'Sven-sation!' read one headline. But the English never understood that for me Germany was a qualifying game like any other. If we had beaten Germany and then lost to Albania in the next game, the Germany win would have been for nothing. I explained that to the players. Four days later at St James' Park in Newcastle, they beat Albania 2–0. I was almost as proud of that victory as the 5–1 crushing of Germany. Almost.

THE WORLD CUP

IT was David Beckham's party. He and his wife Victoria held an auction in the garden of their home outside London. The money raised would go to charity. The party was packed with football players, movie stars and other celebrities. Nancy and I were sitting at the same table as David and Victoria and Elton John and his partner. Joan Collins was at our table also. We talked mostly about football. Elton loved football. He owned Watford FC. I committed a bit of a faux pas when I offered to pour him a glass of wine. I must have been the only person in England who did not know that Elton John had admitted to being an alcoholic and was now teetotal.

After dinner, we were all mingling. I caught David sitting at the table fidgeting with some papers. He was sweating and did not look too well.

'Is everything okay?' I asked him.

'No,' he said. 'I'm so terribly nervous.'

He was going to make a speech and was terrified of making a mistake. To give a speech in front of a big crowd was not something that the most famous person in the world liked very much. At least not then.

I was not the one who made David Beckham England captain. Peter Taylor had already done that when he handed David the captain's armband for the friendly against Italy, England's last game before I took over. But there was never any discussion about David staying on as England captain. He was a born leader. Despite the hysteria surrounding him, he always kept his feet on the ground. That impressed me. But maybe impressed is the wrong word. I have never been easily impressed. I admired enormously his ability not to let the world around him complicate things. David had enormous mental strength.

There was never any doubt about who would take the free kick against Greece in the last minute of the last World Cup qualifying game at Old Trafford in Manchester on 6 October 2001. Teddy Sheringham tried to take the ball, but David would have none of it. We were down 2–1. Germany, on level points with us in the group before the last game, were on their way to drawing against Finland. All we needed to win the group and qualify for the World Cup was to score a goal.

We had not played well. Michael Owen was injured and the crowd booed us when we walked off the pitch at half-time, a goal down. I took off Nick Barmby, who had started on the left, and moved Heskey down there and put Andy Cole up front. That got the team going and in the second half we pushed the Greeks back but without getting the goal we needed. In the sixty-eighth minute I replaced Robbie Fowler, who had started in Owen's place, with Sheringham. A minute later, Sheringham equalised with a header. It was one of those substitutions that makes the manager look like a genius. We thought the Greeks would crumble after that, but a minute or two later, they regained the lead. Time was ticking away and we almost seemed to have given up hope.

But not David. People remember only how the game ended and the role that David played, not that he played the entire second half as if possessed. He was everywhere, tackling, winning back balls, getting every attack going. In injury time, Sheringham won a dubious free kick six or seven yards outside the Greek penalty area. David had missed a string of free kicks earlier in the game and this time Sheringham wanted to take it. David pushed him aside. On the bench we wondered if he would kick it high once again.

I never thought he would score, but of course he did. When the ball curved into the top left corner, Old Trafford exploded with pure ecstasy. Even I threw my arms up in the air and jumped off the bench. I think I hugged Steve McClaren. It was the goal that took us to the World Cup. Later it would be chosen in an FA online poll as the greatest goal England ever scored.

● ● ●

The day after Beckham's heroics I was back at my desk at the FA offices. It was eight months until the next competitive game. In my twenty-five years as a football coach, I had never been away from the bench for more than a week or two at a time, excluding summer breaks. How would I handle this? The last desk job I had was at the state insurance agency in Karlstad. That had not worked out too well.

The truth is I rarely sat at my desk. Most of the time I was travelling around looking at players. I saw as many games as I could, sometimes five or six a week, two in a day even. I could wake up in a hotel room and have no idea where I was. But the people at the FA were masters of logistics. Michelle Farrer was responsible for all administrative matters. Together with two secretaries, Tanya and Anne, she arranged everything. They were amazing. Every time I stepped off an aeroplane, a car and a chauffeur were waiting for me. It was the same when the team came back from playing a game. We could land at Luton airport at three in the morning, and twenty Mercedes cars would be waiting for us. Ten minutes later, players and coaches were all on their way. I was not used to that kind of organisation in Italy or Portugal.

At the FA offices, Tord and I had desks on the fourth floor. Adam Crozier sat on the eighth. Sometimes Adam would come down and knock on my door to ask me if I would like a cup of coffee. He was definitely my biggest ally at the FA. Not that I felt I was opposed or had any enemies there. At least, not to begin with. Everything had gone so well. If there had been some turbulence at the FA with Keegan's resignation, those times were over.

● ● ●

I met Ulrika Jonsson on 8 December 2001 at some party hosted by the *Daily Express*, or maybe it was the *Daily Star*. In any case, I had met the proprietor of the paper before. His name was Desmond. The FA wanted me to travel around to various newspapers to be courteous and meet the editors. I remember that this guy Desmond had a filthy mouth. Every other word was 'fuck'. You expect an edcuated man who is in charge of a newspaper to use better language than that. I visited the *News of the World*, too, and met a woman with big, red hair. I didn't memorise her name.

Ulrika was sitting at a table next to me at the party. She was a good-looking blonde. It was not until later that I realised she was a famous television celebrity in England. Nancy was there with me. I think she had gone to the bathroom when I decided to say hello to Ulrika. The newspapers later wrote that Alistair Campbell, Tony Blair's right-hand man, had introduced us, but I don't remember things like that. Ulrika was very nice to talk to. We exchanged phone numbers, but that was all.

A few days later I called Ulrika and we agreed to meet for lunch at a restaurant in London. It was all very innocent. I was not afraid to be seen with another woman. She was Swedish and we wanted to get to know each other. Why could we not have lunch together? I had no experience with paparazzi in England. Ulrika probably knew that I was in a relationship with Nancy. I did not know if she was married or in a relationship. She said she was single. It did not matter to me.

I believe we saw each other on one occasion at her house, but it was not until we met at some kind of a function in Manchester that anything romantic occurred. I was there with some people from the FA. We were going to answer some questions at a breakfast event. For some reason, Ulrika was also invited. We met at the hotel the evening before and ended up spending the night together. Ulrika said she was writing a book about her life.

'Don't worry, Sven,' she said. 'You won't be in it.'

After that, Ulrika and I met when we could. Not daily, but now and then. It got to be more and more serious. Nancy did not suspect anything. She was travelling to Italy a lot during that time. Once, Ulrika and I went to Portugal together for a few days. Mostly, we met at her house, outside London. No paparazzi discovered us. One time I brought Lina with me to dinner with Ulrika. Lina must have been 15 then. She had come from Italy to visit me during her school holidays. She also came with me to the football matches I went to see.

• • •

Sir Alex Ferguson announced that the 2001/02 season would be his last as manager of Manchester United. He had managed Manchester United for sixteen years and won everything there was to win, including the Premier League seven times. He was getting on a bit and probably wanted to finish on top. Steve McClaren had left the assistant manager position at Manchester United and taken a job as head coach at Middlesborough.

One day I got a phone call from Pini Zahavi. Since he brought Kulkov and Yuran to me at Benfica, Pini had become one of the top football agents in the world. He wanted to know if I could come for breakfast at a club in London the following morning. He did not want to say on the phone what it was about. It was very secretive. 'Sure,' I said, 'no problem.'

When I arrived, Pini was there with Peter Kenyon, the chief executive of Manchester United, and I understood immediately what it was about. Straight off the bat, Kenyon asked me did I want the job as manager of Manchester United as of next season? I didn't think about it.

'Yes,' I said. 'I do.'

I knew it would be tricky. I had a contract with England until the 2006 World Cup and I would be severely criticised if I broke that contract. If you left England, you were a national traitor. But this was an opportunity to manage Manchester United, probably the biggest club in the world. The chance would probably not come around again. I would be able to stay with England through the World Cup. My appointment would not be made official until after the tournament.

A contract was signed – I was Manchester United's new manager. A couple of weeks passed and Pini called again. He wanted another meeting at the same club in London. When I got there, I knew something was wrong. Peter Kenyon explained that Ferguson had changed his mind. He did not want to leave the club after all, but had agreed to stay in the job for another three years.

I don't know why Ferguson had changed his mind. In the papers they wrote that his family thought he would miss football too much. Maybe his U-turn had to do with United's relatively poor season. Before Christmas, they had been as far down as ninth in the table. Surely Ferguson did not want to leave his career on anything but a high. I know that he was made aware that the club had picked me as his successor. Had he vetoed my appointment? It did not matter. He kept his job and I kept mine. But to this day, Pini has the signed contract where it says I was Manchester United's new manager.

● ● ●

On 10 April 2002, with fifty days left before the World Cup in Japan and South Korea, Manchester United played a Champions League quarter-final against the Spanish team Deportivo de La Coruña. The game was still in its early stages when Argentinian Aldo Duscher flew into a reckless tackle on David Beckham, which resulted in a metatarsal bone being broken in David's left foot. The press went ballistic. *The Sun* published a real-size photo of Beckham's foot and urged readers to cut it out and put their blessings on the foot, so that it would be healed quicker than the six to eight weeks that our medical team said his recovery would take. Tony Blair declared that nothing was more important to England's World Cup preparations than the state of Beckham's foot. But soon another matter surfaced that replaced Beckham's foot injury in the sports headlines. It had to do with my love life.

• • •

Two days after Beckham broke his foot I was woken up early in the morning by some commotion outside my house. I went into the bathroom and looked out of the window. On the street outside, maybe up to a hundred reporters were gathered. The Ulrika story had got out. I knew that it was going to happen. Ulrika had called me the night before to say that the *Daily Mirror* were going to publish an article about our relationship. But in all honesty I did not think there would be such a hullabaloo over that.

Nancy's mother called from Italy. She had read the story online – Italy was an hour ahead of England. Nancy was livid. Was it true what the papers said? I said it was nothing to worry or get upset about, or something to that effect. The phone rang again. This time it was Athole. He almost whispered, 'Sven, make sure Nancy doesn't read the *Daily Mirror* today.'

The commotion from the street intensified.

'I think it's going to be difficult to keep quiet about it,' I told Athole.

When I opened the front door it was like walking into a wall of smattering applause, except it was the smattering of cameras firing. I ignored all questions being shouted at me. 'Good morning,' was the only thing I said as I got into the car, which had been driven to my door. The chauffeur closed the door behind me. From the car, I called Adam at the office and said I was coming in. He asked me to come up and talk to him when I got there.

It turned out that Tord had forewarned Adam about the Ulrika story and asked if it would be a problem if it came out. Tord was wise. Adam had replied that it was none of the FA's business. It was my private life. When I walked into his office, Adam asked me how I felt. 'Okay,' I said. 'No problem.' He assured me that I did not have to worry about my job or anything like that. Adam was fantastic. He had brought in a PR consultant, and asked him if the FA could do anything to calm down the media storm. The consultant shook his head.

'No, they've waited for this since Sven came to England,' he said.

It was not as if I had not been warned about the intrusive nature of English media. As soon as I got the England job, the press had started digging in my private life. They had tried to get to Anki and Graziella and even roamed around Torsby to dig up any old scraps that they could find. No one was interested in anything positive, it was just the garbage they were looking for. But I had not given much thought to the press before I came to England. I had never read *The Sun* or the *News of the World* and did not start when I got to England. I asked Paul Newman to give me any newspaper clippings that were relevant to my work.

It had been different in Italy. There, the media focused on the football. The Italian papers had written about Nancy and me when we met, but it was just a short blurb about Eriksson meeting a new woman, nothing more than that. I wonder what the English press would have made out of the story. Nancy was married. When *Il Messaggero* wrote about me and Debora Caprioglio, the Italian actress, the paper was banned by the club from asking me questions. That was not an option in England.

One thing that irritated the English journalists was that they could not contact me privately, something they had been able to do with previous England managers to get exclusive scoops. With me, that was impossible.

If I was going to do something exclusively, it had be set up through the FA. I had no problem with that, but the press didn't like it.

At home, things got a little rocky. Nancy tried to keep up appearances. There was never any talk about her leaving me. Instead, she had got it into her head that nothing had happened between Ulrika and me. To Nancy, Ulrika was little more than a prostitute not worthy of being on the same planet as Miss Dell'Olio. Nancy and I went out to a restaurant, San Lorenzo, to eat, as if nothing had happened. During the dinner, the whole street outside was filled with paparazzi. There were those who believed I should have publicly apologised to Nancy. But it was none of these people's business. I did not feel as if I had anything to apologise for.

What I could not understand was how the affair had been exposed. Ulrika was convinced that it was her nanny who had talked. I did not believe that. I thought that perhaps it was Ulrika herself who had gone to the press. She craved publicity. I am not sure what kind of expectations she had of our relationship. I know that I did not envision any long-term future for us. I don't remember if I talked to Ulrika after that. One week later, I went to see Chelsea play Manchester United at Stamford Bridge. On the short walk from the car to the stadium, some Chelsea supporters, who had probably had a beer or two, shouted 'Sven, how was Ulrika?'

I was told Ulrika was also at the game. I didn't see her there. I do remember that Manchester United won the game 3–0.

● ● ●

On 9 May 2002, I presented my first World Cup squad. Over three weeks had passed since the Ulrika story blew up, but the tabloids would not let it go. I don't understand how they could do it. There was absolutely nothing left to write about. From the start, I had made it clear that I would not comment on my private life. I had not talked to the press about it. But in connection with the announcement of the squad, I had to face the media at a press conference. Paul Newman was nervous. He warned me that the reporters would drag up the Ulrika story. I calmed him down. I would just say what I had said before – no comment.

The press conference room was packed to the rafters. When I sat down behind the microphones, the cameras went crazy. I think the first question was about Ulrika. I said that I would not comment on matters in my private life but they did not give up that easily. Would my affair with Ulrika affect the team's performance in the World Cup? I tried to be polite, but firm. I would not talk about my private life. But it did not matter. The questions about Ulrika kept coming. The tabloids would not give up. It was embarrassing – not for me. I didn't really care. It was embarrassing for the real sports journalists who were there to talk about football. I did not understand why I was expected to answer for something I had done that I didn't think was wrong. I was almost treated like a criminal.

We finally got to football. I had not included any major surprises in the squad. Beckham's foot was healing rapidly and we were hoping that he would be ready for our first World Cup game. There was never any discussion about whether or not he should be picked for the squad. Worse was that Gary Neville, the right back, had been injured and was out. His absence would be huge. Despite injury problems in midfield, I chose just seven midfielders, in order to take an extra forward. One player I left out of the squad was Steve McManaman, the left midfielder. We never really clicked, McManaman and me.

In the last game of the league season, a few days after my official squad announcement, Steven Gerrard had to leave the pitch with a groin problem.

It turned out the injury was so serious he needed an operation and would miss the World Cup. That was a huge blow to us. Gerrard had become a key player in the centre of the field. In his place, I brought in Danny Murphy, another Liverpool player, but later he broke a metatarsal bone, just as Beckham had done. It did not bode well for us in the tournament.

As soon as the league was over, we went for a training camp in Dubai. At the first gathering, I felt I needed to apologise to the players for the stir that my private life had created in the media. The players just laughed.

'Welcome to England!' someone said. I think it was Robbie Fowler.

● ● ●

Nowhere else have I seen the kind of hysteria that surrounded David Beckham in Japan during the 2002 World Cup. Our party stayed at a beautiful hotel on the island of Awaji outside Kobe, and from there we travelled several miles each day to the training ground. People stood along the entire road, stacked like slices of bread, just to see our bus fly by.

'We love you! We love you!' the girls screamed.

It was mostly girls who stood there with their England flags and placards, and it was not the team they were shouting for. They were declaring their love for David Beckham. David remained calm. The other players were used to the circus, too. When we returned to the hotel, they told David to get off the bus first so they could walk into the hotel undisturbed while he signed autographs. I don't know how many autographs he wrote during our time in Japan.

We had been drawn in what was dubbed 'the group of death' – Argentina, Nigeria and our first opponents, Sweden. We had played Sweden once since I came to England, in a friendly that ended 1–1. In England, people thought that we would be able to take advantage of my knowledge of Swedish football. In Sweden, they wrote about where my loyalty would lie. Both were nonsensical issues. I had no magic bullet of knowledge to defeat Sweden, and although I was proud of being Swedish, I was there to win with England. We played a good first half and took the lead when Sol Campbell headed in a Beckham corner. In the second half, Sweden came back and equalised. When it was over, both teams were probably pretty happy with the result.

Our second match, against Argentina, was likely to be decisive – a victory would give us one foot in the second round; defeat would most likely mean packing our bags after the group stage. Argentina had knocked out England on penalties in the World Cup four years earlier after Beckham got sent off. That did not affect my thinking about the game, but I knew the players were extra motivated. Argentina had come to Japan as favourites to win the World Cup.

The match was played in an indoor stadium in Sapporo and the whole arena seemed to be filled with England fans. It was fantastic to hear them. We would repay their faith in us by playing one of the best games during my time as England manager. Just before half-time, Michael Owen, who was magnificent in the match, was brought down just inside the Argentinian penalty area. I have rarely heard a noise louder than the cheer after Beckham scored the penalty. In the second half, play went back and forth. Both teams had opportunities to score, but the 1–0 result stood. We had beaten Argentina, the favourites. When FIFA's technical committee released its report after the tournament, analysing all the games, our match against Argentina was ranked as the best game, tactically, in the entire World Cup.

We played out a nervous and scoreless draw against Nigeria in the last game of the group stage. In the second round, we faced Denmark, who had won their group by beating reigning champions France. It would not be an easy task. Looking back, I don't think we got enough credit for how well we played in that game. We completely dominated the match and at half-time, with the score 3–0 in our favour, it was all over. The mood in the team was perfect. Eighteen months earlier, England had been on their way to missing out on qualifying for the World Cup. Now we had a chance to win it.

● ● ●

In my whole career as a football manager, I have never approached a game thinking we would lose. It was no different as we entered the Shizuoka Stadium in searing heat to play the World Cup quarter-final against Brazil. But the important thing was not what I believed. What was important was that the players truly believed they could win. Had I communicated that feeling to them?

Brazil were favourites. They had the three Rs – Ronaldo, Ronaldinho and Rivaldo. Did Danny Mills, Nicky Butt and Trevor Sinclair really believe that they could not only go toe to toe with these Brazilian superstars, but beat them? Did they believe it after Michael Owen exploited Lúcio's mistake in defence to score for us in the twenty-third minute? I am not so sure. What would have happened if we had managed to keep the lead until half-time? If Beckham had not pulled out of a tackle, Scholes lost the ball, Mills found himself out of position, Cole been exposed by a bit of Ronaldinho magic before Rivaldo equalised in injury time right before half-time? Who knows?

Early in the second half Scholes gave away a free kick in a seemingly harmless position some way outside and to the side of our penalty area.

When Ronaldinho stepped up to take it, everyone expected him to hit a cross. But Ronaldinho's kick was too deep for a cross. Instead, the ball went straight at goal. It sailed over Seaman, who was off his line, and into the top corner. Brazil had taken the lead. Did Ronaldinho mean to aim for goal or was it just a lucky shot? I asked him that in Portuguese several years later. He laughed.

'But, Sven, you know it was a shot.'

'You're lying,' I told him.

I was 100 per cent sure that he did not mean to shoot.

Seven minutes later, Ronaldinho was sent off for a stamp on Danny Mills. We were going to play with a one-man advantage for more than half an hour, which required a tactical re-jig. Our numerical advantage meant we would automatically gain more possession of the ball. At least, it was natural to think that way. However, this was Brazil. No other team in the world was as good at keeping possession. The Brazilians were like the Spanish seven or eight years later. We hardly got a sniff at the ball. We pressed and pressed, chasing all over the pitch. When it looked as though we had closed down Roberto Carlos, the Brazilian left back, he would hit a fifty-yard cross that landed on the foot of Cafu on the right side and we had to start all over again.

I was criticised after the game for my substitutions. People said I was not creative enough, that I should have put on Joe Cole. But Joe Cole would not have made any difference in the game against Brazil. In any case, I had already taken off Trevor Sinclair and put on a creative midfielder in Kieron Dyer before Ronaldinho was sent off. With ten minutes left, I even switched to a three-man defence and put on an extra attacker. It did not matter.

A lot of people felt that it was Seaman's fault that we lost to Brazil.

Seaman himself knew that he had made a bad mistake. Ronaldinho's free kick had not been hit particularly hard. Seaman had time to move his feet and push the ball over the crossbar for a corner. After the game, I patted him on the back. I did not have to tell him anything. The truth was that it was not Seaman's fault that we were knocked out of the World Cup. Brazil were better than us. It was that simple. But we had played a very good tournament and we had a young team. We were not ready yet. It was the next World Cup that we were going to win.

RUSSIAN RUBLES

IN the summer of 2002 I rented a steamboat and invited some friends for an evening tour of Fryken. It was one of those perfect Swedish summer evenings when the sunset lasted for hours. It was late, probably around 11 o'clock, when I asked the captain if he knew of any houses for sale around the lake. I had been looking for a place to buy for several years, without finding anything that I really liked. The captain said he knew of an old convalescent home located by the water, which we would drive past in a few minutes. It was called Björkefors, and he thought it might be for sale. I told him to make a stop at the dock if possible.

The house turned out to be an old country estate, huge but run down. It was beautifully situated on a hill with the grounds sloping down towards the water. The captain docked the boat and despite the late hour I decided to walk up to the house to see if anyone was there. I had probably had a couple of glasses of wine. When I knocked on the door, an older lady answered. I had never seen her before, but she recognised me.

'Svennis? What are you doing here in the middle of the night?' she asked.

I apologised for calling so late and asked her if it was true that the house was for sale. Yes, she said, it was. I explained that I was interested in buying it. Could I come back the following day to look at it? She should not sell it to anyone else, I told her.

'No, I'm not going to sell it tonight,' she said.

The following day I went back and bought the house. It cost 5.7 million kronor. It was almost that simple. Later, I had to obtain a special permit to own such a large summer house despite not living in Sweden permanently. It took two years to renovate the place and cost a fortune. I wanted it to look like a classic Swedish country estate. We stripped the entire interior, took out a few walls to make room for a large kitchen and put in a new floor. The bedrooms and bathrooms were completely redone. The only thing I kept was the elevator.

The garden was so overgrown you could hardly see the lake. I think we cut down so many trees that I would have wood to burn for the next thirty years. I built a tennis court next to the house, but then changed my mind and had it moved to the other side of the property. Where the tennis court had first been placed, I built an indoor swimming pool. I completely rebuilt the boat house and made it into a cottage. I also built a whole new house for my parents. I don't know how much money I spent. It may have been upwards of 50 million kronor in total. My parents did not approve of the purchase. They said the place was too big and too expensive. Nancy was against it, too. But I think the people in the area liked it. I had transformed an old convalescent home into a beautiful country estate. I had acquired a home for myself.

● ● ●

After the 2002 World Cup, Adam Crozier left his post as the FA chief executive. Maybe 'left' is not the right word. He was more or less forced out. Adam was extremely well thought of at the FA, but he had been in constant conflict with the Premier League and its chief executive, Richard Scudamore. The Premier League had grown into the largest and most profitable football league in the world, with the most television viewers and the most supporters. Adam was always fighting for more power for the FA vis-a-vis the Premier League, but it was a struggle I believe he could not win. Adam's leaving meant I had lost my biggest supporter at the FA.

Perhaps I had also lost some of my shine in the media. Something happened after the loss to Brazil in the World Cup. We had surpassed most people's expectations by knocking out Argentina in the group stage but I had been accused of tactical mistakes in the Brazil game. Many in the media were aggrieved that we did not hold a press conference or make the players available for interviews before leaving Japan. It was understandable. The press had a job to do and that required having access to the players. I did not have anything to do with how the media were handled, but I still got some of the blame for slighting them.

The Ulrika story was still not over. She was planning to release a book in the autumn of 2002, just when we were due to play our first qualifier for the 2004 Euros, against Slovakia away. The Ulrika affair may not have helped my image in the media but I don't think most people on the street were especially bothered. Quite the contrary. I got a lot of 'thumbs up' from young men who laughed and said they wished it had been them getting together with a beautiful woman like Ulrika.

I had not spoken to Ulrika since our romance. The people at the FA were nervous about what would appear in the book, as if I might have divulged some state secrets about players to a woman I was seeing. There was no need to worry. There was nothing to tell, which is what I told the media at the press conference in Bratislava before the Slovakia game. The next day we beat Slovakia 2–1 in miserable weather conditions. The press wrote that we had been lucky and that the first half, when we were trailing 1–0, was the worst England had played in years.

There were also a lot of complaints about my experimenting in friendlies. I made too many substitutions. The supporters didn't like it. They wanted to see England's best players for ninety minutes. I could understand that to some degree. But friendlies were the only chance I had to try new players. When else would I do it? The players themselves liked the substitutions. Most of them were with teams in the Champions League and played two games a week. If they got to rest for a half, they were happy.

The debate around the friendlies came to a head when we played Australia in London on 12 February 2003. This time I wanted to change the entire team at half-time. I would play eleven players in the first half, and eleven new players in the second. The people at the FA were against it. David Davies, who had temporarily taken over from Adam, pleaded with me to reconsider. But I had made up my mind. It was a friendly and thus a good opportunity to see as many players as possible.

However, I had underestimated the rivalry between England and Australia. The English took their friendlies seriously, especially against little brother Australia. But the Australians? To them, it was like a World Cup final. At half-time, we were trailing 2–0. I kept my promise and changed the entire team. Our play did not improve in the second half and we lost the game 3–1. I was not too concerned, but in the press it was as if the world had come to an end. After that, the debate over substitutions spread beyond England's shores. It ended with FIFA proclaiming that a maximum of six players could be substituted in an international friendly. I suppose the footballing world has Eriksson to thank for that.

● ● ●

One of the players I used in the second half against Australia was a 17-year-old boy named Wayne Rooney. He was 17 years and 111 days old, to be exact, which means he became the youngest England player ever. Tord and I had been to see Rooney when he played for Everton, and been impressed with the incredible intensity he had shown. He was exactly the kind of forward we needed in 2003. Andy Cole had never done it in the national team during my time. Heskey was up and down. Jermaine Defoe was not ready. Michael Owen was our only truly top-class forward.

I had a hard time understanding Rooney's Liverpool accent, at least in the beginning, so I had to talk to his agent, Paul Stretford, instead. Stretford naturally pushed for his client to be included in the national team. Everton's manager, David Moyes, was not as convinced. There was no discussion about Rooney's footballing abilities, despite his tender age. He was both a physical and intelligent player, a creator as well as a finisher. He did not have an ounce of fear in him. Apparently, he had been a boxer, like his dad, but had to give up on that career after being knocked out one too many times. Moyes was worried that Rooney would not be able to control his hot temper and that he was not ready socially. I had many long discussions with Moyes about Rooney.

But Rooney was ready. After his debut against Australia, a game in which he was the only England player who performed admirably, I decided to select him for the important qualifying game at home against Turkey on 2 April 2003. Rooney fitted into the group immediately. In training he was just as tough as Gerrard and Scholes, who were like machines in practice. The day before the game I told Rooney he would be starting against Turkey.

'Okay,' he said, as if he had been expecting it.

Turkey had finished third in the 2002 World Cup and were our toughest opponents in the qualifying group. The Turkey game was very important. After the opening win against Slovakia away we had managed just a draw at home against Macedonia after a blunder by David Seaman. That was Seaman's last game as England keeper. I brought in David James in his place.

We could not afford to lose any more points at home. Before the game, some of the players had come under criticism in certain sections of the media for lacking passion, which irritated David Beckham especially. We would not be lacking passion against Turkey. David was even cautioned for talking to the referee. We played brilliantly and won convincingly 2–0. Man of the match was 17-year-old Wayne Rooney. Would I have played him against Turkey if I had not seen him play against Australia first? Probably not.

● ● ●

After the league season was over, we had one qualifying game remaining, at home to Slovakia on 11 June 2003. Before then, we travelled with the team to South Africa to play a friendly against the national team. It was a long flight and our doctor, Leif Swärd, the Swede whom I had brought to England after the 2002 World Cup, advised all of us to wear surgical stockings to prevent our legs from swelling up on the plane. I put them on. Tord was sitting across the aisle from me, reading. I fell asleep, as I always did when flying – I don't know for how long – and when I woke up I could not feel my feet. I pulled off the stockings and stood up, which was the wrong thing to do because I fainted. When I came to, Tord helped me up, only for me to faint again. This time I fell awkwardly on to an arm rest and broke my little finger. To this day, it's all crooked. It doesn't really bother me. But I have never worn those stockings on a plane again.

We beat South Africa 2–1. While we were in the country, we travelled to Johannesburg to meet Nelson Mandela, which was a great honour. Back in England, we beat Serbia and Montenegro in a friendly and then Slovakia 2–1 in the qualifying game. That placed us second in the group, two points behind Turkey but with a game in hand. Turkey had won all their games except the one against us. Everything pointed to a decisive game between us in Turkey in the last round of the qualifiers. First we had a summer break. I went home to Björkefors, which then looked like a building site.

One day I got a call from one of the directors at Real Madrid. He said Real were interested in buying David Beckham from Manchester United and he had a question for me. He wanted to know if Real would be buying a playboy or a professional. I assured him that there was no player more professional than David Beckham. I also warned him about the public hysteria that always surrounded David. The director laughed. At Real Madrid, he said, they were used to that sort of thing.

A few days later, David had become a Real Madrid player. Later I received another call from the Real director. I had been right, he said, Beckham was a super-pro. And the hysteria around him was like nothing they had ever seen at Real Madrid.

● ● ●

On 2 July 2003, an official announcement was made that Roman Abramovich, a Russian oil magnate, had bought Chelsea football club for £80 million. Few people knew who Abramovich was. I did. I had already declined two job offers from him.

My relationship with Abramovich began some time earlier, when Pini Zahavi called me and said that a Russian businessman wanted to meet me. When I arrived at London's Les Ambassadeurs Club for the meeting, Pini was waiting there with four Russian men. I had the name Abramovich in my head, but I did not know what he looked like. So I walked up to the first man, who was dressed in a suit and introduced myself. It was not Abramovich. The second person was not him, either. Neither was the third. The fourth man was dressed in jeans and a jacket with a T-shirt underneath. Naturally, that was Abramovich, the man whose fortune was estimated at a cool £10 billion and who would change the face of football.

'Sorry,' I said.

'No problem,' he said and smiled.

We ate lunch and talked about football. Abramovich explained that he was interested in buying a football club in Moscow. He wanted Pini and me to look at four potential clubs for him. So that is what we did. After spending a few days in Moscow, visiting training grounds and such, Abramovich asked me which club I thought he should buy.

'CSKA Moscow,' I said. 'They're the biggest.'

'Okay,' he said. 'If I buy CSKA, will you come to manage the team?'

'No,' I said. 'I can't leave England.'

Soon after that, Abramovich's adviser, German Tkachenko, whom I had met in Moscow, called. German said that Abramovich was now thinking of buying a football club in England instead. He wanted a London team. He was looking at Tottenham or Chelsea. Which one did I think he should acquire?

'It depends on what he wants to do with the club,' I said.

'He wants to win,' German said.

'If he wants to win, it's Chelsea,' I said. 'Then he only has to change half the squad.'

A few days after that, Abramovich bought Chelsea. At that point German called me again.

'Do you want to be manager of Chelsea?' he asked.

It certainly was a tempting offer. But, still, I could not leave England.

'Sorry,' I said. 'It's impossible.'

It was the second time I had said no to Roman Abramovich. But our relationship was still friendly. I was in Sweden when one of his advisers called and asked if I would like to come to Oslo for dinner with Roman. He was going to be there with his yacht for a couple of days. When I got there, the yacht was moored in a special harbour for cruise liners. It was that big. Roman was sitting on the enormous afterdeck with a friend, watching some old football match on a giant television screen. I think there was a player he wanted to have a look at.

His wife at the time, Irina, was there, as was a Dutch scout and a football agent, whom I didn't know. We all had dinner together. Roman had brought in a Norwegian chef for his stay in Oslo. Wine was served with dinner, but Roman himself did not touch alcohol from what I could tell. After dinner, Irina showed me her office on board. She had a computer with a database of all football players in the world. Maybe she was the one who was choosing players to buy? No, I doubt that.

In London, I would meet Roman every now and then at his apartment. One time I was there with Pini. Without our knowledge, a photographer snapped a picture of us as we entered the apartment. It was published in the papers the next day and immediately speculation was rife that I was replacing Claudio Ranieri as Chelsea manager. I had to say publicly that that was not the case. Roman's people advised me to use the garage entrance from then on. You drove into a basement garage and walked up a flight of stairs that led straight into Roman's kitchen.

Abramovich's apartment was both huge and elegant. With his fortune, he could buy whatever he wanted. When I commented to Eugene Tenenbaum, Roman's right-hand man, that the £80 million that Abramovich had spent on Chelsea was a lot of money, Tenenbaum nodded.

'Yes,' he said. 'But that affects Abramovich's finances about as much as if you or I went to the coffee shop and bought a cup of coffee.'

Judging from the way he dressed, it was difficult to believe that Abramovich was so wealthy. He often dressed in jeans and a T-shirt. He was more like a regular guy, polite and friendly. I don't know how much he cared about the expensive art on his walls. When I said something about the artwork, he looked around as if it was the first time he had noticed the paintings.

But he was absolutely crazy about football. I talked only football with Roman and his other friends who came visiting. The talk centered mostly on what players Chelsea should buy. Roman needed advice and I became one of the people he listened to. Among the players I recommended, he bought Joe Cole, Damien Duff, Wayne Bridge, Glen Johnson and Juan

Sebastián Verón. Before the close of the transfer window on 31 August 2003, he had also bought Adrian Mutu, Hernán Crespo and Claude Makélélé. Abramovich spent more on player purchases than he had done buying the club.

● ● ●

If I had a warm relationship with Roman Abramovich, my relationship with Sir Alex Ferguson was a little more turbulent. Ferguson was a genuinely nice man. We met many times and even had dinner together on a few occasions. But woe to the person who threatened or bothered Manchester United in any way. Then Ferguson would not spare his venom. I know, because he often aimed that venom at me. He caused a fuss before practically every friendly we played with England. Friendlies were completely useless, he thought. Players only got hurt. Sometimes Ferguson would call at seven o'clock in the morning, ordering me not to select one of his players for a friendly. The player was injured or else he needed to rest, Ferguson claimed. He never asked if I could possibly be careful with a particular player.

I was not going to let Ferguson bully me. If I wanted a Manchester United player in my squad, I was going to select him. Ahead of a friendly against Croatia on 20 August 2003, Ferguson had, according to the papers, told the media that I should not select Paul Scholes. Scholes had a hernia, Ferguson claimed. I picked him anyway, and played him for sixty minutes only. Ferguson was livid. According to him, Scholes's injury was made worse because of that game. Yet Scholes was okay to play two more games for United before he had an operation just before our two Euro qualifiers against Macedonia and Liechtenstein.

A bigger confrontation with Ferguson loomed on the horizon, featuring Rio Ferdinand. On 23 September 2003, Ferdinand was training as usual with Manchester United when representatives from England's anti-doping organisation came to the United training ground to conduct doping tests on four randomly selected players, among them Ferdinand. For some reason, Ferdinand skipped the test, leaving the training ground and going home. It was viewed as a very serious offence, on a par with testing positive.

The FA took all doping matters very seriously, and they showed no mercy to Ferdinand. A new chief executive, Mark Palios, had been installed and he instructed me not to select Rio for the decisive Euro qualifier against Turkey away on 11 October. I was facing a huge dilemma. I understood the FA's tough stance but at the same time, Rio had not yet been found guilty of breaking the rules. Ferguson, not surprisingly, did not appreciate the FA's actions against Ferdinand. One morning he called me at the crack of dawn. He was aggressive right off the bat. This time he wanted me to select Ferdinand in the squad, directly disobeying the order I had been given by my employer.

'I understand how you feel,' I said. 'But I can't select Ferdinand. You have to call and yell at someone else.'

Many of the players were angry over what they saw as the unfair treatment of Rio, and they threatened to go on strike if Rio were not recalled to the team. I was put in a difficult position. It had not been my decision to drop Rio; it was the FA's. So I told Palios that it was his responsibility to confront the players and explain the decision directly to them. I am not sure things turned out all that well. Palios was not an expert communicator. Finally, however, the players backed down and agreed to play the game. In a written statement to the press, they sternly criticised the FA's actions.

Rio's ban was not the only problem ahead of the Turkey match. Open war existed between English and Turkish football fans. Two Leeds supporters had been stabbed to death in Istanbul three years earlier in connection with a UEFA Cup semi-final between Leeds and Galatasaray. The English authorities ruled that no English supporters should be allowed to travel to the game in Turkey. I was given the unpleasant job of making that announcement to the public. It was not very well received by either the Turks or UEFA.

The atmosphere was filled with rancour when we arrived at the stadium in Istanbul, with not a single English fan among the 43,000 spectators. I think it only helped spur on our players. We were incredibly focused and took control of the game. Towards the end of the first half, Gerrard was pulled down in the penalty area and the referee, Pierluigi Collina, pointed to the spot. Beckham would take it, but just as he was about to strike the ball, it was as if the ground where he had planted his support leg just fell out from underneath him and he slipped. The ball sailed high over the goal. Emotions ran high. The Turkish defender Alpay, who normally played for Aston Villa, put his hand in Beckham's face. There was some altercation in the tunnel at half-time, but it was nothing serious.

A draw would be good enough for us to win the group and qualify for the Euros, while the second-placed team would have to play an extra play-off game. That night we showed what a strong team we were, especially mentally. We were not intimidated by the hostile atmosphere. The defence, with 22-year-old John Terry playing in Rio's place, was immense. Turkey got nowhere. The game ended 0–0 and we were through to the 2004 Euros in Portugal. I was still undefeated in all World Cup and Euro-qualifying games with England. Turkey lost the play-offs to lowly Latvia and missed the Euros. Rio Ferdinand also missed the Euros, because of his no-show at the doping test. On 19 December 2003 he was fined £50,000 and banned from football for eight months.

● ● ●

In the spring of 2004, Pini Zahavi came up with a job offer that I had already turned down once – Chelsea. They had done very well in Abramovich's first season as owner, finishing second in the league. But finishing second was not why Abramovich had got into English football. Only titles mattered to him. Ahead of the next season he had decided to make a managerial switch. He wanted to sack Ranieri, and replace him with me.

This time I was willing to accept the job. After more than three years as England manager I was missing club football. At Chelsea I would have a chance to be part of building a team that could possibly dominate English football for years to come. It was not that I wanted to leave the England job, but at the same time I knew there were no guarantees I would get to stay if results went against us. I wanted to stay with England through the 2004 Euros and then join Chelsea before the next season. That would be the perfect solution, as long as news didn't get out that I would be leaving the England job.

Pini and I met Peter Kenyon in his apartment in London to negotiate a contract with Chelsea. Kenyon, who had once offered me the manager's job at Manchester United when he was chief executive there, had taken the job as chief executive at Chelsea after Abramovich bought the club. The negotiations were straightforward. Chelsea wanted me, I wanted Chelsea. We had a deal and it only remained for the contract to be drawn up.

There was only one problem. From across the street, someone had photographed Kenyon and me inside the apartment. The photo was splashed across the newspapers the next day. We had been sitting behind a thin curtain, so the picture was a little fuzzy, but there was no doubt that it was us. The media went wild. I was accused of betraying the nation. As the England manager, you were expected to sit politely and wait for the day you got fired. If you so much as listened to another job offer, you were considered a traitor.

At the FA, they didn't want to lose me. They were willing to offer an improved contract to get me to stay. In return, I had publicly to deny that I was ever interested in the Chelsea job and affirm my loyalty to England. I felt the pressure to comply. As a result, my contract with England was extended for another two years. It would now run to 2008. I also got a salary raise. I would now be making £3 million a year *after* tax. That was, of course, very nice, but at the same time I had been pressured into committing to England for an even longer period. I knew that the chance of managing a club like Chelsea may never return.

● ● ●

The 2004 European Championship was to be played in Portugal, and I'd had a hand in that. Several years earlier I had received a phone call from the president of the Portuguese FA, Gilbert Madail. He was wondering if I knew the president of UEFA, Lennart Johansson, who was Swedish, and if Lennart and I would be interested in coming to Portugal to discuss the possibility of Portugal hosting the 2004 Euros. Lennart and I knew each other well. I told Madail that we would be happy to come. When we got there, he took us out for dinner and showed us the plans for the tournament. Everything looked good. Lennart wanted a smaller country, such as Portugal, to host the tournament instead of one of the big footballing powers, such as Germany or Spain. But would the Portuguese really be able to pull off hosting such a big event? 'Absolutely,' I replied, being far from sure that they would. Lennart had been won over and I was happy. Portugal was like my second home, although I am not sure where my first home was. I owned houses in four different countries – Sweden, England, Italy and Portugal.

During the Euros, we would be staying outside Lisbon. Our logistical genius Michelle had found the perfect hotel for us. The national stadium, which we were going to use as a training base, was located five minutes away. Everything was perfectly organised, as usual with England. The wives and girlfriends stayed in a hotel next to us, just as they had in Japan two years earlier. It was my absolute conviction that the players should be allowed to spend time with their families during the tournament. You had to be able to trust your own players. Why should they live differently during a championship from how they did otherwise? All other national teams let their players meet their families. In the English press, it was turned into a huge problem.

Unlike the World Cup in Japan, we had no injuries going into the tournament. Only Rio Ferdinand was missing because of his suspension. The big question mark was still the left flank. Beckham would naturally start on the right, but we had no obvious left midfielder. We did, however, have three world-class central midfielders in Steven Gerrard, Paul Scholes and Frank Lampard. Some people suggested that Gerrard and Lampard could not play together. It was an opinion I never understood. World-class players like them needed to be in the starting eleven. Time and again they had proven to be the difference between victory and defeat. Lampard could not play anywhere but in the middle. He needed to be on the ball, plus he was not fast enough to be on the wing. Gerrard had played on the left once or twice, but he was at his best in the middle. And why would they not be able to play together? They were both intelligent footballers. If one player went forward, the other had to stay back. It was not more difficult than that.

I decided to move Paul Scholes to the left, and not because he was a lesser player than Gerrard or Lampard, not at all. Scholes was England's best football player. He had everything, except the ability to tackle without earning a yellow card. It was impossible to take the ball from him, and he never mishit a pass. He did not belong on the left flank, but that is where we needed him the most. He had played on the left in the qualifying campaign, which we had gone through undefeated, and sometimes even at Manchester United. The alternative was to change the whole system to a 4-3-3 formation, but that required two speedy and creative wingers, which we did not have.

A lot of people were not aware that Scholes suffered from asthma. When the international tournaments were played in the summer, it was always too hot for Scholes. When we practised penalties before the 2004 Euros, Scholes stayed on the other side of the pitch. I called him over to ask why he did not want to take part in the penalty practice. He replied that there was no way he would still be on the pitch to take penalties after 120 minutes in the Portuguese heat.

'If I last an hour, that's good,' he said.

Paul Scholes was most at home on a cold February day away to Newcastle.

● ● ●

The 2004 Euros came to be Wayne Rooney's tournament. We had been drawn in a tough group with France, Switzerland and Croatia. The opening game against France was going to be played at the newly rebuilt Estádio da Luz in Lisbon. The old Estádio da Luz, where Benfica played when I was there, had been torn down.

We played very well against France, especially in midfield. In the first half, Lampard scored with a header from Beckham's free kick. When Rooney was brought down in the second half and we were awarded a penalty, it looked as if we were heading towards a relatively comfortable victory. But the French goalkeeper Fabien Barthez saved Beckham's penalty. It would be a costly miss. In the ninetieth minute, France won a free kick just outside our penalty area. Zidane's free kick was unstoppable and suddenly the game was tied. Then, in injury time, Gerrard hit a terrible back pass that Thierry Henry intercepted. He barrelled down on goal, before being tripped by David James, our keeper. Penalty! Zidane made no mistake in converting it and soon after that the referee blew his whistle for full-time. In less than three minutes, we had gone from 1–0 to 1–2.

The loss against France was a bad blow, but at the same time, we had shown that we could play very well. In the second match, against Switzerland, we did not perform as well in the first half. The players were struggling in the thirty-degree-plus heat. In the second half, we got our game going and Rooney became the youngest goalscorer in the history of the tournament. Later, he scored another, and Gerrard added a third.

The Wayne Rooney Show continued with our third game against Croatia. A draw would be enough for us to go through. Croatia took an early lead, but after that we completely dominated the game. It soon paid off when Scholes scored and later Rooney gave us a 2–1 lead. The second half continued like the first. Rooney scored his second, before Croatia got a goal back. Soon after that Lampard scored to make it 4–2, which was the final result. We were through to the quarter-finals. Later I heard it was the first time that England had advanced to the second round of the

European Championship when it was not played in England. I said to the media that I could not recall a player having made such an impact on a tournament as Wayne Rooney had in Portugal since Pelé's amazing achievements at the 1958 World Cup.

Everything was perfect before the quarter-final against Portugal. The day before the match we practised penalties at the Estádio da Luz, where the game would be played. If the game was still tied after regular and extra time, it would be decided on penalties. The last penalty shootout that I had been involved with was Sampdoria against Arsenal in the Cup Winner's Cup in 1995. Arsenal had won that battle after David Seaman saved three penalties out of five. I knew that England had a terrible record when it came to penalty shootouts. The English had been knocked out on penalties against Germany in both the World Cup semi-final in 1990 and the Euro semi-final in 1996. Things had ended just as badly against Argentina in the 1998 World Cup.

The grass round the penalty spot at Estádio da Luz was in very poor condition. I think it was Tord and our goalkeeping coach, Ray Clemence, who pointed it out to the FIFA delegate who was there. If you put your foot down next to the penalty spot, the grass just disappeared. The delegate promised that it would be fixed before the game, and so did the caretaker of the pitch. I don't think it was ever fixed properly, as we would come to see later on.

More Portuguese fans than English fans filled the stadium on 24 June, but not a lot more. And the English fans definitely sounded louder. I know all football managers say that their fans are the best in the world, but there was no doubt in my mind that the English supporters were the most passionate of all national team fans.

We got off to a dream start when Michael Owen exploited a mistake in the Portuguese defence and scored after just two minutes. It reminded us of when he gave us the lead against Brazil in Japan. The Portuguese players were in shock, but Deco, their playmaker, was soon pulling the strings in midfield and Portugal started to control the game. We also had to keep an eye on Portugal's 19-year-old sensation Cristiano Ronaldo, who had arrived at the Euroa after an impressive debut season with Manchester United, although we were probably not as afraid of him as the Portuguese were of the player who would later be his team-mate at Manchester United, Rooney.

Wayne drew two defenders to him every time he got close to the ball. That opened up space for Owen. I was full of confidence, but halfway through the first half, the unthinkable happened. Wayne was chasing a ball into the Portuguese penalty area. He was trying to shake off a defender when the guy stepped on Wayne's foot, causing his shoe to come off. It looked an innocuous incident. Replays later showed that the defender had not touched the ball. If Rooney had gone down, he surely would have won a penalty. Instead, he staggered across the touchline and sat down. Leif Swärd ran over to examine him. It was clear that Wayne would not be able to go on. We did not know it then, but a metatarsal bone had been broken.

I put on Darius Vassell in his place. Darius was a strong forward from Aston Villa, whom I liked. I had given him his England debut in 2002, and he had scored with a phenomenal bicycle kick. But Darius was not Wayne Rooney. No one could replace Wayne Rooney at the 2004 Euros.

Portugal created more and more chances, although we held on pretty well. There was no strategy on our part to pull back, but in the second half I took off Paul Scholes for Phil Neville, who was a more defensive player. Portugal pressed even more, without getting the breakthrough they were looking for. With less than ten minutes to go I took off Gerrard for Owen Hargreaves. Now we just had to hold on. Just a couple of minutes later, it fell apart when Hélder Postiga equalised with a header.

The match was going to extra time when, in injury time, we were awarded a free kick, which Beckham lofted in towards the Portuguese goal. Michael Owen, our shortest player, somehow got his head to it and directed the ball on to the crossbar. Sol Campbell was there to head the rebound into the net. However, the Swiss referee, Urs Meier, thought John Terry had pushed the Portuguese goalkeeper Ricardo just before Sol headed the ball into the net. He disallowed the goal. Replays later showed that Terry had done nothing wrong.

We should have won the game in ordinary time. Instead it went to extra time. By then, many of the players on both teams were spent. Portugal's manager, Scolari, had made all three substitutions, as had I, and we could not influence the game much further. The first half of extra time ended without a goal, but five minutes into the second half, one of Portugal's substitutes, the veteran Rui Costa, collected the ball a little way outside our penalty box, shook off Phil Neville and hit a thunderbolt of a shot into the roof of the net. I could not believe my eyes. Would Rui Costa, who had started his career at Benfica fourteen years earlier when I was manager, finish his international career by knocking England and me out of the Euros? Maybe it was fate.

But even fate can be defeated – with the help of Frank Lampard. With five minutes left of extra time, we won a corner, which Beckham took. Terry headed the ball down to Lampard, who spun around in front of the Portuguese goal and kicked it into the roof of the net. After 120 minutes of play, the result was still tied and the game would be decided on penalties.

We had practised penalties, but I knew it did not matter that much. In the heat of the moment, when it really mattered, it would all come down to individual nerves. As a manager, it was almost impossible to prepare the team for a penalty shootout. You never knew which players would still be on the pitch after extra time. A penalty shootout almost had nothing to do with football. I sat helpless on the bench when Beckham stepped up to take the first one. I was confident that he would score but he blasted it sky high. He turned around and looked at the penalty spot. The ground had not been fixed as promised.

After that, Owen and Lampard scored their penalties, while Deco and Simão did the same for Portugal. Rui Costa missed the target, and we were even again. Both teams continued to score after that, all the way to the seventh round when Darius Vassell stepped up to take his penalty. He struck it well, but Ricardo guessed right and tipped the ball around the post. Darius fell in a heap on the pitch. If the Portuguese scored their next penalty, they would be through. Up stepped Ricardo, the Portuguese keeper. He shot low and hard and even if David James had guessed right he had no chance of reaching it. Portugal had won. We were out of the Euros.

After the game, I was given permission to talk to Urs Meier, who had wrongly disallowed Sol Campbell's headed goal in injury time. I thanked him for the game and shook his hand. What was done was done.

The English press were not as forgiving. They called Meier 'Urs Hole' and 'Idiot Ref'. After an English tabloid published his contact information, Meier received thousands of hate mails and even death threats. His children could not go to school as normal. Meier was placed under police protection after reporters from *The Sun* travelled to Switzerland and hung a huge English flag near his home. When I heard what had happened, I called him and apologised on behalf of the England team.

There was no excuse for that kind of behaviour. I think Meier quit refereeing after that.

I went back to Sweden. Many people were disappointed that we had been eliminated. Of course, I was, too, but we had played a great tournament. Luck had not been on our side. Maybe things would have turned out differently had Rooney not been injured. But there would be other chances. In football, as in life, it does you no good to look back.

UNFAIR GAME

When David Davies called I was in a suite at the Leonard Hotel near Marble Arch in London. David said that the *News of the World* was about to reveal that I was having a romantic relationship with Faria Alam, David's secretary at the FA. David asked if it was true.

'It's nonsense,' I said.

By that I didn't mean it wasn't true, but that the question was nonsense. That was my private life. What David did not know was that Faria was with me in the suite when he called. It was at the Leonard Hotel where she and I met a few times.

• • •

The first time I met Faria was at the FA offices. She sat at a desk outside Davies's glassed-in office. Faria was dark and exotic-looking, a former model, born in Bangladesh. We started talking more and more each time I came by David's office. I was not the only one who liked Faria. At a big dinner, she and Mark Palios, the FA chief executive, had become romantically involved. I found that out later on. No one knew of their relationship.

I think it was in February of 2004 that I called Faria to ask her out for lunch. I was pretty sure she was going to say yes. I booked a hotel room where we had lunch and one thing led to another. Faria was both sexy and smart, just my type. She was very pleasant to be around. We started seeing each other at least once a week, sometimes for lunch at an Indian restaurant where Faria knew the owner, sometimes at the Leonard.

During the Euros in Portugal I had talked to Faria on the phone almost every day. Nancy was with me in Portugal, but she was staying at the hotel for wives and girlfriends. When I went to Sweden after the Euros, Nancy went to Italy and Faria visited me at Björkefors. No one knew that she was there and there was no reason to suspect that we would be discovered. It was after we went back to England that David Davies called me at the Leonard Hotel when I was with Faria.

I had said neither yes nor no to his question if Faria and I had a relationship, and I advised Faria to do the same if she was asked – neither admit nor deny that it was true. It was no one's business. Soon after I got off the phone with David, Faria's phone rang. It was David. She went out of the room and I don't know exactly what she said but when she returned, she was visibly shaken. I told her to remain calm and not do anything drastic. Late that night, she went to her place. I remember that she was worried paparazzi would be standing outside the hotel.

On Sunday, 18 July 2004, the *News of the World* published an exclusive scoop that I'd had an affair with Faria Alam. The article did not contain any irrefutable evidence, however. I was sure that I could ride out whatever storm would follow. I don't think Nancy was in London then.

The following day, I went to the office. When I arrived, Faria had already gone to David Davies to request legal assistance. She had denied that the story was true. The FA threatened to sue the newspaper and quickly issued a public statement denying the accusations. That would prove to be a big mistake. At the FA, they did not know that the paper had in its possession some of Faria's e-mails and text messages in which she described having sex with me. Not only that, the paper knew about her relationship with Mark Palios. When the newspaper informed the FA about the evidence it had, the people at the FA panicked. Suddenly, it was all about protecting Palios. Without my knowledge, our press director, Colin Gibson, tried to make a deal with the *News of the World*. The paper would be supplied with information about my affair with Faria and in exchange Palios's name would be kept out of the story. It was big blow below the belt. I would be thrown to the wolves.

The *News of the World* also demanded an interview with me and Faria. There was no chance of my agreeing to anything like that. I was not interested in defending Palios. He and I had never really got on. I had always thought he was the wrong man for the chief executive's job. Why would I agree to humiliate myself in a newspaper interview so that Mark Palios could get away unscathed? I had never talked about my private life in the media and I was not about to start now.

When the *News of the World* came out the following Sunday, 25 July, Faria and I were still front-page fodder. This time there was no doubt that the story was true. The newspaper published Faria's explicit e-mails and text messages. How could she be so stupid as to write about our bedroom business to her friend? The paper also revealed Faria's affair with Palios. The next day, the FA chairman, Geoff Thompson, called me and said the

FA would launch an inquiry into what exactly had happened. Until that was concluded, Thompson said, it was best if I did not come into the office. In other words, the chairman of the FA forbade me to go to work.

I went home to Björkefors, but it was a zoo. Reporters had laid siege to my house. My parents were distraught. Paparazzi from England and Sweden were everywhere. There must have been at least twenty cars outside the gate leading up to the house. The police put up signs saying 'no trespassing'. One particularly intrusive Sky News reporter walked up to the door and rang the bell. My mother opened it and screamed in Swedish, 'Leave us alone!'

Sky showed that clip over and over again. My mother became semi-famous in England. No one understood what she had said. Later, my father decided to have some fun with the reporters. He put a couple of rubbish bags on the back seat of the car, threw a blanket over them and drove off. At least ten cars must have followed him. The photographers thought I was hiding on the back seat. My dad drove to the dump, removed the blanket and unloaded the rubbish bags. I would like to have seen the faces of those so-called journalists when he did that. One Swedish reporter offered my dad an apology.

It went on like that for a few days. Finally, I left and went to Amsterdam to attend Ajax's annual pre-season tournament. One of the four teams participating was Arsenal. If I could not come back to the office, I could at least watch some football. Sitting on the plane next to me was a young woman who turned out to be a journalist. She desperately tried to get me to say anything about the Faria business. At Schiphol Airport, a BBC crew waited, but I didn't tell them anything, either.

While I was in Amsterdam, I was accused of having yet another affair with an attractive young woman who worked in reception at the FA. Colin Gibson called to ask if it was true. I told him it was none of his business.

He said it had to do with her safety and that he had to ask on behalf of the FA if I'd had an affair with her.

'No,' I said, and it was the truth.

To the *News of the World*, the Faria story was a gold mine. On 1 August – for the third Sunday in a row – the newspaper dropped yet another bomb. This time, the FA was the target. The paper described Colin Gibson's desperate attempts to keep Palios's name out of the spotlight. The paper had recorded the phone conversations with Gibson in which he tried to make a deal with the paper. Now the FA officials, especially Palios, were put on the spot. The FA held a crisis meeting at the Leonard Hotel, ironically, which resulted in Palios having to leave his post. The press chief, Gibson, also had to go.

But not me. There were those at the FA who wanted to see me fired, but I had not done anything illegal. There was nothing written in the bylaws of the English Football Association that said you could not enter into a romantic relationship with another employee. I had never lied, as Palios and Faria had done, and said the accusations were not true. I had not said anything and therefore I had nothing to be held accountable for.

Faria hired Max Clifford, a publicist whom I had also previously met. With his help, she sold her story to the *News of the World* and the *Mail on Sunday*, and on 8 August, the two papers published her account of how I had seduced her. The articles contained quite graphic descriptions of our love-making, but that really didn't matter to me. The story was out anyway. It was said that Faria received hundreds of thousands of pounds to tell her side of the story, but I did not have any problems with that, either. Faria had been hung out to dry in the press and lost her job, so why not make some money off the whole ordeal?

What made me sad was that it was definitely over between us. I liked Faria a lot. I think love had even blossomed, at least from my end. I didn't care what people said, that I should have stopped to think what I was doing. If I liked a woman and wanted to meet her, why should I not be able to? I felt no remorse towards Nancy. She lived in my house, but we were not married and I did not love her. People could say whatever they wanted. I did not regret anything.

• • •

The summer after the Faria story had come out I was in the United States with England to play a couple of friendlies. I was sitting on the team bus in New York, on our way back from training, when I got a message on my phone. It was from Faria. She was living in New York and was wondering if I wanted to meet for a cup of coffee. I didn't respond right away, because I thought I might call her later on. Back at the hotel, Adrian Bevington, the press officer, came up to me in reception.

'Don't do it,' he said.

He had found out that Faria wanted to meet me, but how? When I asked him, he said that he had received a message ten minutes earlier from a journalist.

'You still have some friends in the press,' he said.

I thought it was a publicity stunt. I called Faria and asked her what the hell she was trying to do. Did she want to set me up? She didn't understand what I meant. When I told her, it seemed obvious to me that she had leaked information about our secret meeting to the press.

'I'm sorry you feel that way,' she said. 'I won't bother you again.'

• • •

When I took the England job, the plan was to win the 2006 World Cup in Germany. It was the vision of the English FA. Forty years after England's 1966 World Cup triumph, it was up to a Swedish manager to repeat Alf Ramsay's achievement, this time on German ground. I had been in the job for almost four years, which was a long time for a football coach and almost an eternity for a national team manager. We had played two good tournaments, without getting past the quarter-finals. In the 2002 World Cup, we had been beaten by a better team. In the 2004 Euros, we had been unlucky to be knocked out on penalties when our best player was injured. It was time to go all the way.

First we had to qualify for the tournament. We were handed a decent draw with Poland, Austria, Wales, Northern Ireland and Azerbaijan in our qualifying group. Things did not start as well as we had hoped, however. Once again, it was the goalkeeping question that gave us headaches.

David James did a good job at the Euros, after taking over from Seaman. We had hoped that Chris Kirkland would develop into England's number-one keeper, but Kirkland struggled with injuries.

David James had everything that a goalkeeper should have. He could fly from one post to another, he was big and excellent at handling crosses. But Ray Clemence always warned that you could expect one big mistake from David James in each game. It was a big problem. A goalkeeper cannot make mistakes. It is the kind of thing that loses games.

Our first World Cup qualifier was away to Austria on 4 September 2004. We were on our way to a routine victory, leading 2–0 in the middle of the second half, when Austria got a goal back from a free kick. A minute or so after that, one of the Austrian midfielders had a pop from well outside the penalty area. The shot might have touched one of our defenders, but it should have been a simple save for David

James. Instead, he let the ball slip underneath him and into the goal. Suddenly, the score was 2–2, which was the final result. We had lost two points.

It was the end of David James's international involvement during my time as England manager. Of course, that I would bench him was not something I told the press after the game. To the journalists, I said that James had saved us many times before and that his one mistake was not a problem. It was one of those white lies that a manager has to tell sometimes. You could not always tell the truth. You could not, for example, go to the press and say you wanted to sell a player, because then that player's price tag would plummet. I also had to talk to David first. To his credit, he handled the news as a consummate professional.

The English media went all out in their criticism of James after his goalkeeping howler. One of the papers depicted David as a donkey in one picture. The players did not like that. They supported David James.

Four days later, we were playing Poland away in Chorzów in the southern part of the country. The day before the game, most of the players and I went to visit Auschwitz, which was located nearby. I had never visited a concentration camp. It was a very enriching experience, if you can put it that way, something I will always remember. On the team bus, players usually played music and talked, but on the way back from Auschwitz not a peep could be heard.

A few months later I participated in a major event at Westminster Abbey in remembrance of the Holocaust. I had been asked to give a speech and say something about my visit to Auschwitz. Although I was not very comfortable with it, I felt I had to do it. I had never liked talking in front of big audiences, especially if the subject was not football. When I got up to the podium, I looked out at the guests gathered there. In the front row sat the Queen, Tony Blair, Gordon Brown and a whole slew of famous people. Was I going to give a speech to them? The memorial was being broadcast live on BBC and probably in a bunch of other countries. I remember standing there, looking out over the dignitaries and thinking, 'Svennis, what the hell are you doing here?'

We won the game against Poland 2–1. The players had decided not to talk to the press after the match. In their eyes, criticism of David James had gone too far. They may also have been worried that they would get hammered in the same way the next time they made a mistake. The journalists were up in arms. I could understand them, too, especially the serious ones. After all, not everyone had behaved badly.

● ● ●

I have always said that a football manager's most important job is to create a good atmosphere in the team. As the manager of a national team, you have three or four days to work with the players before a game. There is really not a lot you can accomplish in such a limited time when it comes to coaching. You do a bit of tactical work, but you can't change the players. They must already be the finished product. The most impor- tant thing is to let them play in the positions they are used to from their clubs. They have to feel at home in the England team.

A healthy team spirit is created primarily off the pitch. You have to be able to trust your players. They are grown men. Professional men. It is important to give them freedom, but also the responsibility not to violate that freedom. The England players had never given me any cause to distrust them on this point. So when David Beckham asked, after a World Cup qualifying victory over Northern Ireland in Manchester, if the players could go out to eat and have a beer or two that night, four days before the next game, I told him yes.

The qualifying campaign had gone as planned after the initial setback against Austria away. We had beaten Poland, Wales and Azerbaijan, and demolished Northern Ireland 4–0 on 26 March 2005. We would play Azerbaijan in Newcastle four days later. If the players wanted to hang out and have a beer or two, that was fine by me, as long as they kept it to that. I remember my old playing days at KB Karlskoga. You could not go out partying the night before a game. Everyone in Värmland would find out. I had let the England players have a night out during the training camp in Dubai ahead of the 2002 World Cup and there had been no problems whatsover.

They were supposed to be back by a certain time. I went out for an early dinner with the coaching staff and then went to bed early. In the morning, I was informed there had been problems the night before. One group of players had apparently partied way too hard. Ray Clemence had still been up when the players returned to the hotel, but it was our security manager who told me what had happened. He did not want to tell me the names of the players who had been drunk and disgraced themselves and I didn't want to know who they were, either. That would just have made me angry with individual players. I planned to confront the team. The players had let me down.

I called a meeting before lunch. I was mad. It was completely unacceptable, I told them, that I could not trust the players on the England national football team to behave themselves. If this were repeated, they could find themselves another manager. The players all sat quietly. The mood in the group was a little sour after that. Not everyone had abused my trust in them. At the same time I think most of the players respected that I had not dug any deeper into what had happened, and that I had not pinned the blame on individuals. What was done was done. Three days later, we beat Azerbaijan 2–0 with goals by Gerrard and Beckham.

● ● ●

Everyone knew that Nancy's and my relationship was on the rocks. It had always been on the rocks. But I did not care what it looked like to the outside world. We travelled together, went out for dinners, visited friends. Nancy became close friends with David Dein's wife, Barbara, and David Davies's wife, Susan. We were often invited to David and Barbara Dein's home in London. They had a beautiful house and were amazing hosts. Sometimes Arséne Wenger and his wife were there, too. They lived nearby. At those occasions, it was still nice to have Nancy there. She was incredibly social and people liked being around her.

For the most part, though, I was tired of Nancy. I had wanted to cut ties with her a long time ago. Sometimes I checked into a hotel in London just to get away from her. During the spring of 2005 I decided to buy an apartment where I could be by myself. I had done the same thing in Rome during my last year with Lazio. I had rented a house near Formello to get away from Nancy. It had its own swimming pool. I never told Nancy and it happened that I invited other women there. One woman, a television celebrity, started writing a book about me. *The Gentleman in Football*, she called it. I gave her permission to write what she wanted about football, but she could not write about my private life. The book never materialised. It was just filled with match reports.

Nancy was not the only reason I wanted to get out of the house. I wanted to get away from the paparazzi, too. At times, it was said, I was living in England's most media-scrutinised residence. Some paparazzi would stand outside the house waiting for twenty-four hours straight. Maybe I should have done what Chris de Burgh, the singer, suggested. I got to know him and his wife during a holiday in Barbados. We had dinner together. We were talking about paparazzi laying siege to our houses. He suggested offering them tea and put laxatives in it. Half an hour later, the street would be empty of paparazzi.

People said the constant media attention was something I had to accept, Once I took the job and the money I was somehow fair game. I never understood that, or what was so interesting about my private life. When Lina came to visit from Italy, we would go running together in the park and I ran with my baseball cap pulled down as far as possible. Even Lina was not always left alone. At one point, a newspaper published a picture of her and me with a caption that claimed she was my new girlfriend. I think she was about 16 then.

● ● ●

With the help of Suzanne Bolinder, I bought a nice apartment in Belgravia in central London. It cost £1.7 million and I had to take out a mortgage for most of it. Athole had introduced me to Karl Fowler, a rich businessman who had worked for Goldman Sachs before and now ran his own financial consulting business. His company did not arrange mortgages, so he recommended another financial adviser who did, Samir Khan.

Samir Khan was a short, stocky man of Pakistani origin, around 45 years of age. Samir fixed the mortgage for me without any hassles. I trusted him from the beginning. When he explained that he could help me more broadly with my finances, it sounded like a good idea. I needed the help.

I was not interested in how best to invest my money. I wanted to leave that to an expert, like Samir Khan. I did not know much about his background, so Athole looked him up and everything seemed to check out okay. He had helped Nick Faldo, the golf pro, and he was apparently one of the few financial advisers insured by the City of London. That meant my money would be in safe hands. At some point, I visited Samir at his office in Bond Street.

In time, Samir Khan took over my finances. It made my life much easier to have someone who could take care of everything. He would pay all my bills. I was still building at Björkefors, which was not cheap. Samir also suggested investments that sounded good. I was not interested in details. If he said the investment was sound, I trusted him. I did not read long contracts. Sometimes he would fax a page from a contract that he wanted me to sign.

● ● ●

During my time as England manager, the Premier League had grown into the strongest football league in the world, at least from a financial perspective. The Premier League brand had become a cash cow the like of which the football world had never seen. Millions of new fans, from Asia to Africa, followed English football. The Premier League attracted the best players from around the world. Already, when Lazio played Chelsea in the Champions League in 2000, Chelsea did not have a single English player in its starting eleven. Arséne Wenger's Arsenal featured half the French national team. The foreign players improved the quality of the Premier League, but the trend did not benefit the development of English players. Increasingly, new English talents had difficulty breaking into their own football league, which did not help the English national team. Despite that, there were never any serious discussions about limiting the number of foreign players who could play in each Premier League team.

However, other things could be considered to help England compete internationally, such as introducing a winter break. England was alone among the important footballing countries in Europe not to have a winter break in its domestic league. Statistics clearly showed that when the international championships came around, the English players from the Premier League were more tired and to a greater degree injured than the Italian, German or Spanish players who had played in leagues with winter breaks. During my whole time in England, I fought to introduce a winter break in the Premier League but it was like banging your head against the wall. The English had their traditions. Football had always been played during the entire month of January and that could not be changed. There were, of course, economic reasons for it, too.

I also wanted the league to be concluded at least one month before the start of the big championships. That way, players would have time to recover after the demanding league season, and be able to prepare themselves, both mentally and physically, for the impending World Cup. I knew the Premier Leauge would object to that idea, so I went directly to FIFA. During a breakfast meeting with FIFA chairman Sepp Blatter and his right-hand man Peter Hegarty, David Davies and I suggested that FIFA should issue a decree that all football leagues must end their seasons at least one month before the World Cup. Blatter bought the idea on the spot. He later came to push it as if the idea were his own, which I didn't mind. He did a very good job with this issue.

Time passed and everything was going well when I got a phone call from Hegarty. He said that FIFA had received a written request from the

English FA, seeking a special exemption for the Premier League from the one-month rule that was to be implemented across Europe. No one had told me anything about it. I asked Peter to send me a copy of the fax, which he did. In the fax, the English FA appealed to FIFA to be allowed to run the league until three weeks before the start of the World Cup. The fax was signed by Geoff Thompson, the FA chairman.

During my years at the English FA I had never visited Thompson in his office, which I think was on the top floor. I don't think he ever came down to visit me, either. Sometimes he would come to greet the team before a game. 'Good luck, Sven,' he might say. I didn't have anything more to do with him. But when I received that fax, I was furious, which doesn't happen very often. I took the lift up to his floor, walked straight into his office without knocking and threw the fax on his desk.

'What the hell is this?' I demanded.

Thompson understood why I was mad. The whole thing had been my idea. Just as I had expected, he blamed everything on the Premier League. They needed that extra week to fit in all the games.

The exemption was not allowed, but the whole mess exposed the weakness of the leadership at the FA. It was clear that the Premier League controlled English football. I understood that it was futile to battle the powers that be if my own chairman did not even back me up.

● ● ●

During my whole time as England manager, I lost one qualifying game. There could not have been many other national team managers with a better record than mine. But when that one loss occurred, it was as if the whole world had ended and it was all my fault. The date was 7 September

2005, and we were playing Northern Ireland in Belfast. The Northern Irish starting eleven mostly featured players from the lower divisions of English football. Northern Ireland had no chance of making the World Cup but that did not matter. To Northern Ireland, a game against England was like a World Cup final.

In an attempt to get our passing game moving, I decided to play Beckham as a holding midfielder, in the centre of the pitch, and Rooney on the left. It was unlike me to fudge with my principle of always letting the players play in the positions they were most comfortable in, and the experiment failed miserably. Beckham saw too much of the ball and kept hitting long passes that seldom found their target. Rooney went missing and got frustrated. Lampard and Gerrard got nowhere. It reminded me of when we played as kids back home in Torsby. If nothing worked and people got irritated with each other, the guy who owned the ball could pick it up and walk home with it. Game over. That's what I felt like doing that day in Belfast. I wanted to go out on the pitch, pick up the ball and walk off. In the middle of the second half, David Healy scored the lone winner for Northern Ireland and my first and only qualifying loss with England was a fact.

The English press went ballistic. As usual, I tried not to read the papers, but I knew some people were calling for my resignation. The idea that I should resign after one qualifying loss – my first in five years as England manager – was absurd. We were still on track to qualify for the World Cup. But that did not matter. The papers shouted about English pride and the same old nonsense about my lacking passion. My thought was that the job required the exact opposite. You could not let emotions govern you as England manager. I had made a mistake with the team I picked for the Northern Ireland game. It had nothing to do with passion.

The day after the Northern Ireland loss I was invited to The Oval for the start of the last, and for England crucial, match in the Ashes series. I think the game was starting at 11 a.m. When I woke up and looked out my bathroom window, there must have been fifty reporters standing outside my house. It was like the days of Ulrika and Faria. There was no way I was going to the cricket match. I would have been bombarded by the press. I went to the office instead.

I recognised that the papers wanted to sell copies, and they had a knack for making things sound dramatic. If we beat Argentina in a friendly, we were suddenly the greatest team in the world. If we lost to Northern Ireland, we were worthless. At least they were writing about football this time, not my private life. In Italy I was used to handling criticism when it came to football. I didn't have anything against the media as long as we were talking about football. I had no sympathy for the tabloids and the garbage they put out. At the same time, I had the highest respect for the many serious sports journalists whom I met during my time in England. Many among them were very knowledgeable.

● ● ●

One month later, it was not Eriksson's head the tabloids were after. It was Beckham's. We played a qualifying game at home to Austria and won it 1–0 – an important victory taking us a step closer to our goal of qualifying for the World Cup. However, in the span of just two minutes in the second half, David Beckham had received two yellow cards and got himself sent off. It was unforgivable, according to the press. Beckham had put England in a situation in which we had to play with ten men for half an hour. For that, he should lose the captaincy, the papers wrote. It didn't matter that we had won the game.

Matters did not improve after our last qualifying game, at home to Poland. Beckham was suspended because of the sending-off against Austria and in his place I played Shaun Wright-Phillips, with Joe Cole on the left. Ledley King came in as a defensive midfielder. As a team, we may have played our best game in the qualifying campaign, even though the score finished just 2–1 in our favour. It meant we won the group. Beckham's critics shouted that their argument had been strengthened. Our excellent performance against Poland proved, they said, that Beckham was no longer needed in the England national team, and his time was past.

It was ridiculous. How many times had David won a game for us? I never gave the idea of demoting him a second's thought. Even if I had, what was the alternative? Shaun Wright-Phillips? No offence to Shaun, he was a very good footballer, but David Beckham was a world-class player and one of the best I have ever managed. He was going to lead England to their first World Cup title, forty years after the 1966 triumph. I could feel it.

PENALTIES

IT was thanks to Athole Still that I got the England job and I saw him as my agent, although we had never signed a contract. In that regard, I was no different from most other football managers. You worked primarily with one agent, but listened to others, too, if they came with something to offer. It was, for example, Pini Zahavi who had contacted me about the jobs at Manchester United and Chelsea. If I had listened only to Athole, I would not have received those offers. I was happy with Athole, though. He was a good man, and experienced in the ways of the world. He spoke French, German and Italian fluently. I felt loyalty towards him because of the England job, but also because he was honest and worked hard for me. He would never cheat me.

During the autumn of 2005, Athole asked me on several occasions to go to Dubai. A rich sheikh wanted to see me to discuss how football could be developed in the United Arab Emirates. Each time I said no because I did not have time. Athole was very keen on my going. He and his lawyer, Richard Des Voeux, had visited the sheikh's organisation's offices in Bond Street to confirm that the project was legitimate. He had received authorisation from the FA allowing us to travel to Dubai to listen to what the sheikh had to say. After New Year's I had an opening in my diary. Athole asked me again if we could go to Dubai. This time I said yes.

Athole, Richard and I flew first class from London and a limousine took us to the luxurious Burj Al Arab hotel, which looks like a sailboat. I was given a suite. We were staying for two nights and everything was paid for.

The first night we had dinner with our hosts in a private dining room. The sheikh, a relatively young man, wore traditional Arabic dress. I had not met him before and knew nothing about him, except that he was rich and liked football. I had been told that I was there to listen and give advice, but during the dinner, it became apparent that the Arabs had something else in mind. They had a job for me. They wanted me to take over the whole football organisation in Dubai and the sheikh was willing to pay me an enormous sum of money to do so. I made it clear to them right off the bat that it was impossible. There was no way on earth that I would leave England to take a job in Dubai. It did not matter how much money they paid me. I was not interested.

After that, we talked more broadly about football and, I think, about building football academies in Dubai. But suddenly the sheikh changed the subject. He said he was interested in buying a club in the Premier League. Which club did I think he should buy? I didn't say anything. Athole jumped in and said that Aston Villa was for sale. 'If we buy Aston Villa, would you come to manage the club?' the sheikh asked. I said that if we didn't win the World Cup with England, it might be a possibility because

233

the FA probably would not keep me on as England manager. I made it clear that it was not something that could be discussed now.

I thought the sheikh and his friends had a lot of money but the whole thing about buying a Premier League team was not something I took seriously. The conversation was completely hypothetical. If they bought the club, I would be interested in the manager's job, just as I would be interested in other jobs. I never said that I would go to Aston Villa. They wondered if I would be able to lure Beckham to Villa. I told them that Beckham and I were close, which was true. It was an innocent discussion. There were no concrete offers to consider. They had offered me a job, which I had turned down. Now we were talking generally about football. When the evening drew to a close, they asked me if I was interested in some lady company. It could be arranged, the sheikh's friends said. I declined. I remember wondering what exactly I was in Dubai for.

The next day, we were served a light lunch on board the sheikh's boat out in the bay. Athole, a former Olympic swimmer, couldn't resist going for a swim. I had a couple of glasses of wine, chatting with the sheikh and his people. It was a pleasant day. We picked up from the conversation the night before. They asked me about various players and what I thought of them. At one point, the conversation turned to corruption in fooball. Was it true, someone asked, that some managers pocketed agent's fees? There was no substance to the discussion. It was like a pub chat.

When we returned to the marina, there was no limousine waiting. I think we took a taxi back to the hotel. It had been a strange experience. Had I really travelled to Dubai to talk about hypotheticals? Who was that sheikh, really? I remember asking Athole in the car, 'Are you sure that was for real?'

The idea was that we would meet the sheikh and his people on the second night, too, but that did not happen. I got no explanation as to why. In the morning, when we were travelling back to England, I asked Athole if he had heard anything from the sheikh. 'No,' he said, 'nothing.' We flew home.

● ● ●

I had never heard of the fake sheikh before the Dubai trip. He was, I was told later, a British journalist by the name of Mazher Mahmood, who dressed up as a sheikh to con famous people. He worked for the *News of the World* and had exposed a string of celebrities by using various dirty tricks. Maybe I should have known about him, but I didn't read the papers.

Naturally, it was Mahmood whom I had met in Dubai. He and his companions had secretly taped our conversations and I was first-page fodder again: 'Sven's Dirty Deals!' screamed the headline.

According to the article, I was willing to ditch England to take the Aston Villa job but only if my salary matched José Mourinho's at Chelsea — £5 million. I was also supposed to have said that I could guarantee David Beckham coming to Villa. They wrote that I had called Rio Ferdinand 'lazy' and that Michael Owen had gone to Newcastle purely for the money. There was nothing about my being invited to Dubai as an adviser. It was all a fabrication of what was said in the meetings with the sheikh.

I was angry with the paper but at the same time I didn't take it too seriously. It was, after all, just the *News of the World*. Everyone knew it was a gossip rag and what was said in it was not true. I assured the FA that I had no intention of leaving my job. They were worried about how things looked, however, and asked me to make a public statement saying that I was 100 per cent committed to the England cause. I also called the players I was supposed to have talked badly about. When I explained to Rio Ferdinand that I had not expressed myself in the way the paper described, he just laughed.

'Sven,' he said. 'I know I'm lazy. Don't worry about it.'

I did an interview with another newspaper to deny the accusations laid out in the *News of the World* article and thought it was pretty much over after that. But, of course, it wasn't. The following Sunday I was still on the front page of the *News of the World*. The headline was: 'Sven: The Tapes'. They published transcriptions of the conversations I'd had with Mahmood, but important words and details had been omitted, which meant the meaning of what I had said was distorted. They tried to make it sound as though I had said that Harry Redknapp, Portsmouth's manager, was 'the worst' manager when it came to pocketing agent's fees. But it was the reporters who had said that, in the form of a question. I think I had even questioned their statement.

'The worst?' I had asked.

But in the article, the question mark had been left out. It was dirty. I had not said anything bad about Harry Redknapp. Still, I felt obligated to make that clear to Harry, so I called him. I told him that what was written in the article was not true. Harry understood that. I liked Harry. He was a great guy.

However, this time Brian Barwick, the FA chief executive, wanted to see me the next day. His secretary called me at home on Sunday to arrange it. My relationship with Barwick was okay, but no more than that. He came from television, but he was a football man. At least, he saw himself as that. I don't think he disliked me, but I had not been his pick. Adam Crozier had chosen me for the post and I think Barwick, just like Palios before him, wanted his own man. Football executives were just like football managers. They wanted to choose their own people.

Athole and I met Barwick at his office. Richard Des Voeux was there, too. Barwick was furious. That was immediately clear.

'On Sunday mornings, I want to sleep, not have to sit on the phone and talk about what you have or have not done,' he said.

Athole explained that the second article, like the first, had been a lie, but Barwick didn't want to hear it. He didn't care what was true or not true. He had had enough of seeing me on the front page of the tabloids. It made me angry. Could these stinking rags really be allowed to write whatever they wanted about me without the FA even checking if it were true? That only legitimised what they were publishing.

'I have heard that the *News of the World* rules England, but I didn't know that it rules the English FA, too,' I snapped.

Barwick didn't care.

'I want to finish this story, here and now,' he said.

By that he meant the story with me. I realised it was pointless even to discuss the matter. The decision had been made. I was getting fired.

The rest of that Monday was spent negotiating my terms for leaving. I had a contract with the FA that ran for another two and a half years. If they wanted to get rid of me before then, they were legally responsible for paying my salary for the duration of my contract. But on Athole's and Richard's advice, I agreed to a compromise. I would get paid my full salary for six months upon leaving and then receive half my salary for six months after that. The next day, the FA announced that I would leave the England managerial post after the 2006 World Cup.

Athole was broken-hearted. It was, after all, he who had brought me to Dubai. Pini Zahavi advised me to cut ties with Athole but I did not want to blame Athole for what had happened. He had been deceived, just as I had been. He had got permission from the FA for us to go to Dubai. I still respected Athole, but I think our relationship changed after the story with the fake sheikh.

● ● ●

During my thirty-year-long career as a football manager, I had never been fired from a job. Clearly, I was very disappointed. It was not because of results that I had been forced out of my job. The reason had nothing to do with football. I had been fooled by a fake sheikh. What had I done besides letting my naiveté get the better of me? Nothing.

The media wrote about morals and passion for the cause while at the same time using all their resources to nail the manager of the nation's football team. I could never wrap my head around that. This time, I felt, I could at least hit back. I told Athole to get me the best lawyers he could find and sue the *News of the World* for libel. I didn't care how much it would cost. The legal process took six months and resulted in the news-paper having to pay my costs of £160,000 and make a donation of £3,000 to a charity of my choosing. Also, they had to publish an apology. The important thing was not the money, but that I had been right, even though it was too late.

At the same time, it was an open secret, even before the sheikh mess, that I would most likely leave the job after the World Cup. Five years in the same job was a long time and there were those at the FA who were tired of Eriksson and his scandals. Although Barwick took the opportunity to get rid of me, he must have had support from other people in the organisation, but from whom I don't know and I didn't want to know.

It was a mistake to go public four months before the World Cup, though. I suppose the FA felt they had no choice and had to be seen to act. I urged Barwick not to appoint my successor until after the World Cup. If he did it before, my position would be undermined, especially if the choice was Steve McClaren. Steve had returned as my assistant manager before the 2004 Euros and he was now one of the candidates to replace me. I think Barwick agreed that it was best to wait until after the World Cup, or maybe he just didn't know whom he wanted to appoint.

The media debate over who was going to be the next England manager started immediately. The focus was no longer on the upcoming World Cup, but my successor. Guus Hiddink, who then managed PSV Eindhoven and Australia simultaneously, expressed an interest. The Bolton manager, Sam Allardyce, was of the opinion that the job should be given to an Englishman – him. Alan Curbishley, Martin O'Neill and Stuart Pearce all seemed to want the job. No one at the FA consulted me on the matter, but I had no problem with that.

I don't know how Felipe Scolari's name came up. Some people at the FA must have still been willing to bet on a foreigner as England manager. Scolari was Brazilian. His teams had knocked us out of both the 2002 World Cup and the 2004 Euros. He was still the manager of Portugal at that time and Barwick went there to offer him the job. Scolari seemed to want to take it. The problem was that the news was leaked to the media. In England, the whole foreign-versus-domestic debate started all over again. Every pundit weighed in on the matter. The press began digging into Scolari's private life. One newspaper published a detailed comparison of his relationship with his wife with my relationship with Nancy. Something about how we dressed differently.

That kind of nonsense was nothing new to me but Scolari was not used to it. Suddenly he had twenty reporters outside his door. Within twenty-four hours he publicly declined the job as England manager, citing the intrusive behaviour of the English media as his reason for not taking it. He was not used to that kind of culture, he said, and he didn't want anything to do with it.

Barwick may have panicked after that. Scolari's rejection made the English FA look weak. A few days later, a little more than a month before the start of the World Cup, Barwick, without any notice, appointed Steve McClaren England's next manager – exactly what I had urged him not to do.

I saw the logic in the choice of McClaren. He was a very good coach, especially when it came to the defensive side. He was an Englishman and the plan had been for him or Peter Taylor to be groomed to take over after me. But why appoint him before the World Cup? That just created unnecessary confusion among the players. And would McClaren really be motivated to help me win the World Cup when he knew that he would take over the national team after the tournament? We had discussions about removing McClaren from the coaching staff. I mulled it over but in the end decided that he should stay. It was not his fault that the FA had mishandled the situation. He had been with us for the whole ride. It would not be fair to remove him now.

● ● ●

During my time with England, I had no problems with any of the club managers in the Premier League, except Sir Alex Ferguson. I had a lot of respect for Ferguson. How could you not? He had built so many great teams throughout the years and I appreciated that his teams always tried to play attacking, positive football.

Ferguson defended Manchester United's interests at any cost. It was a good trait to have, but it made my job more difficult. I had already been involved in a few scraps with him, but a bigger confrontation occurred with just a month to go before the World Cup in Germany. This time it involved our biggest star, Wayne Rooney.

It all started with a game between Chelsea and Manchester United on 29 April 2006, little more than a week before I was due to announce my preliminary World Cup squad. It was a busy time, when I was keen to see as many games as I could. Naturally, I was present at Stamford Bridge. Chelsea needed a point to secure their second straight league title under José Mourinho. I liked Mourinho. Outwardly, he was cocky, but he was really a very nice guy. Unlike Ferguson, he never gave me any hassles about his players. If one of them had an injury problem, it was up to me to select him or not. Mourinho never got involved.

Chelsea took an early lead and never relinquished control of the game after that. With ten minutes to go, they were comfortably 3–0 up. The match was over when Rooney, for some reason, threw himself into an unwinnable tackle. I did not see exactly what happened, but Wayne must have landed awkwardly because he immediately grabbed his foot and grimaced. It was clear he had to come off and I watched him being carried away on a stretcher with six weeks to go before our first World Cup game. Our doctor, Leif Swärd, was also at the game. I can't remember if I called him or he called me, but in any case I asked him to go down to the

Manchester United dressing room to check on Rooney. When Ferguson saw Leif outside the dressing room, he pointed at him and said, 'Don't let him in.'

It turned out Rooney had broken a metatarsal bone, just as Beckham had done before the 2002 World Cup. Later, Ferguson called me.

'You can't pick Rooney for the World Cup,' he said.

'Who says that?' I asked.

'My doctor,' Ferguson replied. 'Rooney is injured.'

'Okay,' I said. 'Then I will come with my doctor to talk to you.'

I think it was a Sunday morning when Leif and I met Ferguson and United's doctor at Carrington, the Manchester United training ground. We drank some tea and chatted before talk turned to the subject we were there to discuss, Rooney's injury. He cannot play in the World Cup, Ferguson said flatly. The United doctor brought out some X-rays that he said showed that Rooney's broken bone would not heal in time. Leif sat patiently and listened to the United doctor's argument. Leif was the calmest and nicest person in the world. When the United doctor had finished, there was a moment's pause before Leif looked him in the eye.

'Why do you sit here and lie to me?' he asked.

I thought Ferguson and his doctor would fall off their chairs. I almost fell off my own chair. I had never heard Leif even raise his voice. He was a kind Värmland-native, like me.

'What do you mean?' the guy asked.

'I operate on breaks like that all the time,' Leif continued, as calmly as before. He knew it was not true.

Leif knew what he was talking about. He was one of Europe's foremost specialists on the kind of foot injury that Wayne had suffered. I just wish I could have filmed Ferguson's face, and his doctor's, when Leif calmly proceeded to tell them how things were. He explained that Wayne's break would heal in time for the World Cup. Maybe he would have to miss the first game, but he would be ready for the second, no problem. When Leif had finished, I turned to Ferguson.

'Sorry, Alex,' I said. 'I will pick Rooney.'

The United doctor had said that with that kind of fracture absolutely no weight should be put on the foot, and Rooney had been given a protective boot to wear. One week after his injury, one of the masseurs on the England medical team was getting married. Rooney came to the wedding. Leif did, too. Rooney had taken off the boot and put on his dancing shoes. As Leif had explained, it was no problem to walk on the foot with the kind of fracture that Rooney had.

I don't believe Rooney ever doubted that he would play in the World Cup, but Ferguson did not give up. Before I selected my final squad, he called me again. This time he was screaming into the phone – that was his way of communicating – something about making my life very difficult if I went against him and picked Rooney. Now I'd had enough of his shouting.

'Alex,' I said. 'I wish you a very nice holiday, but I am going to select Wayne Rooney for the World Cup. Goodbye.'

Then I hung up. It was the last time I spoke with Sir Alex Ferguson as the England manager.

• • •

My England squads for the 2002 World Cup and the 2004 Euros had not included any major surprises. This time, however, I thought we needed some kind of a wild card, an attacking player whom I could throw on if needed, who could change a game. A new star. Someone like Rooney in 2004.

Three strikers were definitely coming – Rooney, Michael Owen and Peter Crouch. I considered bringing Jermaine Defoe, the Tottenham striker, as the fourth forward, but Defoe's season at Tottenham had been up and down. He had scored fewer goals than Tottenham's two other strikers, Robbie Keane and Mido. I did not feel that Defoe would give us that something extra in a World Cup.

A young player at Arsenal had piqued my interest. Theo Walcott was just 17 years old and had still not made his debut for Arsenal's senior team. But Arsène Wenger had lavished praise on him. Tord and I went to watch him play for the Arsenal reserves. He was, just as Arsène had said, quick – no, incredibly quick, with phenomenal acceleration. He had that something extra I was looking for. I decided to take a chance on him. When I presented the squad, Walcott's inclusion was greeted with collective shock by the press corps. Most of them had never heard of the boy. Of course it was a long shot, taking Theo Walcott to the World Cup, but I felt I had little to lose.

During the first few training sessions, however, Theo was struggling. At the same age, Rooney had walked into the English national team as if he had always been there, but Walcott was incredibly nervous. He constantly lost the ball and mishit easy passes. I began to wonder if I had made a mistake. But as the days went by, Theo's nerves steadied and I became convinced that he could be the wild card I had been hoping for.

Everything seemed to be falling into place. I was certain that we would play a good tournament and go far in it. I felt as if the time had come to take the next step. As usual, the English press whipped themselves into a frenzy. Suddenly, we were favourites to win the World Cup. Even the players jumped on the bandwagon. Someone said to the papers that we would win the Cup. I had no choice but to say the same thing. The truth was I actually believed it. I had not felt like that before.

●　●　●

Our base during the World Cup was Baden-Baden in southwestern Germany. Michelle and her team at the FA had, as usual, found the perfect place for us. The hotel looked like a fortress and was situated on a mountain top outside town, with a view of the Black Forest. It was just us staying there, together with a few select reporters. Wives and girlfriends were staying at a separate hotel in town. Lina and Johan stayed there, too. And Nancy. The set-up was the same as during previous tournaments but this time the English press went completely haywire. They followed every step that the wives and girlfriends took. The women were like big game to the reporters.

We, on the other hand, lived in total seclusion. The players spent a lot of time in the activity room, which had ping-pong tables and video games. They had plenty of spare time to kill between matches and training sessions. They hated that and became restless, as I did. They wanted to get out and do something. But the mood in the group was still very positive. It was my third tournament with England. This time, it really felt as if it would be our championship.

The teams in our group did not look unbeatable – Paraguay, Trinidad & Tobago and, for the second World Cup in a row, Sweden. By the time of the first game, against Paraguay, Wayne's foot had healed. Leif had even gone back to Manchester with him to allow United's medical team to examine him. It was part of the deal we had made with United and I had no problem with it. Wayne was not match fit, however, so we decided to keep him out of the starting line-up until the third game, against Sweden.

Except for Rooney, we had avoided all injuries. Against Paraguay, I started Peter Crouch up front with Michael Owen. Paul Robinson was our number-one goalkeeper. Gary Neville, who had missed the World Cup four years earlier, was in his right-back position. Together with Ferdinand, Terry and Ashley Cole, he made up one of the best defences in the world. In midfield we had Beckham, Gerrard and Lampard. Scholes had retired from international football but we seemed to have found a solution for the problematic left flank in Joe Cole, who had come off a brilliant season with the league champions, Chelsea. We had a complete team.

If everything felt right when we arrived at the stadium in Frankfurt, it got even better when we took the lead in the third minute, albeit with a Paraguayan own goal. There were no further goals, however, and we did not play particularly well. But a win was a win. It was the start we had hoped for.

Against Trinidad & Tobago, Jamie Carragher took over from Gary Neville at right back. Otherwise, I played the same line-up. Neville had sustained an injury in training the day before the game and we didn't yet know how serious it was. Most people probably expected us to beat Trinidad easily, anyway, but there are no easy games in the World Cup. That is no cliché. To get to the World Cup, Trinidad had knocked out Honduras and Costa Rica. A draw against Sweden in their first game proved that they belonged in the tournament.

I was right. It would not be easy. Peter Crouch scored the first goal in the eighty-third minute. We got another one soon after that and the game ended 2–0. We were through to the second round. If we managed to beat Sweden, we would go through as group winners.

Rooney was back for the Sweden game, but the talking point revolved around his strike partner. In the first minute, we lost Michael Owen. After receiving the ball, Owen was shaping up to pass it when his right knee buckled and he fell to the ground. He crawled across the sideline, obviously badly hurt. Later, X-rays showed that he had suffered a serious injury to the cruciate ligament and would be sidelined for many months.

We played a good first half. Joe Cole scored a dream goal with a volley. We were up both 1–0 and 2–1 until Sweden tied the game in injury time. It didn't matter much. We had still won the group. But we had lost Owen. I tried to keep up a good appearance in front of the media afterwards. We had other players who could partner Rooney up front, I said. But I knew what an enormous loss Owen was. He was our top goalscorer. If there was one thing that World Cup history showed it was the importance of having a healthy, in-form, goal-getting striker on your team. Would Brazil have won the World Cup four years earlier without Ronaldo? We had Rooney, but he had just come back from injury. Peter Crouch was a good football player but, given his height, he was more of an alternative to throw on later in the game to win balls in the air. The last forward I had at my disposal was 17-year-old Theo Walcott. Some people probably felt justified in arguing that I should have brought a more experienced attacker to the World Cup. But, once again, what were the alternatives? The truth is, England needed Owen.

That did not mean that I now thought we couldn't win. Far from it. I was convinced that Rooney would get better the further we went in the tournament. In the second round, we faced Ecuador and, instead of playing with a second striker, I decided to change the formation of the team. I had two attack-minded midfielders in Gerrard and Lampard, who could support Rooney as a lone forward. For cover centrally, I brought in Michael

Carrick as a deep-lying midfielder behind Gerrard and Lampard. It was a 4-1-4-1 system. It was unusual for me to change a system, but I had players whom I trusted to handle it. And they did. We won 1–0 after Beckham scored with a free kick.

I neither read nor listened to what the press said about us. I knew we had not yet played as well as we could but that did not worry me – almost the opposite. A World Cup ran for a month and to stay at 100 per cent the whole way was a tough proposition. The most important thing was to advance from the group stage and then keep improving the deeper you got into the tournament. It was no coincidence that the World Cup was often won by teams that had struggled in the beginning. The best example of that was Italy in the 1982 tournament.

In the quarter-final we would once again face Portugal. It was our third quarter-final in a World Cup or European Championship and the third time that I would face Scolari. His teams had beaten us before. This time, I was convinced we would get our revenge – at least, as convinced as you could be in football. Gary Neville was back in the starting eleven. We had the tournament's best defence. We had kept a clean sheet in three games out of four. I played the same formation as against Ecuador, but with Owen Hargreaves, who had played in Neville's right-back position, as a defensive midfielder. I also hoped to be able to use my wild card, Walcott.

The game was played at a packed stadium in Gelsenkirchen. The roof at the arena was closed and the noise was incredible. As usual, our supporters were completely dominant in the stands. The first half was tight, with few clear goalscoring opportunities, even though we probably had the upper hand. I still felt confident at half-time. The scene was set for a big second half.

We could have had a penalty just a few minutes into it when the ball hit a Portuguese defender in their penalty area, but the referee waved play on. Soon after that, David Beckham injured his ankle and had to be substituted. I put on Aaron Lennon in his place. But the turning point in the game came after a little more than an hour's play. Rooney had, on a couple of occasions, looked frustrated. He always gave everything and wanted to do everything. His hot temper was both his strength and his weakness. This day, unfortunately, it proved to be the latter. After getting entangled with two Portuguese players close to the halfway line, he planted a foot in the groin of Portuguese defender Ricardo Carvalho. The referee was standing right next to where it happened and without any hesitation pulled out his red card. I don't think I have ever seen the incident on television. I don't know whether it was right or wrong to send off Rooney. I just knew what it would mean for our chances in that game.

I replaced Joe Cole with Peter Crouch. With ten men, my attacking alternatives were limited. I still had match winners on the pitch in Gerrard and Lampard but Walcott would have to stay on the bench. The aim first and foremost was not to concede a goal. I hoped that Crouch could maybe nick a header off a corner or a free kick. Owen Hargreaves played the game of his life. He ran and ran. I have never seen a player show such energy as Hargreaves did in that game. With his help, we held on not just in regular time but also during the thirty-minute period of extra time. It was a highly admirable performance by the players. Later, people would forget that we played for a whole hour with only ten men.

• • •

Penalties again. I remained convinced that we could beat them. Jamie Carragher had been brilliant in training. With just a few minutes left of extra time, I made a substitution and put him on so that he could take one of them. We had practised with the players walking from the halfway line to the penalty spot, just as they would have to do in a real game. Decide where you are going to put it, put the ball down, step back, wait for the whistle, hit it. That is what we had told the players. But training was not real life. I knew that. In the final of the 'Little World Cup' against Sunne, I had hit my first four penalties to the right of the keeper. Just before my fifth shot I had changed my mind and gone to the left. The shot hit the post and out. Why had I changed my mind?

Three of our experienced penalty-takers – Beckham, Owen and Rooney – were not on the pitch after 120 minutes. But we had Gerrard and Lampard. And Hargreaves, the man of the match. Among the coaching staff, we locked arms, just as the players did. We watched Simão score the first penalty for Portugal. Lampard was taking our first penalty. Ricardo, the Portuguese goalkeeper who had been the hero at the Euros two years earlier after scoring the decisive penalty himself, guessed right and saved it. All I felt was helplessness. Portugal missed their next penalty, too. Hargreaves scored with a shot that was too hard for Ricardo to handle, even if he guessed the right way and got his hands to it. Portugal missed again, and if Gerrard scored, we would be in the lead. But Gerrard, ashen-faced, hit a weak penalty that Ricardo saved. Hélder Postiga made no mistake for Portugal and now it was Carragher's turn. He put the ball down, walked back, turned around, hit it, and scored. But the referee had not blown his whistle. Carragher had to re-take it. His second penalty was poorly struck and Ricardo managed to push it on to the crossbar and out. If Ronaldo scored his penalty, Portugal would win. He struck it and Robinson went the wrong way.

'I wish to be judged as an honest man who did his best,' I told the media at the press conference afterwards.

Together we flew to England. From there I arranged for a private plane to take me directly to Torsby. Maybe that is when I first truly realised that it was over.

SHOULD I STAY OR SHOULD I GO?

I looked out over Fryken. It was July and the sun was shining in Värmland. The best time of the year. The family had gathered. Björkefors was finally complete. The remodelling had turned out just the way I had hoped. There were no reporters hanging around at the gate. I should have been able finally to relax. But it was impossible.

I had always been able to get over a loss. Johan always said he could not tell by my face after a match if I had won or lost. This time it was different. The second we lost the penalty shootout against Portugal it was over. Not just the one match, or tournament. I would not get another chance with England. Losses you can shake but the end is final.

I kept going over in my head what I had done wrong. I had never done that before. I knew it was a futile exercise but I could not stop. What

Above: At Stadio Luigi Ferraris, home of Sampdoria. In Genoa, I achieved some success with a young and talented team. But my private life was in flux. I got divorced, and Anki moved to Florence.

Right: Standing with Anki, Johan and Lina after Johan graduated from high school in Italy. I was the manager of Lazio then and Anki and I had been separated for several years.

Above: With Roberto Mancini at Lazio. "Mancio" played for me during all my years at both Sampdoria and Lazio. I made him my assistant manager during my last season with Lazio. "Mancio" is a born leader.

Right: Meeting Lina and my mother in Karlstad, Sweden, where we had gone on a pre-season tour with Lazio in August, 2000. I have often taken my teams to Sweden for pre-season training.

With Sergio Cragnotti, the Lazio owner, celebrating the victory that made us Italian champions. I have never seen a more passionate owner of a football team than Cragnotti. He wanted to win the scudetto as badly as I did.

Nancy and I sitting on "Nancy One", the boat she had with her husband, Giancarlo. We went on boating holidays in Greece. I rented that boat without Nancy, too.

My first game with England was a friendly against Spain at Villa Park. The press was curious about England's first foreign manager. I was seen as a bit of a mystery. My struggles with the English press had not yet begun.

The work as England manager is all about watching football. Here I am with Tord Grip, watching West Ham take on Sunderland in January, 2001. It was right after I had left Lazio and taken on the England job full-time.

In England, our demolition of Germany at the Olympic Stadium in Munich is seen as one of the greatest triumphs in English football history. Naturally, I was very happy with the win. Yet it was only one World Cup qualifying game.

Above: David Beckham has just taken us to the World Cup after scoring *that* freekick against Greece at Old Trafford on October 6, 2001. During the game, David had missed free kick after free kick. But he finally got his aim right. In an FA online poll, the goal was voted the greatest England goal ever scored.

Right: The nightmare scenario: Wayne Rooney has just broken his foot against Portugal in the 2004 Euro quarter-final. Wayne had been the tournament's best player to that point.

Looking to the heavens after losing on penalties to Portugal in the 2006 World Cup. As a manager, I felt helpless during the penalty shoot out. At this moment, I knew it was all over for me and England.

Sir Alex Ferguson and I lead our teams, Manchester City and United, onto the pitch at Old Trafford. We were honouring the memory of the Munich plane crash of 1958 in which many of the Manchester United players died.

Above: We finally turned the basement of my house in Portugal into a pool room. Here I am playing with my father against my brother Lasse and Johan, seniors versus juniors. These are serious games. This time, my dad and I won. I'm sure of that.

Left: Giving a speech at the wedding reception of Johan and Amana in Italy, a big moment in my life. I wished them both a happy life and welcomed Amana into the family.

Right: Yaniseth, here together with her son Alcides, and I met in Mexico City in 2008, when I was the Mexico manager. She is a model and dancer. Alcides is a big Barcelona supporter. Yaniseth supports whichever team I'm coaching.

I am giving instructions to Siaka Tiéné and Didier Drogba during the game against Portugal in the 2010 World Cup. Drogba broke his arm the week before the tournament started and had to start on the bench. It was a major setback to not have him available from the start. Drogba is one of the best players I have ever coached and a fantastic person.

Training with Guangzhou R+F on June 21, 2013.

would have happened if Wayne had not been sent off? Not that it was Rooney's fault that we got knocked out.

'Don't kill Rooney, kill me,' I had told the media after the match. 'You will need him. You don't need me any more.'

Trivial things bothered me. In his speech to the players afterwards, Steve McClaren thanked me, and added that I would be invited as an honorary guest when England played the Euro final in 2008. As if he would be able to do what I had not been able to.

I could only imagine what the *Sun* and the other rags wrote about me. During five and a half years as England manager, I had lost three competitive matches in ordinary time. It really was an exceptional record. When I arrived, England had been ranked number seventeen in the world. Five and a half years later we were number four. But it was an argument I knew I could not win. At least, not for a while. The statistics did not matter to the media.

The fact remained that our aim had been to win the World Cup and in that quest we had failed. Three honorable quarter-final exits were not enough. Twice we had been beaten by Portugal on penalties. The margin between success and failure was razor thin. Yet only the results mattered in the end. I knew that better than anybody.

I should have brought in a coach to help the players prepare mentally for penalties. I should have done it after the exit from the 2004 Euros. Why did I not do it? Maybe I thought that players such as Gerrard, Lampard and Beckham, who had been there before and who took penalties for their clubs, had the experience to handle the pressure. Perhaps I did not want to bring in a specialist to prepare us for something that may not happen. Whatever the case, I had made a mistake.

I sat on the couch and looked out over Fryken.

• • •

The England job had been the best I'd ever had, despite the press and the politics, the scandals and shootouts. It was the biggest football job in the world. Everyone in England was a fan of the team that I managed. It was an amazing feeling. The passion for the game in England was unrivalled. Sometimes I wanted to go into a pub and sit down and chat about the game with other football supporters. It was a shame I never got to do it.

I wanted to stay in England to coach a Premier League team but there seemed to be a curse on former England managers. Hardly any of them had got a job at a big club in England after leaving the national team. Many were forced to go abroad. Even the great Bobby Robson had been shunted to Holland after he left the job in 1990. No one wanted to touch an ex-England manager.

I hadn't thought about it during my time in the job, or immediately after I left the post. I was a big-name manager, only 58 years old. I had many years ahead of me. Of that I was sure. I could not by happenstance have become a bad manager.

But the days went by and nothing happened. Time used to fly by. One match led to another and that is how it went on for eleven months. For the first time in my career I was without a job. I should have enjoyed it. My parents were close by. But the days were too long. I invited people I had not seen in a long while to Björkefors. I exercised, ran and swam. A few times I went to Björnevi and watched Torsby play. But the more time passed, the more anxious I became. Lina moved to England to start college in Norwich. The autumn season was about to begin. It was clear that it would start without me.

● ● ●

One positive consequence of my leaving the England job was that things finally ended with Nancy. I don't even remember if she was with us on the plane back from Germany. She did not come with me to Sweden. I don't remember if we spoke on the phone after the World Cup. There was no confrontation. I should have ended the relationship years earlier. In the end, it just fizzled out.

During the trip to Dubai in January of 2006 I had met Roxy, a singer and former gymnast from Romania. She had a very pleasant personality. I liked her quite a lot. We had met a few times during the spring. After the World Cup, she came to see me in Värmland. Once I went to Bucharest. We met in Portugal, too.

I could not bear sitting in Björkefors waiting for the phone to ring. It made me fidgety. I wanted to get back in the world. A couple of times I went to Israel to visit Pini and his wife. We swam in the Dead Sea. Katarina, a Swedish woman who worked for Scandinavian Airlines, came with me on one of those trips. We were photographed at a restaurant and the picture wound up in the Swedish papers. There were paparazzi in Israel, too.

I was not a registered resident of Sweden and was therefore not allowed to stay in the country for more than 180 days in a year. I was careful not to exceed the limit. My friend Lars Sternmarker and I travelled to Hong Kong and Thailand on a publicity trip for some real-estate project. Nothing came out of that. I went to Beijing, too, for another real-estate deal. I don't think anything happened with that, either.

A year after the fake sheikh incident I was invited by the Qatari

Football Association to talk about taking over the Qatari national team. I went to Doha with Athole and Samir, another sheikh I had met in Dubai. Qatar had won the Gulf Cup of Nations a couple of times, the last time in 2004. Their goal was to qualify for the World Cup, something they had never been able to achieve. I met the technical committee several times, but I did not get an answer about whether they wanted me or not.

During our stay in Qatar, we were invited to a royal dinner. I was sitting at a table with a group of English people when a waiter came up to say that I was wanted at a different table. I told him that I was comfortable where I was but Samir told me to do what the waiter had asked. The royal princess of Qatar had requested my company. I spoke with her for a while. She told me she travelled regularly to London to shop and watch football. She was an Arsenal fan.

The next evening we were invited to another royal gathering. It began with an auction that raised millions of dollars. Another dinner followed. I think that was held in the royal palace. I had never seen such riches – gold everywhere. Towards the end of the dinner a man approached me and once again Samir came to my aid. This was the Royal Prince of Qatar himself. We exchanged a few pleasantries. He asked how long I was staying in Qatar and I told him that I would be flying back the next morning. 'When?' he asked. 'Very early,' I replied. That was too bad, he said. It would have been nice to speak more. We said goodbye. When Samir heard what had happened he was appalled.

'The Crown Prince asks how long you are staying in the country for and you tell him you're leaving early in the morning?' he said.

Apparently, the answer should have been, 'How long do you need me, Your Highness?'

The prince probably had a say in who the next manager of the Qatari national team should be. But I had been in the country for several days and nothing had happened. I flew home without getting an answer.

● ● ●

Around this time I started thinking about writing a book. Several books had been written about me, but they were all very bad. They had been written without my participation by people who did not know me. During my time as England manager, I had been offered big money to write a book but I was too focused on my job. Now I had time but still it did not feel right. I would want to write the truth, and someone would always be offended by it. Maybe I was not ready to tell my story, especially the stuff off the football pitch.

One day David Beckham called me. Fabio Capello had taken over as manager of Real Madrid, where David was playing his fourth season for the club. Capello had benched him. Beckham complained about not getting enough playing time. He asked me what he should do.

'Ask Capello why you are on the bench,' I said.

David did that and Capello answered him, 'Because I can only play eleven men.' He was not an easy man to deal with, Fabio Capello.

Towards the end of the 2006/07 season Pini called. He had a job offer for me in Ukraine, as manager of Dynamo Kiev. We went to Kiev to meet the president of the club, Ihor Surkis, and his brother, who happened to be the president of the Ukrainian Football Association. The plan was for me to take the job at Dynamo Kiev and, after a few years, move over to the national team. It had just been officially announced that Ukraine and Poland would co-host the 2012 Euros.

We met at the stadium. A breakfast buffet was served that was out of this world, with all kinds of shellfish and caviar. And vodka, of course. I was not used to drinking vodka for breakfast, but my hosts insisted. I got the impression they really wanted me as manager. One guy, I think he was a vice president of the club, said he would be willing to be my chauffeur and drive me in his Bentley if I took the job. When I just smiled he pulled out his wallet and showed me a photo of his girlfriend. She had been Miss Ukraine two years earlier.

'You can have her, too,' he said.

It was a joke, naturally. I was very close to taking the job. It was a big assignment. Yet it still felt like a step down. Ukrainian football was not as strong then as it is today. But the main reason I told them no was because another job had come up, a job that would take me back to England.

• • •

I had never heard of Thaksin Shinawatra before he bought Manchester City for £80 million in June 2007. Later I was told that he had been prime minister of Thailand. One day I was contacted by Jerome Anderson, an agent whom I had met before. Thaksin had consulted him on his purchase of City, and Anderson had put up my name as a candidate for manager. Now he wanted to see me in London.

We met at the Hotel Leonard. I went without an agent. Anderson represented the club. Manchester City wanted me as their new manager. Was I interested? Of course I was. Manchester City was a classic English club with a large supporter base. It was always said that in Manchester more people were City supporters than United supporters. It had been a long time since Manchester City had been a top team in England, but that was going to change with Thaksin's help. A substantial amount of money was available to spend on new players.

I said yes immediately. It never occurred to me to check up on Thaksin Shinawatra. His purchase of Manchester City had been finalised and approved by the Premier League. That was all I knew and it was good enough for me. I negotiated my own salary. It was nowhere close to what I had earned as England manager, but it was still good. The job was exactly what I had hoped for. I signed a two-year contract. On 6 July 2007, it became official. I was the new Manchester City manager, and the first non-British manager in the club's history.

● ● ●

Manchester City had been in the Premier League for five years. Kevin Keegan had taken them from the First Division and brought them back to the top flight after he left the England job. Since then, things had taken a turn for the worse. Under Stuart Pearce the season before I came, Manchester City had just about avoided relegation, managing just 11 wins in 38 matches. The squad was too thin and filled with mediocre players. The season was starting on 11 August. I had five weeks to build a whole new team.

My first priority was to put a management team together. Naturally, Tord was the first person I called. We needed new players and there was no better scout in the world than Tord Grip. The club had a scout, Derek Fazackerley, who had been assistant manager to Pearce. I did not want to sack anyone so I gave Derek his old job back as assistant manager. It would help with continuity. Derek proved to be a very good coach. Like most English coaches, he was excellent at giving instructions. That was something I valued highly.

I also wanted a Swedish assistant. Tord, who knew everyone in Swedish football, recommended Hasse Backe, who was very experienced, working mainly in Scandinavia. I had met Hasse twenty-five years earlier, when he completed his coaching badges in Sweden. I was the manager of Gothenburg then, and had come to speak to Hasse's class. Hasse came to Portugal during my first year at Benfica to do another coaching course and later came to visit me at most of the clubs where I had been. Yet I think he was very surprised when I asked him if he wanted to join me at Manchester City. He said yes right away. Who did not want to come to the Premier League?

We needed up to ten new players, so, although there was money to spend, we could not afford to blow the whole transfer kitty on one or two big stars. I came to rely on Tord a lot, but perhaps even more on Hasse. He had worked in television and travelled around Europe. He knew a lot of players. We did not have time to go to watch players, and there were hardly any matches to see in July, anyway. So we were stuck with viewing a lot of videos. It was total chaos, but one of the most invigorating times I had experienced. It was fantastic to be building a whole new team.

One week after my appointment we announced our first signing, Rolando Bianchi, an Italian striker from Reggina. The English press had no idea who he was, even though he had finished as the fourth top scorer in Italy the season before. The next day we presented another signing, Gelson Fernandes, a young Swiss midfielder. After that we travelled to Sweden for a training camp. My old school friend, P.G. Skoglund, put the tour together in record time. No one at Manchester City had thought about pre-season training before I got there.

Back in England we continued buying players. I brought in the Brazilian Geovanni on a free transfer from Cruzeiro and the Bulgarian Martin Petrov from Atletico Madrid. We sold Joey Barton to Newcastle and Trevor Sinclair to Cardiff. Other players were loaned out. A week later we presented three new signings in one day – Corluka, a Croat; Elano, a Brazilian; and Garrido, a Spaniard. The Bulgarian Bojinov arrived the following day. We held press conferences every day, it seemed. The media called me 'Spend' Eriksson. They wondered how we were able to find all these players, and how did we expect them to fit together as a team?

It was a good question. I was not so sure myself how it would work. I was good at creating a harmonious feeling in a team but we had up to twenty different nationalities in the squad. It must have been one of the most international football teams in history. Most of them I had not seen play a competitive match before the season opener on 11 August, away to West Ham. It could not have gone any better, though. Bianchi scored an early goal and after Geovanni sealed the win with a second, our stunned supporters sang 'What the fuck is going on?'

The next week we beat Derby at home. A bigger challenge awaited us in the third week – Manchester United. To the City fans, it was by far the season's most important game. After my first press conference as City manager, a City supporter had come up to me and told me that I should just forget all that talk about finishing as high up the table as possible and getting into Europe. Beating United, and preferably twice, was the only thing that mattered. Everything else was secondary.

I wanted to beat United, too – especially Ferguson – but United dominated the match. Less than ten minutes from the start, Bojinov was seriously injured and had to be substituted. United created a slew of goal opportunities and should have won the match in the first half hour. Then, suddenly, Geovanni got the ball in the United half, advanced and hit a speculative shot from outside the penalty area. The ball was deflected slightly off a United defender and went in at the bottom of the post. The

City fans went nuts. United continued to dominate, but we defended extremely well and the game ended 1–0 to us.

After the match, Ferguson and I had a glass of red wine together, as was the custom in England. He showed no bad feelings and congratulated me. I would be lying if I said I did not feel an enormous amount of satisfaction. We had won the first derby. We were top of the league after three matches with nine points and no goals conceded. I was awarded Premier League manager of the month. A huge poster of me was put up in the city with the words 'Old blue eyes is back'. City fans were offered free Thai food in Albert Square. Everything was almost too good to be true.

● ● ●

Thaksin Shinawatra knew nothing about football. That quickly became clear. He would call before a match to remind me to tell the players to play aggressively. To Thaksin, that constituted good advice. It was something new for me to have an owner who did not know the game. In Italy and Portugal the club owners lived for football. Businessmen such as Thaksin believed that football was like any other business. Big investments would automatically lead to big results. But it was not that simple.

A lot of rumours were circulating about how Thaksin had made his money and how much he had actually invested in the club. I knew that he was a controversial figure, but I didn't know, for example, that he was suspected of tax fraud after selling this telecom company in 2006, when he was still Thailand's prime minister. I didn't know that Thaksin had been deposed in a military coup in the autumn of 2006, while he was in New York. Thaksin did not return to Thailand after that, but took up residence in England.

At the club, we didn't talk about Thaksin's finances, at least not in the beginning. It was said that his assets were frozen in Thailand, but we all got paid. It was not our business to investigate Thaksin's affairs. I focused on the football. The plan was to finish in the top ten in that first year. At the same time, we wondered why Thaksin had bought the club. Did he want to make money? Was it to enhance his standing in Thailand? Was the footballing business a cover for his other affairs? We never got an answer to that.

I had been to Thailand on holiday but had never worked with Thai people before. They were delightful, polite and generous. In the beginning, Thaksin often called and wanted to talk football. Most of the time he stayed in London, but he would come to Manchester for the games and sometimes show up at training. Afterwards he would buy dinner. He surrounded himself with a large clan. There could be fifteen, twenty people at those dinners. Everyone wanted to talk about the match. It was amazing how football seemed to get everyone buzzing.

Thaksin seemed like a regular guy but you could tell he was used to having his way. He often brought his wife with him. His right-hand man, Pajroj Piempongsant, was always there. Pajroj had acted as adviser to several prime ministers in Thailand. I developed a very good relationship with him from the beginning, even though I was not entirely sure what his job really was. Another lady was there, too. She was older and married to the former Thai ambassador to Britain. She came to the matches as well.

Everything was great, as long as we were winning. In our fourth match, away to Arsenal, we played an excellent game but conceded a late goal and lost 1–0. After the game I had a glass of wine with Arsène Wenger. He wondered how it had been possible for us to field almost a completely new team and still dominate Arsenal away. That was great praise coming from Arsène. Thaksin was not so impressed. He called me after the game.

'Schwen,' he said. Thaksin had difficulty pronouncing the letter s in Sven. 'Last week, you were very good. This week, you're very bad.'

● ● ●

Six years had passed since I last managed a club side and I realised how much I had missed everyday life in a football club – the routines, training sessions, close proximity to the players. You simply did not get all that as manager of a national team. I enjoyed talking to the caretaker and the kitchen personnel. I didn't do it for show. It was in my personality to treat everyone the same. It came from my parents.

But my philosophy had changed over the years. Maybe it was something that happened unconsciously. I was always on the pitch during the training sessions, but I let Hasse and Derek take care of much of the coaching. As a manager, I was more easy-going. I did not demand the same rigid structure and organisation from my players as I did at the beginning of my career. Perhaps it came from working with some of the best players in the world for so many years. I realised I had to give them freedom. Most of the time they knew what to do.

Manchester City had not been known for their beautiful football. There was a lot of hoofing the ball up field before I got there. I wanted to change that. I wanted to play football. Most of the new players we brought in were technically very skilled. Elano was one. Corluka had great technique despite being a defender. Petrov had a wild temperament, but he was quick and had a lethal left foot.

At the same time, it was important to have leaders in the team. I inherited the best leader I could have asked for in our Irish captain, Richard Dunne. Richard was not the fastest centre back in the world, but he always put in 100 per cent effort. It didn't matter whether it was a training session or a Premier League game. To the others in the team, Richard was something to hold on to when things got rough. I also had Didi Hamann, our German midfield maestro. Didi had probably left his best years behind, and in training he didn't move very much. Derek would say jokingly that Didi didn't have to shower after training because he never broke sweat. But no one could accuse Didi of not taking matches seriously. He was one of the most intelligent players I have ever managed. He hardly ever misplaced a pass.

I had also inherited several young and promising players, including Micah Richards, a 19-year-old defender who had everything. He was by far man of the match in the win against United. In midfield I had Michael Johnson and Stephen Ireland. Later, both of them encountered problems off the field, but in 2007/08 they were brilliant.

Our main problem was scoring goals. The season before I came to the club, City had five forwards who had combined for a paltry thirteen goals. One of the them was Darius Vassell, my old England striker. I kept Darius at City. Bojinov had torn his cruciate ligament against United and was out for the season. The big goalscorer was supposed to be Bianchi. I had spoken with Mancini, who was then in his fourth year managing Inter, about Bianchi. Mancio was certain that Bianchi would be a hit in England but it did not work out that way. Bianchi scored in the opening game, but it was all downhill from there.

Another dilemma I had was more pleasing – too many good goalkeepers. When I arrived, Andreas Isaksson, the Sweden number-one keeper, was going to be our first choice and the club also had two young, promising keepers in Joe Hart and Kasper Schmeichel. In pre-season I had put Isaksson in goal. He was a solid keeper, but he had one problem – he was too quiet.

One day I was talking to Richard Dunne in my office and I asked him about the goalkeeping situation. Dunne said Isaksson had a problem communicating with his defenders. When a cross came in, he would just run out and try to punch the ball away.

'Sometimes I get hit in the back of the head,' said Richard. 'It hurts.'

Before the season started, both Isaksson and Hart were injured. That made my choice easier. I put Kasper Schmeichel in goal. He was the son of the legendary Danish goalkeeper Peter Schmeichel, who had played for Manchester United for many years but had finished his career at City. Kasper had the same hot temperament as his father, but he was extremely quick on the line and had good feet. He started the first seven games. In the 1–0 defeat by Arsenal he was man of the match.

After the Arsenal game, all three goalkeepers were fit and available for selection. I had to make a first choice. Thaksin wanted me to continue playing Schmeichel. His blond good looks had apparently won over the ladies in Thailand. That was obviously not something I would take into consideration. One person I listened to, however, was Eric Steele, our goalkeeping coach. He wanted me to give the nod to Joe Hart. Joe was big and tall, and very agile. He was better than Kasper at crosses.

I decided to follow Eric's advice and make Joe our first-choice keeper with Andreas as his back-up. I explained my decision to Andreas and, to his credit, he took the news very professionally. Andreas was not someone who complained. We sent Kasper on loan to Cardiff and later to Coventry. He was young and needed experience. It was probably the right decision to make Joe Hart our first choice. He later developed into one of the best goalkeepers in the world and England's number one for many years to come. But I always had a soft spot for Kasper Schmeichel.

● ● ●

I loved life in Manchester. The weather was terrible, of course. During the first training session in July I had to wear my winter jacket. The wind was always whipping around at Carrington, the City training ground, but I could not complain about my living conditions. I was staying in a suite at the Radisson Hotel in the centre of town. It had two bedrooms and I used one as a changing room. The personnel at the hotel treated me like a VIP. Whatever I needed, they got for me, and a ton of restaurants were right outside the door. I remember meeting a guy there who was a huge Manchester City supporter. He said he was a singer. Noel Gallagher was his name. I had never heard of him or his band, Oasis.

'How's the singing going?' I asked.

'Pretty good,' he said.

Hasse and Tord lived in apartments not far away. They usually came to pick me up at the hotel and together we travelled to Carrington. If I wanted to go somewhere else, for example, to see the reserves play, the club would send me a chauffeured car. Sometimes they would send a Rolls-Royce. It was a little embarrassing to show up in Newcastle for a reserve game in a car like that.

I had also met a woman, Malin. We met at the Grand Hotel in Stockholm, where she worked. Malin was Swedish and a really nice woman. She visited me often in Manchester. She was more independent than other women I had known, and liked to be in control, which did not always suit me. I also think she could see a long-term future with me but I was not interested in a steady relationship. It happened that I met other women, too.

One day Nancy showed up in Manchester. I had met her in Italy at the end of May when I went there to celebrate Johan's birthday. She had written a book that had just come out. She had assured me that I would not be featured in the book, but of course I was. I didn't read it. Apparently, she described our relationship as blissful throughout. It was laughable. And when she came to Manchester, it was definitely over. We needed to come to some kind of financial agreement.

Nancy and I had never been married, but we had lived together during my entire time as England manager. British laws on co-habitation meant that she was entitled to financial support. I did not have a problem with that. I had money, she didn't. I had sold the Regents Park house, but I still had the apartment in Belgravia. The agreement that I thought we had reached was that Nancy would receive a cash sum, less than a million pounds, and the beach house in Italy, which I still owned. In addition, she would stay rent-free in the London apartment for two years. It was a generous settlement. Perhaps I still felt a moral obligation towards her. Most of all, I just wanted to end things once and for all.

● ● ●

We won the first game of 2008, beating Newcastle 2–0 away. After twenty-one games we were fourth in the table, the last Champions League spot. Manchester City had never been placed that high in the table that late in the season since the Premier League was formed in 1992. When the transfer window opened, I sent Bianchi on loan to Lazio. It was a huge disappointment to me that he had not done better in England. Towards the end of the transfer window I brought in two new forwards, Felipe Caicedo and Benjani Mwaruwari. Benjani was Zimbabwean and came from Portsmouth. That spring, he turned out to be our leading scorer.

But we did not win any of our four games following the victory against Newcastle, drawing two and losing two. Losses were a big problem for Thaksin. He could not handle them. To Thaksin, losing a football match meant losing face. He would ignore me after we lost a game. I would pass him in the hallway and he would not say hello or even look in my direction. It was very strange.

Our self-confidence had been bruised before the biggest game of the year on 10 February – away to Manchester United. After a poor start to the season, United had played some brilliant football and steamrollered their way back up to second place in the table. In Ronaldo, Rooney and Tevez they had the most potent attacking trio in the Premier League.

The game at Old Trafford took on extra significance because it was played on the fiftieth anniversary of the Münich air crash. In February 1958, the plane transporting the Manchester United team ran off the runway in Münich and crashed during a storm, killing 23 out of the 44 people on board, including eight players. The tragedy was due to be commemorated with a ceremony and a minute's silence before our game.

United and City were bitter enemies. In the week leading up to the game, everyone at the club was nervous that our supporters would not behave with respect during the ceremony. But we had no reason to worry. As Alex and I walked on to the pitch and placed two wreaths in the midfield circle, the entire crowd applauded respectfully. After that, the minute's silence was immaculately observed. You could have heard a pin drop in a stadium filled with 75,000 people. I was incredibly proud of our supporters. The whole ceremony was a very emotional event.

We had beaten United at home. At Old Trafford they were almost invincible. They had not lost a game there that season. Until they faced us. We pulled off another huge upset. Darius Vassell scored and Benjani, who had a fantastic game, scored a second. United managed a consolation goal late in the game, but we won 2–1. It was the first time since 1969/70 that City had beaten United twice in a season.

After the game we went to share a glass of red wine with the United coaches, but Ferguson did not show up. His assistant, Carlos Queiroz, explained that Ferguson had had to rush off. He told Hasse that United had lost because the occasion had been too big for their players.

● ● ●

By this time, Samir Khan was handling all my finances. I trusted him. While I was still England manager, Samir had suggested that I invest in a technology company called Lucidiom. The company was going to be acquired by Hewlett Packard and stood to make a lot of money. It sounded like a good investment. Samir explained that I did not have to invest any of my own money, but that he would be able to borrow the money needed at a very low interest rate. I agreed to invest almost a million pounds with borrowed financing. Athole borrowed a large sum as well.

About a year and a half later, the company had still not been sold. By that time I had invested in yet another project of Samir's. This time it involved a real-estate deal in Portsmouth known as the Southsea Development. The main investor in the project was Portsmouth manager Harry Redknapp. Athole had consulted Harry's people about the viability of the project and everything seemed sound. I don't remember how much money was involved.

One day Athole received a phone call from Harry Redknapp's accountant, who asked if Athole knew anything about a project called Pier 24. Apparently, Pier 24 was Samir's company in which I was a shareholder. It was through Pier 24 that we had invested in Southsea. From what the accountant said, it seemed as though Samir Khan's Pier 24 project was a scam. I called Samir and told him that I did not want to be part of it. No problem, said Samir. He would get me out of it. But later I ran into Harry. He was complaining about the Southsea project and said that Samir Khan was a crook. Harry said that I was still part of the project. Angry, I called Samir and asked him why he had not pulled me out of the deal. He made some excuse about the time it would take to process my withdrawal, but promised me that it had been done. I did not give the Southsea business any more thought.

It was not the only financial issue I had to deal with. One month when I received my pay slip, a large sum of money, between £50,000 and £100,000, had been deducted from it. For what, I had no idea. It turned out that the money was an agent's fee that had been paid to Jerome Anderson, who had brought me to Manchester City. But as far as I was concerned, Jerome had represented the club, not me, but when I queried it he said it was all stipulated in the contract. There was nothing I could do about it, but it didn't seem fair.

● ● ●

After the United game, we won just one game out of seven, against Tottenham at home. Thaksin stopped calling. I had no contact with him. He had finally been able to return to Thailand to visit, but I knew he still faced serious legal problems. His assets were still frozen. After a while, we had begun wondering exactly how much money Thaksin had invested in the club. It appeared as though he had mainly borrowed money from the television rights to finance the purchases of players. It was not his money.

One day I was called to a meeting with Thaksin at the Radisson Hotel where I was staying. It must have been the day after a game, maybe one and a half months before the end of the season. When I arrived, Thaksin was there with Pajroj and the woman who was married to the former Thai ambassador. Her name was Sasin. I was not worried before the meeting. We had not played well recently, but we were still in the top half of the table and the goal had been to finish in the top ten. We had defeated Manchester United both home and away. The fans were over the moon. Against all odds we had managed to build a brand new team. I expected that Thaksin wanted to talk about his plans for the following season.

I was wrong. I don't remember what was said at the meeting, but it was nothing productive. When I left I knew there would not be a following season for me with Manchester City. When I saw Tord and Hasse, I told them, 'We're going to get fired.'

We won the next two games, away to Sunderland and at home to Portsmouth. Yet Thaksin did not call. In the third to last game of the season we lost at home to Fulham, where Roy Hodgson was now manager. By that time, my imminent sacking had leaked out in the press. The players were not happy. I am 100 per cent sure we would not have lost that game to Fulham if the news about me had not leaked out and the players had not had their focus turned. The win helped Roy Hodgson's Fulham stave off relegation that year.

I had still not heard anything official from Thaksin. But I knew I was a dead man walking. I was going to lose my dream job, all because of a Thai businessman and former politician who knew nothing about football. Among our supporters, very few thought I deserved to be fired. During an away game at Liverpool, they sang Pink Floyd's song 'Another Brick in the Wall' with some new lyrics:

'We don't need no Mou-rin-ho,

We don't need no Sco-la-ri,

Hey, Thaksin, leave our Sven alone!'

● ● ●

Before the last game of the season, away to Middlesbrough, Richard Dunne came into my office. He told me that the entire team were going to refuse to play the match. I told Richard to sit down, and I put an end to that kind of talk right away. I told him that I appreciated that they would show such solidarity to their manager, but they were professional football players who had a job to do, which was to play the game.

They did play the game, but barely. Fifteen minutes into the match Richard received a red card for a clumsy tackle that gave Middlesbrough a penalty, which they converted. I knew the game would be my last with City, so I did not want to lose it. But the players were not interested in playing. They wanted to show their disgust about the whole situation. Middlesbrough scored a second before half-time.

The second half was a complete disaster. Middlesbrough did whatever they wanted, and the goals flew in, one after another. Our best player was Andreas Isaksson, who was goalkeeper in that match. It finished 8–1 to Middlesbrough. But despite the humiliation, our 2,000 fans sang from start to finish: 'One Sven-Göran Eriksson, there's only one Sven-Göran Eriksson'.

● ● ●

But the season did not end there. Thaksin had arranged for a post-season promotional tour to Thailand. We were going to play the Thai national team. The players refused to go, and once again I had to convince them that they had a job to do, which included participating in the promotional tour. I had not been officially sacked, which meant I had to come as well. It was not something I was looking forward to, but I had no choice.

We were in Thailand for a few days. I don't believe Tord came with us. One night in Bangkok, Thaksin invited the coaching staff to a karaoke club. I was still the club's manager. After dinner, a bunch of suggestively dressed women appeared. I assumed they were for hire. Thaksin brought one of them with him up on stage to sing karaoke. There, he stood, a glass of tequila in one hand and his other arm around the woman. He had said to me once that one should drink tequila, not red wine. I don't know where he got that from. Thaksin was a good singer. He fancied himself as Frank Sinatra. After a couple of songs, he said, 'Schwen, this song is for you!' The song that started playing was the Clash's 'Should I Stay Or Should I Go?' Thaksin came off the stage to stand right in front of me, singing:

'Come on and let me know.

Should I stay or should I go?'

● ● ●

When Thaksin returned to the stage, Eric Steele, the goalkeeping coach, leaned across to me and told me to pinch him. He thought he was dreaming. I don't know how long the night lasted. I went back to the hotel and went to bed, still the Manchester City manager.

The next morning the axe fell. I met Thaksin and Alistair Mackintosh, the City CEO, for breakfast in a private dining room at the hotel. Thaksin thanked me in his own special way, but said that unfortunately he had to let me go. I asked him why. We had done so well that year. He said it was a feeling he had. Alistair would take care of the details. I had a year left on my contract and would receive 50 per cent of my annual salary as severance pay. There were no big discussions about that. After we finished, Alistair left me and Thaksin on our own. That's when I asked Thaksin again why he had decided to sack me. This time he said, 'I don't know.'

Later, I asked Pini and Pajroj if they knew why Thaksin had fired me. They said it had something to do with my missing a training session once. It was true that I had missed one training session, but that was when I went to Sheffield to apply for a work permit for Bojinov.

I didn't buy that for one second. There were all sorts of rumours but I really don't know why I was fired or who was behind it. There must have been a plan somewhere because just two days after I got the sack, Mark Hughes was announced as the next Manchester City manager.

Two months later, Thaksin sold Manchester City to the Abu Dhabi United Group, a consortium controlled by the royal family of Abu Dhabi. Suddenly, Manchester City became the richest football club in the world. They were able to spend hundreds of millions of pounds on new players. Thaksin, meanwhile, was charged with corruption in Thailand and once again had to flee the country. His wife, Potjaman, received a prison sentence for tax fraud. Mark Hughes lasted one and a half years as manager of Manchester City before he was fired and Roberto Mancini took over. In 2012, Mancio won the Premier League title with Manchester City, the first time in fifty years that the club had won the league.

Of course, it occurred to me that it could have been me in Mancio's shoes, if Thaksin had sold the club before he fired me. I am convinced that the new owners would not have got rid of me. But I never lost any sleep over it. You had to accept that it was all part of football. A lot of it was very professional, but a lot of football was controlled by men who knew nothing about the game.

THE ART OF WINNING
AWAY

17

THE year without football was the worst of my life. I wanted to avoid repeating that at all costs. But what could I do except wait for another job offer? As a football manager, you did not look for work. You waited for work. Once agents heard that I was going to get fired from Manchester City, I received a number of calls about various jobs. There was some talk about Lazio and Fenerbahçe, but nothing concrete. One day, however, Rui Costa, who was then the sporting director at Benfica, and Filipe Vieira, the Benfica president, came to Manchester to offer me the job of managing Benfica again. I was tempted. I had my house and roots in Portugal, but it felt a bit like old hat going back to a club where I had already spent two tours. Toni Oliveira also warned me that Benfica might not have the resources to compete with Porto. So I said no to the job.

After the tour to Thailand with City, I was contacted by a young Mexican agent, Juan Carlos Padilla Jr, with another offer – manager of Mexico. I already knew Carlos because he had brought the Mexican midfielder Nery Castillo to Manchester City. I did not know anything about Mexican football, though, only that Mexico always qualified for the World Cup. So this would be an opportunity to be involved in another World Cup, and I had never had a job outside of Europe. I was open to trying something new. So I thought why not?

I met the Mexican delegation, led by the president of the Mexican Football Association, Justino Compeán, at a hotel in London. They explained that their first choice had been Mexican manager Javier Aguirre, but Aguirre already had a job, as manager of Atletico Madrid, and was not available. I had always been first choice for my previous jobs. At least, I think so. I would be taking a big risk accepting a job when my prospective employer actually wanted someone else. At the same time, it would be a challenge to prove that I was the right man for the job. I had never said no to a challenge.

Once again, I negotiated the contract myself. It was pretty straightforward. Carlos had informed the Mexicans what I was looking for in monetary terms. I was offered a contract that would run over the 2010 World Cup and would pay me an annual salary of almost two million euros. That was more than I had been paid at Manchester City. I was also going to get paid bonuses based on results. The main aim for the Mexicans was to play a fifth game in the World Cup. In other words, I would get a bonus if I took Mexico to the quarter-finals. With England, I had been fired for that same result.

I signed the contract on 3 June 2008 and I flew to Mexico City the same day. I was going to be introduced at a press conference the following day. It was held at the Mexican FA's headquarters and almost as many journalists were there as there had been when I was introduced as England manager. Obviously, I wanted to make a good first impression. That meant I had to speak Spanish. I didn't know Spanish, but I had bought a Spanish grammar book, and Portuguese was pretty close to Spanish, so I figured I would be able to pull it off. And I did, sort of. I had trouble understanding some of the questions, but I think I snapped up most of them. I was mixing Spanish and Portuguese, and I probably threw in some Italian, too. The people at the FA helped me translate when things got too far off track. The press liked it. My appointment had not been received with unanimous enthusiasm by the Mexican press corps, but they were nice to me at the press conference. No one asked me for the name of the left back of some Mexican team.

After that I went home to Björkefors where I sat and watched DVDs of Mexican football, which Carlos had given me. I was impressed with the high technical standard. The organisation did not seem as good as that in European football, but I was looking forward to working on that. Both Tord and Hasse were coming with me. Tord was going to work as a scout and watch Mexican players in Europe. Hasse was going to work with me in Mexico. I also wanted a Mexican assistant and found Paco Ramírez, who had worked as an assistant manager with the national team before. I quickly came to develop the same good chemistry with him as I had with Toni at Benfica.

Hasse and I travelled together to Mexico City for our official unveiling. At the airport, the reporters and photographers went crazy when they spotted us. Hasse was shocked. We had to be shepherded out through a back door. After the presentation, we travelled on to the United States, where Mexican club teams went on pre-season tours. Tord joined us there. We saw as many games and players as we could. I went to Washington, while Hasse went to California. I think Tord went to Chicago.

Hasse and I returned to Mexico in time for the start of the league season. The league in Mexico was split into two separate seasons, as it was in Argentina. The autumn season was called *Apertura* and the spring season was called *Clausura*. Thus two league winners were crowned each year in Mexico. We flew around the country to scout as many players as possible. The quality of football was at a higher level than I had expected, and interest in the game was enormous. Around the clock, people talked about football. I don't know how many TV channels exclusively showed football. There were a lot. Everyone was extremely friendly towards me and I received the red-carpet treatment wherever I went.

Mexican football was organised very differently from the way it was run in most European countries. The Mexican Football Association was essentially controlled by the clubs. In England, the league and the FA may have been in constant conflict but at least the FA had its own officials who were supposed to be acting in the best interest of the national team. In Mexico, the owners of the clubs sat on the Football Association's board. It was more or less the club owners who decided how the national team should be run. At least, that is how things had worked before I got there. It was something new to me. I had never had an owner or director tell me whom I should play or what tactics I should use.

I had been in the job for about a week when I was called into my first meeting with the board. In the meeting room, a table was set up like a U. Behind it sat all the club owners. In front of the table were placed two chairs, one for me and one for Hasse. Hasse whispered something about it looking like an execution hall. It would have been interesting to know which of these men had been opposed to my selection as Mexico manager. But of course everyone was nice to my face. It was, after all, an introductory meeting.

In Mexico City, Hasse and I were invited to visit Bora Milutinović, who had coached Mexico at several times. He lived in the capital with his wife. Bora gave me a book about the character of the Mexican person, which was pretty helpful. The Mexicans were an enormously proud and patriotic people. That, I had understood. They were also very polite, which was something that stood in stark contrast with the negative image of Mexico that is generally broadcast around the world.

Concacaf, the football organisation of North and Central America, had three World Cup spots available. Mexico and the United States were always favourites to nab two of them. After the first two elimination rounds, the World Cup qualifiers were organised into a third round of three groups with four teams each. The top two teams in each group advanced to the fourth round in which the six teams played each other twice and the top three teams in the table qualified for the World Cup.

We were drawn in a relatively tough third-round group with Honduras, Jamaica and Canada. Honduras, especially, had a strong team. And it was Honduras we would play in our first qualifying game on 20 August 2008. At home at the Azteca Stadium in Mexico City, Mexico had lost just one qualifying game since the stadium was built in 1961. But I did not think about what would happen if we lost a second. As it happened, we won all three games. I had achieved the same perfect start as I did with both England and Manchester City. Life was good. I liked it in Mexico.

● ● ●

When I first arrived I stayed in a hotel, but with Carlos Padilla's help I soon found an apartment to rent in the upmarket neighbourhood of Polanco. The apartment was located in one of the three towers that

Coca-Cola had been allowed to build in Mexico City. Two of the towers had been sold and turned into apartments. Every taxi driver knew where 'Coca-Cola Tower' was. My apartment was huge, seven-hundred square metres. It took up a whole floor on its own. I had a terrace that wrapped around the whole building. From there, you could see half of Mexico City.

I had to pay for the apartment myself and it was expensive. The rent included a butler, a Mexican named Pablo, about 35 years old. He had worked for the young lady who owned the apartment. I met her a few times. She had inherited it from her grandmother, but it was too big for her so she had decided to rent it out. Pablo was brilliant. He cooked and cleaned and did the laundry.

There were a lot of restaurants and shops in the neighbourhood, everything you needed. Hasse lived nearby. When Tord came to Mexico, he stayed at a hotel in the vicinity. On the other side of the street was a park with a great cinder track to run on, over half a mile long. I would run five or six laps, but one day when I came back, a policeman was waiting and he said that I must absolutely not run in the park on my own. It would be just a matter of time before I was kidnapped. In Mexico, I had to have a bullet-proof car. The doors alone weighed a ton.

At eight o'clock in the morning every day, a Swedish guy named Andrés came over to give Hasse and me Spanish lessons. His mother had worked for the Swedish Football Association during the World Cup in Mexico in 1970 and had stayed in the country. After that, we would go to the office. I got on well with the people there. We generally spoke English. Hasse, Paco and I would discuss players and plan what games we would see that weekend. In the afternoon, we would go back home and work out in the gym before heading out for dinner in the evening.

One night, after dinner Paco and I met some friends in a bar for a couple of glasses of wine. It was probably pretty late when we left the bar. Outside, two ladies came walking towards us and when one of them saw me, she burst out, '*Dios*! *Es el*!' Oh, my God, it's him!

It was dark and the woman was wearing some kind of shawl. Her eyes and her white teeth glimmered in the moonlight. I could tell she was very good looking, and she was very excited to see me for some reason. She eagerly shook my hand and rattled off something in Spanish. I was speechless, and not just because I could not understand what she was saying. Paco had to translate. The woman said her name was Yaniseth and that she worked as a dancer at a restaurant and nightclub not too far away. She invited me to come and watch her when she danced.

This might have been on a Monday. On the Wednesday, Hasse, his fiancée Sofia and I went to the restaurant that Yaniseth had told us about. Sofia was visiting from Sweden, where she worked at a correctional treatment facility. The restaurant turned out to be quite luxurious. The waiters all recognised me. We grabbed a table and ordered dinner. I think we had almost finished eating when a band started playing in the bar next to the restaurant. You could not see it from where we sat, so I asked Sofia to go and see if Yaniseth was there. I described her to Sofia as dark-skinned, pretty, with big eyes and bright white teeth. A short while later, Sofia returned to our table.

'Yes,' she said, 'I think it's probably her dancing and singing.'

After dinner we all went to the bar. A man was playing the piano, a girl was singing and two women were dancing some kind of salsa. One of them was Yaniseth. She was scantily clad and a real beauty. When I came into the room, she saw me immediately and suddenly stopped dancing. She just stood there for a moment, before resuming her dancing. We sat down at a table and watched the show. I bought a bottle of champagne and as soon as there was a break in the performance, I walked over to the table where Yaniseth and the other artists were sitting and asked if I could offer her a glass of champagne. She was excited to see me. She could not believe that Mister Eriksson had really come to see her perform. We spoke in Spanish for maybe ten minutes before it was time for her to get up on stage again. She gave me her telephone number and asked me to call her. After that, Hasse, Sofia and I went home.

The next day I called Yaniseth and asked her over for dinner in my apartment. Pablo cooked the meal. Yaniseth was impressed. My apartment was the biggest she had ever seen. It might have been the biggest apartment I had ever seen. Yaniseth came from Panama. Like many other people in Central America, she had moved to Mexico City to earn better pay. She loved football and had worked as a hostess at several football clubs. Her mother also lived in Mexico City, she said. But she didn't say anything about having a son. I found out about that much later.

• • •

Mexico had one huge problem – the team never won away. At home, the Mexicans were practically unbeatable. But away, they appeared to have some kind of mental block and transformed into a different team. We had won our first three group qualifiers at home and needed just a point or so to make sure of advancement to the next round. But it had been made very clear to me when I took the job that it was not enough to win just the home games. It was up to me to get Mexico winning away, too.

In the autumn of 2008, our three remaining away games in the group started against Jamaica, in Kingston. It was a disaster. The grass had not been cut and the pitch was full of holes. The Jamaicans knew we were technically superior. It was impossible to get our usual passing game going on such a poor pitch, which was exactly what the Jamaicans wanted. We lost the game after Ricardo Fuller, who then played for Stoke, scored the only goal of the match. Four days later, we played Canada in Edmonton. It didn't go much better. The Canadians went ahead 1–0 and 2–1 before we scored an equaliser and at least salvaged a point.

Around this time the club presidents started to get involved, showing who really controlled the national team. The FA president said I had to go and visit with various club owners. The idea of Adam Crozier telling me to explain to Manchester United's owner why the national team had lost was unthinkable. But that's how it worked in Mexico. I met some of the big club owners and they all had different opinions about what had gone wrong. Why had I chosen Paco Ramírez as my assistant manager? Could I not bring in someone else? And why did I not convince Blanco – a 35-year-old footballing icon in Mexico, who had retired from the international game, and not before time – to make a comeback?

It was absurd. I could not report to several different people who all had different interests. I had always been clear that I wanted to report to one person. What that person did with the information I gave him was up to him. But that is not how it worked in Mexico. There, it was important to make allies with the people high up in the football establishment. As if that would help the national team win games!

The situation was made worse when we lost our last match in the qualifying group 1–0 away to Honduras. We had scored an own goal and had two players sent off in the dying minutes. It meant we finished second to Honduras in the group, on equal points with Jamaica. We had advanced to the next round on goal difference, and we had not managed to win any away games.

The people at the FA started to get worried. They sent me to Europe to look at some Mexican players. Tord and I travelled around everywhere. We were in England and Holland. In Spain, we visited several clubs, including Barcelona where Rafa Márquez played. During our visit, we watched two of Barcelona's training sessions. Both Tord and I were very surprised at how little actual work was being done in training, and hardly anything tactical. The manager, Pep Guardiola, was not involved at all. It was a completely different managing philosophy from what we were used to.

After that, I went to Sweden to celebrate Christmas. Sometimes Christmas was the only time of year when the whole family were gathered, and it required quite a bit of logistics. We met at Björkefors on Christmas Eve, or the day before or the day after. Lina and Johan were going to their mother's, and Lasse's kids were visiting their mother. That Christmas, Yaniseth came to Sweden for the first time. Otherwise, it was a Christmas like every other.

● ● ●

The first of our matches in the fourth and decisive qualifying round was scheduled for 11 February 2009 against our big rivals, the United States. You would think the venue chosen would have been in California, or Florida maybe, somewhere with a warm climate. But no, the US Soccer Federation had different ideas. It had scheduled the game in Columbus, Ohio, where the average temperature in February barely crept above zero degrees Celsius. They knew that our players would have a tougher time than the Americans in those cold conditions.

That is how things were done in Concacaf. In Mexico, my Football Association had used the same dirty tricks by scheduling our home game against Canada in sizzling hot Chiapas. Now we got a taste of the same medicine. When we arrived in Ohio, the temperature had dipped below zero. The day before the game, just as we were about to start training, it started snowing. We were re-directed to some grass patch that looked like a parking lot. That is where we were supposed to train ahead of a World Cup qualifying game. I was furious.

'Have you heard of fair play?' I asked Sunil Gulati.

Gulati was the president of the US Soccer Federation. He had tried to recruit me as manager of the United States' team before the 1994 World Cup. The job had gone to Bora Milutinović instead. Gulati claimed that it was not his decision to schedule the game in Ohio. He blamed sponsors. It was bullshit. He even said that Ohio had been picked because a lot of Mexicans lived there.

At kick-off, it was windy and ice-cold. They had warned about tornadoes. We started strongly and created several good opportunities to score. But the US worked its way back into the game and in injury time, hit us on the counterattack, scoring a second goal with a shot from long-distance that our keeper should have saved.

My position back home was not secure, and not just because of the loss against the United States. A week or so before that, Javier Aguirre had been sacked by Atletico Madrid and so was available. The Mexicans had wanted Aguirre from the very beginning. Now they had me. And my results had gone downhill ever since the brilliant start.

I returned to Mexico to more meetings with club owners. In Guadalajara, where I met the president of Chivas, it was almost as if I was answering accusations at some kind of tribunal. Why had we kept the goalkeeping coach? He was obviously not up to the job since our goalkeeper had let in such a simple goal. Why did we stay at the hotel we had stayed at? Each question was dumber than the next.

Hasse was convinced that our position was untenable. He felt we had too many people against us. I still thought we could turn things around. After all, we had played well against the United States, especially considering the circumstances. The more we played the new, young guys, the better we would become. But even I, the optimist, had to acknowledge that we could not afford to lose again. Our next game was at the Azteca Stadium, against Costa Rica. We won easily, 2–0. I had earned a little breathing space.

But only for a few days. Honduras were next, in San Pedro Sula. The stadium was packed and the atmosphere electric, as always when Mexico came to visit the smaller countries in Central America. There was nothing better for nations such as Honduras than to beat big brother Mexico in football. The fans' enthusiasm spread to the Honduras players. They ran us ragged. We could not resist. They scored two goals in the first half. In the second, they added a third before we finally got one back. The game ended 3–1.

Even I knew what to expect. It was over. Hasse was almost relieved, we would leave these impossible jobs. No one at the FA wanted to talk to me after the game. However, one of the players, I think it was the captain, Pável Pardo, had heard whispers from higher up that I would get the sack the next day. And that is what happened. I was called into a meeting with the president and those close to him. He said that unfortunately they had to let me go. I told him they were making a mistake. I was convinced that we could still qualify for the World Cup. We had Honduras and the United

States to play at home. But it was too late. I had to go. The next day, Aguirre was announced as the new manager of Mexico.

This was the third time in a row that I had been fired, but I could understand why they wanted to get rid of me. The away results were simply not good enough. I had not managed to turn that negative trend around. Yet it was the off-the-pitch games that had got the better of me, the behind-the-scenes stuff. I had enemies in Mexican football from the first day to the last. Who they were, I don't know, and it doesn't matter.

I don't regret taking the job, but I was disappointed. I liked Mexico. I wanted nothing more than to take Mexico to the World Cup. They went on to qualify, just as I had expected, beating both the United States and Honduras at home. But they lost away to El Salvador and only managed a draw against Trinidad & Tobago away.

I went home to Sweden, but since it was the end of April and the end of the season and I had nothing else going on, I decided to go back to Mexico. I still had my apartment there. Yaniseth and I went out for dinner for the first time. A few months earlier I had finally met her son, Alcides, who was almost six years old. His father was also from Panama and worked in Mexico, but he did not see his son. When Alcides later moved to Panama with his mother, he started calling himself Eriksson at school.

The day after Yaniseth and I went out to eat, a newspaper published a photo of us. I didn't care. They could write and do whatever they wanted.

●　●　●

Sometime during the spring of 2009, Athole called and said that he and Ian Turland wanted to see me. Ian was my banker at Coutts bank, which I had used since I first came to England. Athole was worried that we had lost our investments in Lucidiom. He had contacted Ian to check on Samir Khan's business dealings. As it turned out, Ian was already suspicious of how Samir handled my finances. Samir had moved large sums of money from my holdings at Coutts and invested it in other projects that he claimed were more profitable but which Ian deemed very risky. Together, Ian and Athole had confronted Samir. It was allegedly a heated meeting.

Now, Athole and Ian warned me that Samir was swindling me out of my money, but they did not have any concrete proof. Or maybe I just didn't want to listen. 'Okay,' I said, 'I will handle it.' But I didn't. At least, not right away. The truth was I still trusted Samir Khan. When he said he acted with my best interests at heart, I believed him.

It was not just Athole and Ian who warned me about Samir. My friend Lars Sternmarker, who headed the IMG sports management agency in Scandinavia, also had his suspicions. His colleague Mats Björkman had started looking into Samir's dealings and found a lot of discrepancies. Mats was in contact with Lasse, my brother, and told Lasse to talk to me about Samir and the money. Lasse did, but I didn't listen to him, either. Quite suddenly, it transpired that Mats was seriously ill. The doctors said he had acute leukaemia and only a short time left to live. My brother later said that the last thing he heard from Mats was a text message in which Mats once again asked Lasse to talk to me about Samir.

Samir had mortgaged my house in Björkefors and invested the money into different projects. After that, Samir wanted to mortgage my house in Portugal to invest in some real-estate project in the Caribbean. That made me suspicious. Sometime in June, when I was in Portugal, Samir showed up with a paper for me to sign. A lawyer in Portugal had already drawn it up, regarding the Caribbean investment and the house mortgage.

That is when I decided to put an end to things. On Athole's recommendation, I contacted the accounting firm Deloitte to see exactly what Samir Khan had done with my money. I told him that until I knew what was going on, he was not allowed to touch any of my funds.

18

THE FAIRY TALE

IN June of 2009, Lina was going to graduate from the University of East Anglia in Norwich, where she had studied international development. I was very proud of her and her achievement and, naturally, wanted to attend her graduation. But when I called and asked her if I could come, she answered, 'I think it's best if you don't.' I understood why.

Lina was seven years old when Anki and I separated. She moved to Florence with her mother and spent all her school years there. From the beginning, everyone knew who she was. Or, rather, everyone knew who her father was – Sampdoria's manager, then Lazio's. Lina was popular among the boys. They wanted autographs and football jerseys and bombarded her with questions about what line-up I would use in the coming game. The girls were not as impressed with her.

Lina would come to visit me in Rome when I was managing Lazio. By the time she started high school at the American School in Florence I had moved to England and she would come to visit me during school holidays. She travelled with me to league games. Lina had always been interested in football. But she did not like the attention she received when she was with me. I understood that later. At the time, I never thought about it. For me, it was natural to have television cameras pointing at me all the time.

At the same time, Lina and I were very similar. We didn't show much emotion. She had a hard time talking about personal matters. But in the family she was very much the golden child, just as I had been when I was young. She was the apple of my father's eye. Maybe it was because they had a similar disposition. Neither of them talked too much, but rather, observed what was happening around them.

When Lina graduated from high school in Italy, Nancy and I were there. I was still the England manager then. It was a year or so after the Faria business. The paparazzi had somehow got hold of the news that I was attending the graduation and it was a disaster. A horde of photographers crammed around us on Lina's big day. I have no idea how the paparazzi got to know about it. All the attention landed on Lina and me, even though many other students were also celebrating their achievements. Lina was very hurt. I could understand that.

After graduating from high school, Lina could not wait to get out into the world. She was already an international citizen. She had never lived in Sweden, but to move 'home' was out of the question. Instead, she went to Brazil and worked in a home for orphans and HIV-infected children. She travelled to Thailand where she worked for several months at a hotel. After that she began her university studies in England. It was not difficult to see why she would focus on international development. When she was 14 or 15 years old, she had gone to Nicaragua with a Catholic organisation to help poor people there.

Lina started at university in the year I left the England job. Everyone was discussing the World Cup and why England had been knocked out in the quarter-finals. A lot of the English students were angry with me. They thought that I had messed up. Lina did not tell the other students who her father was, except for a couple of people. She came to visit me in Manchester, but I never went to visit her in Norwich. I knew she would not feel comfortable with that. So I was not surprised when she answered the way she did when I called to ask if I could come to her graduation. It still made me sad.

● ● ●

Later in the summer of 2009, Athole called. He had a new club for me – Notts County.

'Notts County?' I thought. 'Where are they in the league?'

Among clubs still active, Notts County are the world's oldest football club, founded in 1862. Their arch rivals were Nottingham Forest, but since being relegated from the top division in the late 1980s, Notts County had plummeted through the divisions and now they were stuck in League Two. The previous season, they had barely avoided relegation from there. Athole explained that Notts County had just been bought by a consortium from the Middle East and the new owners were planning to invest huge amounts of money to bring the club back to its former glory. They wanted me as the director of all footballing matters.

'At least come and see these guys,' Athole said.

The guys were English, Russell King and Nathan Willett, and we met at the Dorchester Hotel in London. I had not heard of either of them. They didn't look like football people. King, who was very fat and needed a cane to move around, was more interested in Formula One than football. Willett was tall and big, and actually turned out to know a lot about football. He was talking about players in the lower divisions whom I had never heard about.

They were both charming and well spoken, obviously educated men. They confirmed what Athole had told me, that they represented the royal family of Bahrain, and explained that their company, Munto Finance, was indeed going to invest large sums of money in Notts County. The plan was to take the team to the Premier League within five years. It was an ambitious goal, but Munto had the resources to do it. Their presentation was very convincing, and I was not the only one who thought so. Athole was equally won over.

Athole had checked up on Munto Finance and had it confirmed that they had backing from a large London bank called First London. The purchase of the club had not yet been ratified by the English Football League. But when I called the president of the Football League, he told me that it was just a formality. Everything appeared to be in order. I also called Sir Dave Richards at the FA. He said the same thing.

But I had been the manager of the England national team just three years earlier. Could I really take a job at one of the lowest-placed teams in English football? What would happen if we didn't succeed with the ambitious plan to bring Notts County to the Premier League?

At the same time, it was a great opportunity to build a football club from the ground up, and not just any club – the world's oldest football club. I was 61 years old. Perhaps it was time to retire from coaching and try something new? I had no other offers. At Notts County they offered me a five-year contract. I would get paid in shares that were potentially worth more than I had made in my last jobs. Most of all, it was an opportunity to build a legacy. On 21 July 2009, I signed the contract.

● ● ●

When I started the job, just two weeks remained until the beginning of the season. The people in Nottingham were very enthusiastic. The club had been in the doldrums for so long. Now they had wealthy owners with ties to the Middle East, and me, the former England manager, as football director. Everyone was buzzing about what players we would be able to attract.

After Mexico, it was great to be back in England. Here I would not have to deal with all the politics. I could be my own boss. At a meeting with the supporters, old fans came up to me and said how grateful they were that I was there to help the club. It was very touching. I felt at home.

I was going to work together with the chairman, Peter Trembling. Peter had worked for Everton as commercial director. He had a similar financial deal to me. We would both receive small salaries, almost nothing, in exchange for stock options in a company called Swiss Holdings, which was connected to Munto. Swiss Holdings were about to go public, and the money raised would be used to finance the club.

I immediately brought Tord to Notts County as an adviser and scout, and also to work on youth development. The manager of the senior team was Ian McParland, a Scot and former Notts County player. King and Willett wanted to fire him, but I said absolutely not. I did not want my first action to be the firing of the head coach. That was not me. I wanted at least to give him a chance to show what he could do. The chemistry between us was not right, though. I made it clear to him that I would not get involved with team selection, but I don't think McParland appreciated having me there. He was a grumpy man.

However, it was my job to bring in new players. To begin with, we didn't sign any big names. The season started well. We beat Bradford City at home 5–0. Lee Hughes, a new player who came from Oldham, scored a hat-trick. Shortly afterwards, we presented our first big signing – Kasper Schmeichel.

Kasper still belonged to Manchester City, but he had been on loan to a string of clubs. He was 22 years old and, in my opinion, on his way to becoming a world-class keeper. It was not easy to convince him to come to a club in the Second Division, and I had to convince not only him, but also his legendary dad, Peter. After King and Willett also talked to him, Peter gave his approval. I believe we paid £1.4 million for Kasper. It had to be the highest transfer fee ever paid by a League Two club.

McParland was against the signing. He said the team already had a good keeper. Kasper was too short and too much of a hothead, he claimed. The first game after Kasper was cleared to play, McParland benched him. Peter went crazy. He had come to England to watch the game in person, along with Kasper's girlfriend. The team lost. In the next game, Kasper made his debut and we won easily. After that there was never any talk about whether or not Kasper Schmeichel should be the first-choice goal-keeper.

I felt we needed another big signing to lift the club and spark the imagination about what we could do. Soon, the perfect name came up – Sol Campbell. I knew Sol well from my time as England manager. He had 73 international caps and had been a stand-out player both in the World Cup 2002 and the Euros 2004. He was 34 years old, but I was convinced he had several good years in him still. He was also without a club, having left Portsmouth. When I called him and asked him if he would be interested in coming to play for us, he immediately said yes.

Notts County was on everybody's lips. The first few weeks with the club had been like a fairy tale. The whole city was behind us. To be part of creating something long-lasting was very exciting and inspiring. We planned new training grounds and academies. The new owners had grand visions. I could see myself ending my career at Notts County, in the Premier League. Would that not be the perfect ending to the story?

● ● ●

Russell and Nathan spent most of their time in London, but when they came to the matches they would usually stay in Nottingham for a few days. They were always in the office then, coming in early and staying after I left at the end of the day. At the weekends, we spent time together. Tord and I each had our own apartment in a complex on the outskirts of Nottingham, ten minutes from the stadium. Russell and Nathan had an apartment there, too. In the apartment above me lived the former owner of Notts County, Derek Pavis, who had been made honorary chairman of the club.

On Sundays, we sometimes ate lunch together, either at Tord's or at Russell and Nathan's. Nathan cooked typically English food, including Yorkshire pudding. The topic of conversation was usually Notts County, but we talked about everything from politics to cricket. Nathan had a near-photographic memory. He could rattle off every old result, it didn't matter if it was football or cricket. Russell and Nathan were both very social, which is why it was a little odd that Russell seemed so averse to being seen in public. At matches he usually tried to hide away. He never spoke to the media.

But it was not something that preoccupied me. I had other things to think about. Sol Campbell had finally made his debut for the club in an away game that we had lost. Sol had requested a day off after that. When he came back to training the following day, he suddenly left in the middle of the session. I was watching the practice. I didn't understand why Sol just walked off, but it was not my place to get involved. After training was over, I went to the dressing room and was told that Sol had gone home. I called him on his mobile, but he did not answer.

Sol did not show up for training on the following day. I continued to try to reach him on his mobile number, but he never picked up. I couldn't carry on chasing him. It was obvious that he did not want to speak with me. Three days after the one game he played, Sol announced that he would leave the club. Peter Trembling tried to keep up appearances to the media and said that Notts County would be fine without Sol Campbell. But obviously it did not look good when our biggest name quit the team after one game. I still don't know why Sol left. I have met him a few times since then, but I have not wanted to ask him about it.

●　●　●

It is hard to pinpoint exactly when things started not to add up at Notts County. Maybe it was the day I heard we had not paid the milk bill. We had a big problem with cash flow. Russell and Nathan assured me and Peter that it was a temporary problem. As soon as the shares were issued, our finances would be resolved. The Football League had approved the purchase of Notts County. The club had fulfilled all the financial requirements. It was all taking longer than expected because the league had complained that the new owners had not wanted to identify themselves initially. But Russell and Nathan assured me there was nothing strange about that. The Bahraini royal family just did not want any publicity, they said.

The managerial position had been an issue from the outset. Russell and Nathan and also Peter wanted to get rid of McParland and new names were always being put forward. I realised the situation was untenable and thought of my good friend Roberto Mancini. He had been sacked by Inter at the same time as I was fired from Manchester City, and had not worked in over a year. Perhaps he would be interested in coming to Notts County? I called him and he said, absolutely, he was interested. To Russell and Nathan, Mancini was exactly the kind of big-name manager who matched their ambitions for the club.

We met at a hotel outside Nottingham sometime at the end of September – Tord, Peter, Nathan, Russell, Mancio and his agent. Mancini was still under contract to Inter, where he was making around six million euros per year. That did not not deter Nathan and Russell. They were willing to pay the same salary and asked Mancini how long a contract he would be looking for. When I left the meeting, I definitely thought we had found our new manager. Mancini wanted to come to Notts County.

At the same time, we already had a manager – McParland. After the strong start to the season, results had been starting to go against us. The team had racked up three losses when, on 11 October, we managed only a draw against Torquay United at home. At that point, we were fifth in the table. After the game, Russell or Nathan called Peter from Bahrain. It could not go on any longer, he said. McParland had to go.

The next morning Peter came to my office and explained the situation. We decided to call in the assistant manager, Dave Kevan, another Scot and a very nice guy, to make him caretaker manager. We were talking to Dave when suddenly McParland barged in. He demanded to know what we were talking about behind his back. Peter told him straight up – he was getting the sack. When he heard that, McParland completely lost his head. Rarely have I seen a manager behave as badly as McParland did that day. He screamed and accused me of orchestrating his dismissal, despite the fact that I was actually the one person who had defended him from the start. A long time later I met McParland at some event and offered a handshake, but he refused to take my hand.

● ● ●

A couple of months after I had joined Notts County, I got a call from Lars-Åke Lagrell, head of the Swedish Football Association. He wanted to know if I would be interested in the job of Sweden manager. Sweden had failed to qualify for the 2010 World Cup and the manager, Lasse Lagerbäck, had left the post. I basically had a long-standing offer to take the Sweden job if it became available. Many years earlier, Lagrell had come to my parents' house in Torsby to offer me the job. At the time, I was with Lazio and could not leave Italy. Lagrell had told me the job was mine the day I was ready to do it.

I still felt very honoured when he called with the offer to take the biggest footballing job in Sweden. I had not worked in Sweden for almost thirty years, but I was a proud Swede. I had hoped one day to lead the Swedish national team. The problem was I had just signed on to the big project with Notts County. I was going to build a football club from the ground up. I could not all of a sudden just up sticks and leave after a couple of months. I asked Lagrell for some time to think about it.

A couple of days passed. Lagrell had told me I could take the Sweden job and still keep Notts County but I knew it was impossible for me to do both jobs. I had learned that with England and Lazio. I knew myself; while I was in Nottingham, I would be thinking about Sweden, and vice versa. I knew the demands of the job as national team manager. It involved an endless amount of travelling. I would not be able to give 100 per cent to both jobs. There was only one answer.

I called Lagrell and said I was sorry but I would have to decline the Sweden job. I could not leave Notts County. We agreed not to comment on our discussion in the media. A few weeks later, it became official that Erik Hamrén would take over as Sweden manager. For some reason Lagrell then came out in the press and said that I had never been offered the job. That wasn't true. He had offered me the job and I turned it down to stay at Notts County. That would prove to be a huge mistake.

● ● ●

One day Nathan came into my office to tell me that Swiss Holdings, the company connected to Munto in which I held stock options, were in the middle of negotiating some big business deal in North Korea. It had to do with mineral resources in that country. Nathan and Russell were going to North Korea to conclude the deal with the government there.

'We want you to come with us,' Nathan said.

I was puzzled. What did I have to do with their business in North Korea? Nathan explained that my name would help open doors. Plus, the North Korean Football Association needed some advice. I would be inspecting training grounds and talking to football people in the country.

I was very sceptical. What would happen if it came out that I was in North Korea? It would not look good. Could they even guarantee my safety? Foreign policy was not my area of expertise, so I called someone

I knew who was involved with government security policy, Ann Taylor, to ask her for advice. Ann was a huge Bolton fan. She strongly advised against my going anywhere near North Korea. But when I told Nathan the next day what Ann had said, he told me it was in the club's and therefore my interest to come with them to North Korea.

'The club's future depends on this deal,' he said.

I felt I didn't have much choice. I also received some reassurance from the Swedish foreign ministry. When I contacted them, they told me it would be no problem for me to visit North Korea. Sweden had an embassy there. I was given the name of the Swedish ambassador, and his phone number, so I called him. He said I would be welcome to North Korea and he hoped to meet me for lunch. I decided then that I would go. Having taken that decision, I wanted to look at the trip in positive terms. After all, not a lot of people get to visit North Korea.

Russell, Nathan and I were not the only ones going on the trip. The delegation also included a member of the Bahraini royal family, named Khan, and a woman whose name I don't remember but whom I had met previously. I believe she was some kind of director at Munto Finance. Two mining specialists were joining us as well, one from Canada and one from Australia. We all met in Beijing and from there travelled on to Pyongyang.

When we arrived, we were met by a North Korean delegation. Lily introduced herself as our interpreter and said she would stay with us for the next four days. From the airport I expected them to take us directly to the hotel but we were taken to a huge statue of Kim Il-Sung. Everyone was expected to lay flowers and bow and pay respects to the former 'Great Leader'. Only after that were we taken to the hotel, a large, very elegant villa where, I believe, Bill Clinton had stayed. Both the food and the service were impeccable. Mobile phones, on the other hand, did not work. We had to use landlines. I suspected they were bugged.

The hotel was situated in a park and I asked the woman in our delegation if she would like to go jogging with me. She agreed and we started off along a road inside the park. When we came to the park's end, I suggested we continue down the road, which ran beside a river. I should not have done that. Just as we were about to leave the park, two North Korean men holding machine guns jumped out of the bushes. They shouted at us to turn around. We did, very quickly.

The Swedish ambassador ate lunch with Russell, Nathan and me at the villa, which was very pleasant, but our stay in North Korea was filled with curious episodes. We were taken to visit a pig farm outside Pyongyang and on the way there, we saw hardly any other cars, but there were quite a few people, even though we seemed to be in the middle of nowhere. Some rode bicycles, but most walked. I don't know where they were going. I did not see any houses. In the city, there were no traffic lights. Instead, women in tight-fitting uniforms directed traffic. When we passed in our government cars, street cleaners bowed deeply. I was driven in a huge, white limousine.

The chairman – at least, I think he was the chairman – of the North Korean Football Association accompanied me to watch football matches and inspect training grounds, as well as the manager of the North Korean national team. They were extremely proud of the fact that North Korea had qualified for the 2010 World Cup in South Africa. It was the first time in forty-four years that the country had succeeded in reaching the World Cup finals. The manager was a former player who had played for the North Korean team that knocked out Italy from the 1966 World Cup, one of the biggest upsets in football history.

I think it was on the second day they took me to see some youth game. I was sitting next to the chairman and the manager, and Lily was sitting behind us. She translated as the chairman told me that he had his own team with the best players in the country. He'd had the players measured somehow to determine who was of the exact dimensions needed to reach maximum speed and strength.

We had promised to provide assistance to the North Koreans in the form of footballs and supplies, and, I think, shoes for some youth teams as well. The chairman was very grateful. He said there was also another way for us to help them. He would like me to help them earn a favourable draw for the World Cup.

'What do you mean?' I said.

Since I knew people at FIFA, could I not help make sure that North Korea ended up in an easy group?

I could not believe my ears. What were they thinking? That I would call up Sepp Blatter and tell him to fix the draw?

'It's impossible,' I said. 'You must understand that.'

The chairman nodded, but he did not seem convinced. He seemed to think it was absolutely possible for Mr Eriksson to help them rig the World Cup draw.

On the last day we attended a huge meeting in the government palace. I believe we were to meet the people just below the president, Kim Jong-Il. We walked into a large hall with marble and glass everywhere, very elegant, and also television cameras. The meeting was going to be televised live. I did not want to be shown on television, so I made sure I was always behind the cameras.

Russell and the female delegation member did the talking throughout the visit. Nathan did not say a word in public during the whole trip. At the meeting, Russell was received like a king. I did not know anything about the business deals they were making but I understood that big money was at stake. Amid a lot of pomp and circumstance, Russell handed over a number of certificates to the North Koreans, stock options in Swiss Holdings equivalent to two billion dollars. When we returned to the hotel, the handover of the certificates was being shown on television. I was not seen on camera.

After that it was time to go to the airport, where we were ushered into a VIP waiting room and strange things started to happen. Russell and Nathan were acting very oddly. They were worried. I asked what the problem was, but could not get a straight answer. It had something to do with an oil delivery from China to North Korea. From what I gathered, it was to be some kind of a gift. The delivery was supposed to have taken place during our time in the country but apparently that had not happened.

The time when we were supposed to board the plane came and went. Lily said something about a problem at customs. It was hot in the VIP room and I wanted to get some air. So I walked off towards the main entrance to the airport but a woman in one of the tight uniforms stopped me. I was not allowed outside. I went back to the waiting room and was given an escort, so I could walk up and down outside for a while. When we returned to the waiting room, there were no developments. Nathan was frantically talking into a telephone. Russell was sweating. At this point, we were a couple of hours behind schedule. I asked Lily if we would be able to leave.

'Well, you will be able to leave,' she answered with a smile.

I am not sure what happened after that, but some kind of decision was made and we were told we could all leave. Russell flew out of his chair. I have never seen him move so fast. We flew to Beijing. From there I travelled on to London. Russell and Nathan were going somewhere else, Bahrain maybe. But they had some kind of issue with their plane tickets. As I left them at the airport, Russell was screaming at some poor woman behind a counter. It was the last time I ever saw him.

● ● ●

To this day, I don't know if the oil was ever delivered to North Korea. Russell's and Nathan's strange behaviour as we left the country had been disconcerting, but the deal for the mineral rights seemed to have been finalised. I had watched with my own eyes the stock certificates being handed over to the North Korean government. Yet the company had still not gone public, and there were no signs of when that would occur. The club were still struggling with a huge cash-flow problem.

Mancini still wanted to come to Notts County, but I was having second thoughts about whether it was such a good idea. It was obvious that the club could not afford to bring him in before Swiss Holdings went public. I did not want Mancio to give up his big salary, which he was still receiving from Inter, to come to Notts County and then not get paid. I would feel very guilty. I called Mancini and told him not to come to Notts County.

Instead, I brought in Hasse Backe as the new manager. He was definitely a cheaper option than Mancini. We had worked together well at Manchester City and in Mexico. Hasse was a very good manager, full of enthusiasm and energy. On 26 October 2009, his appointment was made official.

I still believed in the project, but the financial situation was far worse than anyone could have imagined. The club could not pay their bills. Even worse, they could not pay the players' salaries. When a club can't pay their players, the club is in big trouble. Unbeknown to me, Peter had paid the players' salaries for October out of his own pocket. I did not find that out until he made the payments out of his own pocket again in November.

We didn't see either Russell or Nathan. One day I received a call from a director at BMW's Formula One team. He introduced himself and said we had never met, but he just wanted to warn me about Russell King. Russell had been negotiating to buy the Formula One team but the deal had gone bust when Russell lied about the money that was going to be invested. With help from my friend Peter Hegarty at FIFA, I checked up on Swiss Holdings' finances in Switzerland. It turned out that practically the whole company was a fraud.

On 8 November 2009, the *Sun* published an article about Russell King and Nathan Willett. The headline read: 'Key Notts County Man is an Ex-Con'. Many years earlier, Russell had apparently been convicted of insurance fraud and sentenced to prison for lying about a sportscar worth £600,000 having been stolen. Russell and Nathan had done some other shady deals together, according to the *Sun*. It also came out that Peter Trembling had worked with Russell and Nathan before the Notts County project. Those deals had also gone bad and ended up in court. There were those in and around the club who began to wonder where Peter stood in this whole mess.

I was certain that Peter had nothing to hide. Russell and Nathan had deceived him, just as they had deceived me. Peter had the same financial arrangement as I had. He was going to receive shares in Swiss Holdings. He was not stealing money from the club – quite the opposite. Peter had paid the players' salaries out of his own pocket. Peter claims that Russell and Nathan stole half a million pounds from him personally. In December, Peter received help from Derek Pavis, who stepped in to pay the players' salaries for a month.

Meanwhile, the team was not playing well. Hasse had probably realised the mess we were in and had, to all intents and purposes, given up. On 15 December, he left the club to take up a job in New York. It was different for me. I had a moral responsibility to try to save the club. I could not let supporters and players down. It was my project. We reinstated Dave Kevan as head coach. A few days before Hasse left, Peter had bought the club for £1. The plan was for him and me to find new owners for Notts County.

I had never gone around chasing money before. In London we had meeting after meeting with potential buyers. Some were serious, others were pretty shady. Peter did most of the talking. He presented the short- and long-term vision for the club. I did not say much. The business side of things was not my strong suit. But it was important that I was seen to be supporting Peter. We were open about the fact that Russell and Nathan had scammed the club. Some potential buyers approached us but Peter was suspicious. He did not want to sell the club to someone who would just let it go into administration.

Around the new year, I contacted a Norwegian agent whom I knew worked with a Norwegian businessman, Idar Vollvik. He put me in touch with Vollvik and I called to pitch him the Notts County project. Vollvik invited Peter and me to Oslo to talk about it. Vollvik had made big money in the telecom business and had at one time been one of Norway's richest people. But he had made some very bad investments and lost practically his entire fortune. Now he had started a new telecom company. He was interested in Notts County, but wanted to think about it.

After the visit to Oslo, Vollvik invited me to Spain where he had a villa. I went with Gary Townsend, the club's chief executive. It was a nice trip. Unfortunately, it ended with Vollvik passing on the deal. He told me that had I come five years earlier, he would have bought the club. Now he could not afford it.

In January of 2010 we seemed to have found a buyer who was not only willing to purchase the club, but also invest money in it. His name was Sukhi Ghuman and he owned a security company in Nottingham. He had put together a consortium willing to buy Notts County for a ten-digit figure. But for some reason Peter was against the deal and it fell apart.

Another group of buyers, led by local businessman Ray Trew, was interested in the club. Trew and his colleagues had been lurking in the background during the whole process. We knew they did not have the resources to invest in Notts County to make the club as competitive as we had hoped to make it, but Peter finally realised that he had no other choice but to sell the club to Trew's group. The club was penniless and in danger of being put into administration if new owners were not found. On 11 February 2010, Peter sold the club to Ray Trew for a pound.

As part of the deal, Peter and I agreed to our contracts being cancelled. We would not lay claim to the large amounts of money that the club actually owed us. Trew was grateful for that. According to the deal, I would get 5 per cent of future shares in the club. I was not counting on ever seeing any money from that deal. The club was £7 million in debt and forced to sell its best players, among them Kasper Schmeichel. Yet the club did well after we left. Notts County won League Two, ten points ahead of Bournemouth, and was promoted to League One.

One year later, BBC's *Panorama* made a documentary about the whole Notts County affair. I participated in the film, which was very informative and revealed things about the Notts County business that I had not known. Among other things, it was said that the mysterious Khan, who had travelled with us to North Korea and who had been presented to me as a member of the Bahraini royal family, was actually an English business associate of Russell's on the run from the British authorities, suspected of large theft.

The reporter interviewed a representative of the Bahraini royal family, who said that neither Russell nor Khan had anything to do with the Bahraini royals. But I am still not convinced. In the documentary, it was confirmed that Russell King had actually lived undisturbed in Bahrain long after being revealed as a fraudster. I would not be surprised if Russell and Nathan did have some backing from someone connected to the Bahraini royal family, and the royals dissociated themselves from the whole thing after the article in the *Sun* came out. Many people were fooled by Russell and Nathan, and not just the ones working for the club.

Perhaps I was unable to confront the bitter truth when it stared me in the face. The truth was I'd been had, and it cost me dearly. But I am convinced that Russell and Nathan believed in what they were saying and selling. Why else would they get involved with Notts County? There was no money to be taken out of the club. To this day, I maintain that Notts County could have been a dream project, and if it had all worked out, I would have been at the club today.

● ● ●

During the months I was trying to save the club's finances, my own finances were in free fall. In the summer of 2009, I had hired the accounting firm of Deloitte to investigate what Samir Khan had done with my money. What they found came as a shock to me.

Without my knowledge, Samir had invested millions of pounds in projects the world over. He had bought a house in Barbados and financed it by taking out a huge loan on Björkefors. Apparently, it was located next to Wayne Rooney's house. He had started a magazine, *Icon*, in which I was the main investor. He had spent lavishly on renovations for his own house, using my money, and bought exclusive art for his office. I had not been there, but it was said to be extremely luxurious. The accountants estimated that all together Samir had embezzled at least £10 million of my assets. There was hardly anything left.

On the recommendation of Deloitte, I hired a law firm, Onside Law, and finally took legal action against Samir Khan. His insurance with the City of London would ultimately not cover any of the losses, because his actions were deemed criminal rather than negligent. In May of 2010 the case was sent to the courts for the first time.

AFRICA

19

JOHAN had been always been drawn to Africa. He had a special connection with Africans. I'm not really sure where it came from. When he was younger, he wanted us to adopt an African boy. He wanted a brother of the same age but why the boy had to be African, I don't know. There was no adoption. But when Johan grew up, he found his way to Africa and African football.

Johan was a mummy's boy, unsurprisingly. I was the one who had left Anki and moved away from the family. When he was younger, he was probably angry with me at times. It could not have been easy to have a famous football manager as a dad. After Johan graduated from high school, he went to the United States to study sports psychology and stayed in America for six years. We met at Christmas time and during the summers in Sweden. When Johan returned to Europe, he lived in Norway for a couple of years and worked with professional golfers, but it was not always easy to find clients. It was probably inevitable that he would end up in football. I could help him with contacts, although Johan wanted to stand on his own two feet. That probably had something to do with his interest in Africa.

At the end of 2006, he moved to Nigeria to work for a club team as an assistant manager. Johan had known the manager, Roger Palmgren, since the days when Roger came to see me at Sampdoria. Roger had established himself as a coach in Africa and been the manager of the national teams of Sierra Leone and Rwanda. When Roger and Johan had been in Nigeria for four months, I received a call from the Swedish Embassy there. They had received warnings that Johan risked being kidnapped. He and Roger left the country immediately.

Around the same time, I went to South Africa at the invitation of Dan Olofsson, a Swedish businessman and philanthropist who owned a five-star luxury lodge in a game reserve called Thanda, which was located a few hours north of Durban. Dan was involved with the Swedish football club Malmö FF, and we talked a lot about football. When I suggested to Dan that he should start a football academy at Thanda, he immediately took to the idea. I told him that Johan and Roger could run the academy, together with Dan's son, Johan Glennmo, who was with us there in South Africa.

Things moved quickly after that. Johan and Roger got the job and went to South Africa to start the project. Dan bought a professional football club that was based outside Johannesburg with the idea of moving it to Durban and tying it in with the academy. Roger and Johan would manage the team. Problems arose when the person from whom Dan bought the club did not want to hand over all the players. For the first game, against South Africa's biggest club, Kaizer Chiefs, they were hardly able to get eleven players together and had no footballs to warm up with. Still, they only lost 2–1.

Things got better after a while. Johan Glennmo took over as director of the club. He and Johan became good friends. The club made a deal with the Zulu king in the region and took the name Thanda Royal Zulu FC. Against all odds, they managed to stay up in the South African top division that first year.

Nothing happened with the academy, however. Johan and Roger were very disappointed. The club also had difficulty drawing supporters. The second season was tough. Dan found it more difficult to run the club than he had expected, and one day he decided to pull the plug. New owners took over and Roger and Johan were bought out of the club.

Johan moved to London with Amana, his fiancée. At Notts County, there was talk about bringing Johan into the organisation, but that did not materialise. He started working with Pini Zahavi as an agent's assistant, but Johan wanted to get back to Africa. He went to the Ivory Coast where he started a football academy together with a local partner, and was asked to manage a club there.

Amana was worried about moving to the Ivory Coast, a country that had been ravaged by civil war just a few years earlier. She did not want to tell Johan that he could not take the job in Africa, however. Instead, she asked him if he would really feel comfortable leaving her alone while his team went away to play matches. Johan knew the answer to that. He declined the offer to manage the club in the Ivory Coast. I am not sure I would have done the same in his position.

● ● ●

In the summer of 2010, the World Cup was to be played in Africa for the first time, in South Africa to be exact. I was still disappointed that I would not be taking Mexico there. This would be the first World Cup without me since 1998. I was also out of a job after the whole Notts County affair. That is when Athole called me with a new assignment – manager of Nigeria's national team. Nigeria was one of the five African teams to qualify for the World Cup. Maybe I would still be part of the tournament after all?

I had long been curious about African football. I remember how impressed I had been when watching Nigeria almost knock out Italy in 1994. Two years later, Nigeria won the Olympics. During the past ten to fifteen years, African players had flocked to Europe and many had established themselves at the highest levels in the European leagues. No African team had managed to get beyond the quarter-finals in a World Cup. Perhaps it was time for one of them to take that next step?

But many problems plagued African football. Economic resources were lacking at grassroot and élite levels. Corruption was said to be widespread and planning often non-existent. After Nigeria lost the semi-final of the African Cup of Nations, the Nigerian FA had sacked the team coach, despite just four months remaining before the World Cup, in order to bring in a European replacement. Like many other African countries, Nigeria did not trust the domestic coaches.

I flew to Abuja, the Nigerian capital, to meet the Nigerian FA and, I thought, negotiate the job as Nigeria manager. I knew the Nigerians had also shown some interest in the coach of the Egyptian national team, but I assumed the job was mine if I wanted it. I should not have made that assumption.

We met at the Hilton Hotel in Abuja. In the meeting room, perhaps ten people were sitting, as if on a panel, behind a table. Right away, they started asking stupid questions. Which formation was I planning to play? Why was I the right man for the job? How could I help Nigeria win the World Cup? This was no negotiation, it was an interview. I had been around in the football business for too long to have to sit there and be interviewed about a job, especially by people who did not know anything about football. It was also clear that they had done no research about me or my background. All they knew was that I had been in England.

After the meeting, an agent whom Athole worked with locally explained that half of my salary would be deposited into a special bank account. It was not too hard to figure out that the special bank account would involve someone else taking a piece of my pie if I got the job. There was no way I would agree to that. I never received an offer of a contract, and it was just as well. Not long after that, Lasse Lagerbäck, the former Sweden manager, was appointed manager of Nigeria. When I met Lasse later, I asked him if he had also been 'interviewed' by the Nigerian Football Association. He had.

● ● ●

I thought that I had passed up the only chance I would get to go to the World Cup, but back in London Athole called me about another job, again in Africa – manager of the Ivory Coast national team. Ivory Coast had also sacked their manager after the African Cup of Nations, where the team was knocked out in the quarter-finals. Ivory Coast was regarded as the best team in Africa. They had easily qualified for the World Cup and had such superstars as Didier Drogba and the brothers Yaya and Kolo Touré. I was very interested in the job.

I met the president and vice-president of the Ivory Coast FA in connection with a friendly the country was playing at Queens Park Rangers' stadium in London. Things were much more straightforward with them than with the Nigerians. I felt immediately that I was dealing with real football people. I think Johan's partner in the Abidjan academy had also put in a good word for me. The day after the friendly, we met again at a hotel in London and I signed a contract to manage Ivory Coast until the end of the World Cup. I was given a salary of 100,000 euros per month, plus bonuses if we advanced in the tournament.

● ● ●

I knew it was going to be tough. Ivory Coast had been drawn in what was dubbed 'the group of death'. We were going to play five-times world champions Brazil, as well as the semi-finalists from the 2006 World Cup, Portugal. The fourth team in the group was North Korea. Apparently, their plan to fix the World Cup draw had backfired.

Despite the tricky draw, expectations were high in the Ivory Coast. Football, I would quickly come to realise, meant the world to people in the country. In 2006, Ivory Coast had qualified for the World Cup for the first time. The year before, the civil war between the mainly Muslim north and the mainly Christian south had split the country in two halves. The combatants, it was said, had called for a truce when the national team had played its World Cup qualifying games. How true that was, I don't know. The war was over now, but there was still a lot of tension between north and south. In football, though, the country was united.

Only two months remained until the start of the tournament. Was I really going to be able to put together a team in such a short time-span? First, I needed to have a look at as many players as possible. For that, I needed help. Naturally, I brought Tord with me to my new job, but I also needed an assistant manager who could speak French, the language of the Ivory Coast. I believe it was Tord who suggested Benny Lennartsson. Benny had a long managerial career in Sweden behind him, but now he lived in Paris and spoke fluent French. He would scout France, while Tord took care of Germany and Switzerland. I would handle England. The Ivory Coast FA rented an apartment for me in London. My own apartment was not available. Nancy was still living in it, even though she was supposed to have moved out a year earlier according to our agreement.

My first stop was Chelsea, where Didier Drogba was the striker ace. From my time with England and Manchester City, I had good knowledge of Drogba. I assumed that he had put in a good word with the Ivorian FA about me. Superstars like him definitely had a say when it came to the choice of national team manager. As a player, Drogba was like an ox. That season he had been in sensational form and finished as top scorer in the Premier League. For his country, he had scored 44 goals in 69 games.

Chelsea was managed by Carlo Ancelotti. I met with Drogba at Carlo's office and we talked about preparations for the World Cup. I told him that we were planning a training camp in Switzerland before the tournament, which he thought sounded good. I was also looking for advice about players and showed him a list of thirty, which the FA had helped me put together. It was not Drogba's job to select our World Cup squad but why not seek his advice? He knew about all the players who were in contention for a spot in the squad.

We talked briefly about the team and I explained how we wanted to play. Drogba said that although the Ivory Coast was the best team in Africa, they had a tendency to make one or two big mistakes in each game, which meant that a weaker team, such as Egypt, was allowed to win the African Cup of Nations. If we could avoid making such mistakes, Drogba said, we could go far in the World Cup.

During the month that followed, I flew around like a madman, watching games, watching players. Tord and Benny did the same. I went to Spain to look at someone there, and I asked Toni to scout a player in Portugal. It reminded me of the time when we were looking for players for Manchester City. It was hectic, but I loved it.

I also brought in Johan to help us. He knew a lot about African football. He was very good with languages and could make himself understood in French. Just like me, Johan is very goal-oriented and focuses on his task, whatever it is. It is an important attribute to have. Johan would assist us and, like Toni, analyse our opponents and provide scouting reports. I knew that Johan would do a good job. I would never have given him the assignment if I did not think he was the best person for it. That would not have looked good.

● ● ●

The training camp was held in the Swiss Alps. When we got together on 24 May, it was the first time that I had met many of the players in my preliminary thirty-two-man squad. We had selected players from twelve different leagues. Just two played in the Ivory Coast, and they were both back-up goalkeepers.

Before and during my two previous World Cups, I lived with the England team. It was a completely different experience living with Ivory Coast's team. The English players were calm and quiet. The Ivorians were loud and boisterous. They could sit and talk and laugh about everything and nothing. Suddenly, they would break out into song or dance. At the long dinner table, people would be sitting at the far end from each other and shout across the table. Emmanuel Eboué, who played for Arsenal, would tell jokes that made everyone laugh. I didn't understand a thing. At one point I felt compelled to apologise to the hotel director for the noise. He just laughed and waved off my apology.

'No, no, we haven't had this good a time in the last twenty years,' he said.

Warm-ups were a sight to behold. I told our physio to lead the warm-ups for a few minutes, but then to let the players handle it themselves. Eboué would lead the group. The players sang while they performed this perfectly choreographed dance. It was pure art. Bam-bam-bam-boom! No one missed a beat. They had probably performed the same routine in the academies and knew it by heart.

Training sessions were a delight. The players were true professionals, polite and friendly and open to new ideas. Once in a while, though, something would happen and in an instant things would change. Someone said something, and suddenly chaos erupted. I didn't understand what was happening. I had to stop training twice. I tried to find out what had happened. It was something minor. But maybe there was something bigger underneath the surface? Was it because of religion? Or because they had gone to different academies? I never got an answer. It was not something that affected the team, however. On the bus home, all the players were happy and acted as if nothing had happened.

Logistics were different with Ivory Coast from logistics with England. On 30 May, we were playing a friendly against Paraguay in the small French town of Évian-les-Bains. Our dressing room at the stadium was relatively small and filled up very quickly when thirty players poured into it, singing and dancing. But it was not just players who had made their way into the dressing room. Other people were pouring in, too – people from the Ivorian FA and men in suits I had never seen before. I counted at least fifty people in the dressing room.

One person missing, however, was the kitman. The players had no kit to put on. I asked the FA vice-president Sory Diabaté where in hell the kitman was. He's coming, Sory assured me. And finally, he arrived, carrying two large bags, which he threw into the middle of the room. Immediately, the players started rummaging through the bags looking for their shirts. Numbers were called out and shirts and shorts went flying across the room. I had never seen anything like it. It was as if we were a division-five team, not a national team about to play in the World Cup. Benny and Tord looked at me despairingly. I told them we should go and have a cup of tea. Benny was confused. Should we just leave the chaos and sit down and have a cup of tea, forty-five minutes before kick-off? Yes, I said, that mess was not something we were going to be able to do anything about today.

When we came out on the pitch, I saw Eboué walking around in his socks. He had not found his shoes, so he couldn't play. The next day I asked the players how they could be so disorganised. This is not how things worked in their normal clubs, I said.

'No,' they replied. 'But this is Africa.'

The next day I called in the officials and everyone who had travelled with us. I told them who was allowed in the dressing room before the match, and who was not. If you had no position with the team, you had to stay outside. I told the kitman that he had to arrive in the dressing room at a certain time and had to put out the kit *before* the players got there. It was not more complicated than that. We never had a problem again. Before the next match, all the shirts were neatly hung up when the players arrived.

I had a tougher task than sorting out the dressing-room situation, however, and it was not one I cherished. I had to eliminate an additional seven players from the squad. All football players dreamt of representing their countries in a World Cup tournament, it didn't matter if they came from England or the Ivory Coast. I had to crush that dream for seven of these players. What made things harder was I'd had just a week to evaluate them personally. It was important to make the right decision. I met with the seven players individually and explained how things were. I thanked them for their efforts. One player, Abdoulaye Méïté, a defender with West Bromwich Albion, took the news particularly hard. He had been part of the national team for seven years.

I now had my final squad. We had no injuries. Everything felt great ahead of our departure for South Africa. We had just one more warm-up match to play, against Japan.

● ● ●

Before I met Didier Drogba, my impression of him as a person was not particularly flattering. He seemed like a cocky guy with an inflated ego. I was proved wrong. Drogba was a superstar, but he was also one of the most awe-inspiring individuals I have ever known. The more I heard about what he did to help his people in the Ivory Coast, the more impressed I became. He had spent millions building hospitals and supporting charity projects in his home country. There, he was seen as the nation's saviour.

His commitment to the national team's cause was just as strong. He was the captain and the undisputed leader. Drogba had talked a lot about how important the World Cup was to the people of Ivory Coast. It was also important for him personally. Drogba was 32 years old. He knew it was probably the last time he would get the chance to play in a World Cup.

The friendly against Japan was played in Sion in Switzerland on 4 June, exactly one week before the start of the World Cup and eleven days before our first game. I had picked my strongest starting eleven, with Drogba up front. Early in the game, he gave us the lead when he scored from a free kick. Soon after that, he and a Japanese defender collided. It looked innocuous, but we realised immediately that something bad had happened because Drogba screamed in agony and grasped his arm. Mats Börjesson, the Swedish doctor whom I had brought into the team, ran out to check him. It was serious. Drogba had to come off. As it turned out, his arm was broken.

Drogba had brought his own doctor to Switzerland. He and Mats confirmed that a bone was broken near the elbow. Together, they got a hold of a Swiss specialist on that kind of break and an operation was performed the next day. I think they implanted some kind of splint in Drogba's arm, which was then placed in a protective casing. There was no chance that it would heal before – or even during – the World Cup. Drogba's participation was now highly doubtful.

Drogba himself was adamant – he was playing. There was another problem. Drogba played for Chelsea. Chelsea did not want him to risk further injuries or incur any permanent damage. A lot of money was involved. Chelsea's doctor told Mats that Drogba could not play. The situation was similar to the one we'd had with Rooney in 2006. Mats called Leif Swärd to ask him for his advice. Since the Rooney incident, Leif had become an expert on insurance questions related to expensive football players. He warned Mats that he would take a big risk if he cleared Drogba for play. If Drogba then got hurt, Mats could be sued for millions. It was a risk he could not take. Drogba solved the problem himself. He went

straight to Chelsea and said that he would personally shoulder the financial responsibility. It did not matter if his arm was broken or not, said
Drogba. He was going to play in the World Cup. That was that. When we
got on the flight to South Africa, Drogba was the first one on board.

● ● ●

Our base during the tournament was a hotel located an hour's drive from
Johannesburg. There was nothing wrong with it, although it was hardly of
the same class as the hotels we stayed at with England during championships. Just like with England, however, the wives and girlfriends stayed at
a separate hotel not far from us. Yaniseth and Alcides stayed there, and
Lina, too.

One day, I was going to visit them. I had planned to take a taxi there,
but that turned out to be impossible. No one was allowed to leave the
hotel without security guards. I had to request a car and a chauffeur. I
am not sure if the directives came from the South African Football
Association or possibly from the South African government. The South
Africans were very strict with security during the tournament. They were
afraid that something similar to what had happened during the last African
Cup of Nations would happen there. In Angola, Togo's team bus had come
under attack by armed men and three people had been killed. At one
point, some of our players wanted to go out shopping but it turned into
such an ordeal that they only did it once.

As an African team, we were warmly received in South Africa. For the
players, it was understandably very special to come to Africa and play in
a World Cup. Initially, I had thought we would go far in the tournament
but I was no longer so sure. Drogba's injury had given me second thoughts.

The training went very well, but when we met the press every question was about Drogba and his arm. His injury was quite possibly a greater talking point than Beckham's and Rooney's foot injuries had been ahead of my two World Cups with England. Finally, it became clear that Drogba would not be able to play the first game, at least not from the start.

It was a huge loss. The first game was against Portugal – a tough task, even with Drogba. It would be very difficult to advance from the group if we lost our first game. It would mean that we would have to beat Brazil in our second game. The opening game was played in Port Elizabeth, on the southeast coast of South Africa. Benny Lennartsson was pessimistic beforehand. We'll never pull this off, he said. But that was Benny. He was from Fjugesta outside Örebro. There, he said, people were negative.

I chose an attacking line-up with three forwards – Kalou, Gervinho and Dindane. It was obviously important to not lose, but we also wanted to win. If we needed a goal in the last twenty minutes, I had Drogba on the bench to throw on. After the warm-up, the players returned to the dressing room. Before it was time to go out again, we gathered in a huddle in the middle of the dressing room. There we stood, players and coaches, arms around each other, listening first to Drogba saying a Christian prayer, followed by Kolo Touré doing the same thing according to his Muslim tradition.

Portugal's big threat was, naturally, Cristiano Ronaldo. A few minutes into the game, he struck the post, but after that, neither we nor Portugal created much in the way of clear-cut scoring opportunities. Despite my attacking line-up, the players were too cautious, which is typical of an opening game of the tournament. In the middle of the second half, I put on Drogba. The crowd roared its approval. But not even Drogba could change the game. It ended 0–0.

'Neither of us wanted to lose,' I told the media afterwards.

The truth was we had more to lose from a draw. Brazil had, as expected, beaten North Korea, but only by 2–1. I had sent Toni and Johan to watch that game. We would need at least a draw against them. Otherwise, Brazil and Portugal would be able to play their final game with the previous results in mind and both be able to advance at our expense.

I had watched Brazil playing a warm-up friendly. They were not as good as in the 2002 World Cup. But with Dunga, my old Fiorentina player, as manager, they had eased through the South American qualifiers and also won the Confederations Cup the year before. They were clear favourites. But we had Dider Drogba back in our team.

Soccer City in Soweto was packed with 85,000 spectators. Drogba started alone up front with Kalou and Dindane on the flanks. We had Yaya Touré and Eboué centrally behind Drogba. We knew that Brazil would probably keep most of the possession. We also knew that they were vulnerable on the counterattack.

Things did not turn out the way I had hoped. In the middle of the first half, Luís Fabiano exploited a defensive error on our part and scored for Brazil. It was exactly what Drogba had warned about. Just before half-time, Fabiano scored a second, even though it should have been disallowed for a hand ball right before he scored. We could not exert any serious pressure on Brazil. They were fully in control. Later, Elano added a third. Drogba got a goal back, but by then it was too late.

I refused to accept that it was over, however. We still had a chance to advance. We needed help from the North Koreans. They had played a brilliant game against Brazil. Maybe they would be able to do the same against Portugal? Maybe they would be able to snatch a point this time? A win for us against North Korea in the last game would likely put us through then.

We met in my hotel room to watch the game on television. It started promisingly. The North Koreans, spurred on by their strong effort against Brazil, went on the attack, but Portugal countered and scored. I think we left for our training session after that. On the bus we heard that Portugal had scored a second and a third goal. By the time we arrived at the training pitch, Portugal was up 5–0. The game ended 7–0.

That made it virtually impossible for us to advance beyond the group stage. Brazil would have to beat Portugal while we beat North Korea by more goals than Portugal had put past them. I tried to keep up a stoic appearance before the team. I told the players that all they could do was focus on the game, and not try to score a barrage of goals as quickly as possible. The truth is, I didn't believe we could do it. No one else did, either. And we didn't. We beat North Korea 3–0 but Portugal and Brazil drew 0–0. We were out of the World Cup.

● ● ●

I flew back to the Ivory Coast with the team. Yaniseth and Alcides flew with us on the plane. I did not know what kind of reception we could expect in Abidjan. People would probably be as disappointed as the players that we had been knocked out. I was not aware of what had happened several years before, during the war. Upon failing in the African Cup of Nations, the national team had returned home to Ivory Coast, only to be put under house arrest by the government. It was probably just as well that I had not heard that story.

I did not have to worry, however. We were given a fantastic reception at the airport. Tons of people were there to thank us for our efforts. The next day, the country's president and other government dignitaries participated in an event held for us at a hotel. We were treated as heroes. It was strange. We had not reached our goal, to get out of the group stage, but our efforts were not seen as a failure. Drogba gave a speech, in French, so I didn't understand. He had told me that he wanted me to stay as Ivory Coast manager. The Touré brothers wanted me to stay as well. The Ivorian FA offered me a new contract. I wanted to accept it, but the salary was way too low and I had to decline the offer.

The next day we went by a boat to an island to have lunch at the home of a French guy who was friends with one of the directors at the FA. The island was filled with beautiful houses. Lunch was served in a swanky garden. We sat there and watched England getting pummelled by Germany, 4–1. I felt bad for the English players. At the same time, it was difficult not to feel a certain amount of satisfaction. Fabio Capello was discovering that maybe the England job was not that easy after all.

Mexico failed to reach a fifth game in the World Cup. Later that same day, the Mexicans lost their second-round match to Argentina 3–1. Aguirre, who had brought Blanco back into the team, was heavily criticised for his team selections during the World Cup. Three days after Mexico was knocked out, he resigned from the managerial post.

MY NUMBER-ONE FAN

TOWARDS the end of summer 2010, my mother started getting sick. Her stomach was hurting. At the beginning of September, she was admitted to Torsby hospital and tests showed that she had an expanded gall bladder. She was allowed to go home. A week later, her pain was so bad that she had to be taken back to the hospital. This time, the doctors concluded that her gall bladder was infected. A few days later, it was removed. The gall bladder, I learned, stores bile but is not necessary for the body to work. The operation did not sound serious and for the first few days, my mother felt better. But soon the pain in her stomach returned. She was sent to a hospital in Uppsala. It was around the same time that I received an offer to return to England.

Pini and Pajroj called to ask if I would meet them in London. It was about a job in Indonesia. I said okay but when we met, it turned out they wanted to talk about a managerial job in England, in Leicester to be exact.

I don't know why they had not said anything about it on the phone. Perhaps they thought I would not consider a job with Leicester.

Leicester had yo-yoed between the Premier League and the Championship, where they were now stuck at the bottom. Before the season had started, Leicester had brought in Paulo Sousa, who once upon a time played for me at Benfica, as manager. Pini had done that deal. Shortly afterwards, a Thai consortium led by Vichai Raksriaksorn, a rich Thai businessman whose company, King Power, owned duty-free shops at Thailand's airports, had bought the club. With Sousa at the helm, Leicester had won just one match out of nine. They were bottom of the table and Sousa was about to get fired. Did I want to take over from him?

I was not sure about joining a team in the second division of English football, especially one that was languishing at the bottom, but I preferred to see the positive side of things. The Thai owners would make major investments and turn Leicester into a big club again. Also, I had no other offers.

On 1 October, Sousa was fired. Two days later, I was unveiled as Leicester's new manager. The day after that, I travelled with the club to Bangkok to play a friendly against the Thai national team and do some PR for the club in Thailand. I had not yet had a single training session with the team.

The airport in Bangkok was plastered with advertisements for King Power. Vichai was well known in Thailand, and was a man with a great deal of influence. The day before the match, we trained at the stadium. The traffic in Bangkok was so bad that it had taken us two hours to get there from the hotel where we were staying. But Vichai guaranteed that on match day, it would take fifteen minutes. I was not convinced, but I figured I had to trust the owner. He was wrong, however. It didn't take fifteen minutes to drive to the stadium. It took less. All the roads had been closed off. There was not a car on the streets.

The transfer window had closed, so we could not make any new signings, and although we had a good blend of young and older players, we were weak in attack. I got wind of the fact that Darius Vassell was out of contract and looking for a club, so I brought him in. On the coaching side, I brought with me Tord as the chief scout. Derek Fazackerley, with whom I had worked at Manchester City, became my assistant manager. Chris Powell, the left back whom I had once selected for England, was already on the coaching staff at the club. He would assist me, but mainly take care of youth development. I also kept Mike Stowell as goalkeeping coach. I was very happy with the make-up of the coaching staff, and I was enthusiastic about the job. It didn't matter that Leicester were not a Premier League team.

With a new manager, the team got a boost. It was natural. Part of my job was to instil a winning attitude among players who had started to think in negative terms. I wanted them to find the joy of playing football again. In training, I tried to use as much encouragement and praise as possible. We managed a draw in my first game, at home to Hull. Three days later, we beat Leeds away. We continued on the right path and won four out of six games.

Vichai had some strange ideas about how we could continue winning. Like most Thai people, he was a Buddhist. One day before a game, he came knocking on my door. His son was with him, and five yellow-clad Buddhist monks. They wanted to give me a blessing before the game. The monks wrote something on my desk and gave me a piece of paper to stick in my pocket. Vichai was convinced that we would win after that. But we didn't and I never saw those monks again.

● ● ●

During the autumn, my mother's health problems continued. She was moved between hospitals and was eventually operated on in Karlstad. It turned out that she had a lot of bile in her abdomen. I went to see her in Karlstad together with Yaniseth. It must have been sometime in November. I had a few days off from work. My mother was sick, I knew that, but the doctors seemed optimistic that the operation had been successful. She was down, but totally clear in her head. Before Christmas, she was moved back to Torsby hospital but she got worse and worse, and had trouble breathing sometimes. Finally, she said she did not want any more done to her.

I was not able to come home that Christmas. We had a busy schedule with four games in nine days. On Boxing Day, we drew against Leeds at home, 2–2. Two days later, we lost to Millwall, but then we beat both Hull and Swansea. On 9 January 2011, we played in the FA Cup at home to Manchester City, where Mancini was now the manager. Manchester City were huge favourites. They were leading 2–1 when a goalkeeping error by Joe Hart allowed us to equalise. The game ended 2–2, which was a great result for us. The replay was in Manchester nine days later, on 18 January. As usual, the team stayed in a hotel the night before – the Radisson in central Manchester, my old home. I was there on the day of the match when my brother Lasse called me. He said that our mother was very sick and I should try to get home as fast as possible.

'It's soon over, Svennis,' he said.

I talked to my dad, and to my aunt Astrid. We agreed that I would fly home as soon as possible the next day.

When I walked into the stadium in Manchester that night, I was received with warm applause by the Manchester fans, who still appreciated me because of my time at the club. It was very nice to hear. Unfortunately, we could not pull off another surprise. Manchester City beat us 4–2. In a BBC interview after the game, I explained how proud I had been of the players for their efforts.

The next day I flew home. I had not been able to get a direct flight to Oslo, so I had to make a stop in Amsterdam. I was there, walking to the next gate, when Lasse called. He had bad news.

'Mother has passed away,' he said.

Later I was told that Lasse had got in his car to drive to Oslo to meet me when our father had called him from the hospital. He said Lasse should come to the hospital immediately. Our mother was almost gone. Lasse had not driven very far when Dad called him again, this time to tell him that mother was dead. Lasse went to Oslo, picked me up and we drove the two hours back to Torsby, straight to the hospital. My mother was still lying in her hospital bed. The staff had prepared her and she was beautiful. My dad and aunt Astrid were there. My father cried and Lasse shed a tear as well. Me too.

Had I known that our mother had just a few hours to live I would have gone home before the game. I don't think anyone realised how close she was to passing. At the same time, my dad had said for weeks that she was not going to make it. She had probably told him that she was not going to fight on. I don't know if I had accepted what he was saying to me. I did not believe my mother was dying.

Her funeral took place a week later, on 26 January. Before then, I was back in England. We played against Millwall at home and won 4–2. The funeral was small, with only family and a few close friends. I think that is how Mother wanted it. I gave a speech in which I talked about my mother, how she'd had the energy to worry about everything and everyone. If it was cold in England, she worried that I had the right shoes on. I said that she was always supportive, even when I did something wrong. Afterwards, Lasse and I walked up to the casket. He was crying and could not speak. I said, 'Well, Mother, now I have lost my greatest supporter.'

● ● ●

Soon after I had won the scudetto with Lazio, Lasse called me. He said that he was selling his house and moving to Portugal with his wife and three children to sell golf trips. I was shocked. Lasse had two jobs, as a fireman and supervisor of the local sporting facilities, and a very nice house in Torsby. Why would he give up all of that and move to Portugal? Did he think he was going to be able to compete with the large travel agencies? Someone who didn't speak a word of Portuguese? But Lasse had made up his mind. He was convinced that his plan would work.

It didn't. A few years later, he and his family moved back to Sweden. He bought a house outside Hagfors, in a place called Uddeholm, 25 miles from Sunne. It was in the middle of nowhere. Why on earth did he want to settle there? But Lasse did not want to go back to Torsby. He was tired of being known as Svennis' brother.

All these years he had lived in my shadow, even when we were little. I was the special one to my mother, even though she did not want to show it outwardly. When people around town asked her how her son was doing, she always replied, 'Which one? I have two.' But it was me they talked about. Every day at the fire station, the guys asked Lasse about me. They talked about my football, my women and my money. Lasse came to visit me wherever I worked, in Portugal, Italy and England. Then he went back to Torsby. I talked to my parents every day on the phone, but it was Lasse who had coffee with them. If Lasse did not show up one day, my mother would worry that something had happened. Once every six months, I showed up. The big man. And stole all the attention.

But when mother fell sick, it was Lasse who became the most important person in the family. He took care of her. Even more importantly, he took care of our dad. He would sit for hours with Dad at the hospital. I would have come home more if I could, but I had the football to take care of. It was Lasse who had to carry the heavy load.

We suspected that the medical treatment killed my mother. How could she develop some stomach pain and four months later be dead? She did not have cancer and she died completely clear in the head. No autopsy was conducted, which meant the cause of death could not be established. But my father did not want to argue. He is like me. He hates confrontation. The chief of the hospital in Torsby was an old family friend. My dad did not want to get involved in any dispute with the hospital. My mother was gone anyway.

Aunt Astrid was not so willing to let things go. She had worked as a head nurse at Karlstad hospital and had practically lived with my mother during the time she was sick. Off her own bat, she filed a complaint with the National Board of Health and Welfare. A year later, she received a reply. The investigation had concluded that the operation to remove my mother's gall bladder had not been necessary. After that, the doctors had committed a string of mistakes. They called my father from the hospital in Torsby and talked to him about the report. They said that the hospital would look over how things were done in the future.

• • •

Johan probably thought I was drinking too much alcohol, and he may have worried about me. One day he came up with the brilliant idea that he and I would take a 'white' month without drinking. I don't know if he doubted that we would make it, but to make things more interesting he said we would be allowed a glass if Leicester won. I said okay.

At that point, Leicester had won five games in a row. We were seventh in the league, one point off the Premier League play-off spots. We had made an incredible recovery. Leicester had been stuck in the relegation zone when I came to the club. But the white month began with us losing away to Cardiff, 2–0. There was no drink after the game. The next game we tied at home to Coventry. No drink after that match, either. After that, we lost two more matches, away to Queens Park Rangers and at home to Norwich. I didn't have a single glass of alcohol the entire month.

One day I was having lunch in Leicester when I suddenly started feeling sick. I had to go to the bathroom. I took a couple of steps, but fell to the floor. I don't know what happened. A few days later, I asked the doctor at the club to check me over to see what was wrong with me. He suspected something heart related and sent me to a heart specialist. The tests showed that my heartbeat was irregular. The doctor said it was probably nothing serious, but at the same time warned of the chances of a stroke. I was given blood-thinning tablets, which I still take to this day.

Maybe it was because I could drink wine again or maybe it was because of the weak opposition, I don't know, but we won our next game away against relegation-threatened Scunthorpe United. The white month was a closed chapter. It had not helped my heart and it had not helped us to win. Johan never proposed that brilliant idea again.

After the previous month's poor results we were five points off a play-off spot with nine matches to go. During the winter transfer window we had brought in Nigerian Yakubu Aiyegbeni, one of Pini's clients, on loan from Everton. Yakubu was a big success from the start. Against Middlesbrough away on 2 April, he scored a hat-trick, although we only managed a draw. We beat Burnley at home, but did not win the following two games. The small chance we had to nab a play-off spot was gone. We finished tenth in the table, eight points behind Nottingham Forest in the last play-off spot.

I went to Sweden as usual for my holiday. Johan came, too, but Lina had to work and could not come home that summer. After the 2010 World Cup, she had lived and worked in Swaziland. Johan and I got an idea. If Lina could not come home, we might as well go to see her in Swaziland. We called her up and said we were coming and a couple of days later we went.

Swaziland was one of the countries hardest hit by the AIDS crisis. Lina worked for a small charity that sponsored orphans and vulnerable kids with school fees and school materials. Her English boyfriend, Tom, whom she had met at university, was also working in Swaziland. Johan and I stayed at their house, which was beautifully situated by a river. We used to take exercise, running along the river bank. We had a very nice time. It was always great to see Lina. I liked Tom, too, even though he was not a football guy. He played rugby.

● ● ●

I didn't know much about the phone-hacking scandal in England when I met two investigators from Scotland Yard at the Mayfair Hotel in London. It had come out that the *News of the World*, the newspaper that had nailed me with the fake sheikh, had illegally intercepted famous people's voicemail messages in order to obtain private information about them to publish. The scandal that ensued resulted in the closure of the newspaper in the summer of 2011.

I was stunned. Suddenly, it all became clear. It explained a lot of things that I had wondered about, not just how the newspapers had found out about my relationship with Faria. I had wondered how a photographer who had taken a picture of me picking up Malin at the train station in Karlstad had known that I would be there. I had even suspected Lasse of tipping off the newspapers. It was clear that he didn't. They must have hacked my phone.

I thought back to the episode with Faria in New York. I thought that she had tipped off the press about our meeting. Adrian Bevington had advised me not to go, saying that I still had friends among the press. But it was not Faria who had tipped off the press. My phone or her phone, or maybe both our phones, must have been tapped. I was angry. At the same time, I felt stupid. I had thought the worst of those women.

● ● ●

Before the 2011/12 season, Leicester's goal was clear – win promotion to the Premier League. To succeed, we needed to sign new players. It was my job to identify the players we should sign, and then the club would have to make a decision about whether or not it was possible to buy them.

At one point, I was invited to a dinner arranged by the BBC. David and Victoria Beckham were there, too. David had been playing in Los Angeles for four years. Half jokingly, I asked him if he wanted to move back to England and come play for us at Leicester. David said it sounded interesting, which was typical of David. He never wanted to say no to me. But Victoria looked at me as if I was mad.

'Sven,' she said. 'Could you see me in Leicester?'

David laughed and said, 'When we lived in Madrid, it was not posh enough for my wife.'

A more realistic signing was Kasper Schmeichel. Many people were critical of Kasper. They said he was too short to be a goalkeeper and that he was too hot-tempered. But I liked Kasper and we bought him. We bought a string of other players, too, among them Paul Konchesky from Liverpool and Sean St Ledger from Preston. Vichai said that he expected us to be leading the league after ten games. I didn't pay too much attention to that. I knew what was required of us – winning promotion to the Premier League. If I didn't succeed in that, I would not keep my job. The important thing was where we were in the table when the season was over, not after ten games.

The problem was strikers. I had hoped to keep Yakubu, who had done a very good job for us, but he was too expensive. He went to Blackburn Rovers in the Premier League on the last day of the summer transfer window. Before then, I had tried to bring in the Irish striker Shane Long from Reading, but he was also too expensive.

Just a few hours remained before the transfer window closed, and we were desperate for a forward. We had one name – Jermaine Beckford. He was a former Leeds player who had played at Everton the year before and scored eight goals. I had called David Moyes, Everton's manager, to ask for his advice on Beckford. I was not totally convinced that Beckford was the type of player we needed. But the longer it went, the more desperate we became. Finally, we had no choice. We bought Beckford just a few hours before the window closed. He turned out to be a poor buy.

The season started badly. We won the first game, but lost the next two. After nine games, we had won just three and were eleventh in the league. I did not hear from Vichai. He had not come to the last game. It was a repeat of what had happened with Thaksin at Manchester City. Vichai's son, who was called 'Top', said to the media that he expected us to win promotion to the Premier League. The message was clear. I tried to focus on my job. What else could I do? I was still optimistic. I had a good relationship with the players and I was convinced that we would soon climb the table.

My dad and Lasse came to visit. They saw us beat Watford at home, 2–0. They were there four days later, too, on 23 October, when we played at home against Millwall, who were mired in the relegation zone. We dominated the game, but could not take our chances. Instead, we let in two goals in the first half and another one in the second. I understood that a 3–0 defeat at home by a bottom-placed team was a real problem for me. The decision to sack me was probably taken right after the game, but no one informed me of it. I felt that was very cowardly. Instead, they let me hold another training session the next day. Dad and Lasse had returned home. I went through the video of the match with the team and I was angry. I told the players that if I were the club owner and saw my team that uninspired, I would consider firing the coach.

I was then informed by the club's sporting director that Vichai's son wanted to see me after training. I understood immediately what was going to happen. Top was polite and perfectly nice. He said the results had not been good enough. We were not at the top of the table after ten games, which, according to Vichai, I had promised that we would be. It was also said that my dismissal had to do with Thai politics, which is something I found very difficult to understand. It was whispered that Thaksin was angry with Vichai for having hired Sven-Göran Eriksson. How much truth was in that, I don't know.

It took thirty years as a football manager for me to be fired for the first time. But after my exit as England manager, I had not been able to hold on to a single job except Ivory Coast, but that was a short-term contract. Now I had been fired from a Championship team in England. I knew it would be almost impossible to get another job in England, maybe even in Europe, especially since we were only two months into the season. My name was not exactly on top of anyone's wish list. Perhaps it was time to widen my horizon.

ASIAN TIGERS

IN December of 2011, Glenn Schiller, my old Gothenburg player, who now worked as a football agent, called me about a job in China. A club called Shandong Luneng were looking for a manager. I went to Jinan, where the club were located, to meet the owners. Nothing came of it, but it opened my eyes to China as a footballing country.

I had been in China before, with Sampdoria in 1994. The country had changed enormously since then, especially the economy. But in the football world, China was still seen as something of a dumping ground for old players and managers from Europe. That had probably been my own view of it, too. But Chinese football, just like the football in the rest of Asia, had made incredible progress over the last few years. The standard of play in the Chinese Super League, the highest division in China, was improving with every year. China was no longer a place for footballing has-beens.

One person with big visions for Asian football was Pajroj. He came up with a proposal for us to start a business together with Pini, based in Bangkok. We would buy and sell football players, and also buy a football club in China. One of Pajroj's friends, Dr Chanchai Ruayrungruang, a very wealthy Thai-Chinese business tycoon, wanted to buy a Chinese club. It sounded very exciting. We started the company and called it Empire Sports. Pajroj, Pini and I, as well as our three sons, were the principals in the company. I think I was made president.

We travelled around China looking for a club to buy, often in Chanchai's private plane. Chanchai smoked a pipe and on the plane, an assistant stood behind his seat, ready to add tobacco when needed. I liked Chanchai. He didn't speak much English but I think he liked me, even if he was no football lover. Pajroj had got him curious about football. Chanchai's big passion was opera. On one trip he took us to the opera house in Beijing, which he owned, and treated us to a very luxurious dinner there.

We flew back and forth across China, looking at different teams in cities I had never heard of where millions of people lived. The plan was to buy a club in the first or second division and move it to Kunming, the biggest city in Yunnan province. That was deemed better than starting a new club, because then you would have to start at the bottom of the league system.

In Kunming, we were received like kings. Chanchai reached an agreement with the local political leaders and everyone was very enthusiastic about us bringing a football club there. The idea was that I would start as a sporting director of the club and later take over as head coach, if that's what I wanted. It would be a new chapter in my life.

At the beginning of the summer of 2012, I was in Sweden when Ian Turland called from Coutts bank. He said I was on the verge of bankruptcy and that he would no longer handle my assets. My business with the bank would be handed over to a woman I had never met or even heard of.

The problem was not just the money that I had lost. I also had big tax debts. I had invested in several so-called film schemes. They were common in England. You could invest in these film schemes to lower your tax burden. It was perfectly legal and many other football managers and players made similar investments.

I knew that I had invested in two film schemes, but in reality I had invested in five. When the authorities began looking closer at those film projects, it turned out that some of them, including mine, had violated the regulations governing them in some way. I never knew anything about the projects themselves. But suddenly I owed tax on the money that I had invested. The amounts were huge, over a million pounds.

I needed to lower my fixed expenses drastically. But first I had to establish what they were. Lasse started digging. He discovered a lot of discrepancies. I had been paying to lease a car that a former girlfriend was driving. That was a trivial expense compared to some of the other things that I had unknowingly been paying for every month. Lasse estimated that I had fixed expenses of about £30,000 a month. It was untenable, especially since I did not have a job. The only solution was to sell some of my properties. They were my main assets.

But that was easier said than done. Nancy still lived in the apartment in London, three years after she should have moved out according to our agreement. The legal costs for the Nancy and Samir cases had started to skyrocket, without anything moving forward. The house that Samir Khan had bought without my knowledge in Barbados had been rented out, but the rent did not even cover the mortgage I now had on it. I wanted to sell the house in Portugal, but the Portuguese economy was so poor that it would be difficult to find a buyer. Lasse had started looking into selling Björkefors. He was probably more worried than I was about my finances.

For me, the most important thing was to find another job. I went back to Asia.

• • •

I was very enthusiastic about the China project. Kunming was the perfect city to bring a football club to. The climate was excellent. We just needed to find a club to move. Several months had passed since Chanchai had made the deal with the people in Kunming and nothing had happened. After a while, we heard that the Chinese league – or it might have been the Chinese government – wanted Chanchai to bring a team to Beijing instead. Suddenly, the focus was on Beijing. Pajroj was talking about starting a football academy with David Beckham in China, so I contacted Beckham's people and there was talk about bringing David to China, too.

But there was nothing concrete. Everything seemed to have stalled. Most of the time, Johan and I sat in the office in Bangkok and twiddled our thumbs. Johan was working as a football agent, and did some business. He brought several African players to Thailand. But I had nothing to do. I just sat there and waited. I was restless.

One day we were invited to attend a football match in Bangkok. The team playing, BEC Tero Sasana FC, was owned by Brian Marcar, a rich Thai who also owned a TV company in Thailand. We met in the VIP box at the stadium. Brian was a very nice guy with a big heart for football. He asked if I could come and help the team for a few months, until the end of the season. The club had fired their manager. At first, I didn't take his offer seriously. But a day or so later, Brian contacted me and Johan again. He was serious. Once again I thought, why not? I was just sitting around waiting for something to happen in China. This was something that I could do in the meantime. I said yes.

I would be a technical consultant for the team. Brian had told me I could pretty much do whatever I wanted. The club had a general manager, Robert Procureur, a Belgian with many years' experience of Thai football. The club's physio, Mirko Jeličić, had been leading the team for the last few games. Brian wanted to me to coach the team. I also wanted to coach. But I didn't want to sit on the bench during the games. Mirko could do that.

I had seen a lot of Thai football since I came to Bangkok. The standard of play in the Thai league was lower than in other Asian countries. Thai players were technically skilled, but lacked the physical attributes. They did not seem to have heard of tackling and, compared with European players, they were tactically inferior. They had problems reading the game. I suppose that had to do with the lack of a footballing culture in the country. Young people started playing later. They had not grown up with playing football every day since the day they could stand up.

I was staying in a suite at the InterContinental hotel in the middle of central Bangkok. The hotel was not far away from the stadium and the training pitch. Due to the heat, we had to train late in the afternoon. I think we started around 4.30 p.m. The biggest problem was not the heat, however, but the rain. It rained several times a day, and not just a little. The pitch became unplayable in minutes, it rained so hard. Most of the time it rained in the afternoon, so I tried moving the practices to the morning. But it started raining in the morning, too.

Despite that, I was happy to be back on the football pitch. Almost a year had passed since I had left the coaching job at Leicester. We kept up a high tempo during the training sessions. The players worked hard. My salary was far from what it had been before, but it didn't matter. I didn't do it for the money. I did it for the joy of football. It was hard to sit in the stands during a game and not be able to influence things, though. I went into the dressing room before the match and at half-time, but I didn't want to take over too much. I wanted to let Mirko do the talking to the team. But he talked too much.

One day, Brian asked me what I had done to Thaksin Shinawatra. 'I don't know,' I said. Apparently, people close to Thaksin had called Brian and questioned why he had hired a man whom Thaksin had fired. The same thing had happened at Leicester, according to the rumours, where Thaksin's people had supposedly questioned Vichai. I think it had to do with Pajroj. Pajroj and I were friends. But Pajroj and Thaksin had fallen out, badly, after the Manchester City year. It had to do with politics that I did not understand. But it was apparent that Thaksin Shinawatra still had much to say in Thailand, from behind the scenes, especially since the new prime minister was his sister, Yingluck Shinawatra.

'I can live with having people around Thaksin calling me and complaining,' Brian told me. 'But if the sister calls me, it's a little trickier.'

The sister never called. But soon my time at BEC Tero Sasana FC was over. We finished third in the league, which was a good result. Our Brazilian forward Cleiton Silva finished top scorer in the league. The China project was on perpetual hold. It was time for me to go home to Sweden.

●　●　●

It was late in the year and I did not think I would get another job that season. That is why I decided to write this book. At least it would keep me occupied. I had always wanted to write my own book. There was so much that had been written about me, and most of it was garbage. I wanted to tell my own story. I had been offered big money to write a book during my time in England, but always turned it down. A book was something you wrote when you were finished. But was I finished? I refused to believe that.

At home in Sweden, the newspapers wrote about my taking over the Ukrainian national team but that was mostly agent talk. I needed an official invitation from the Ukrainian FA first. Different agents called constantly and claimed they could seal the deal. Some of those deals did not seem entirely legitimate. One agent texted me that I would get an annual salary of 2.8 million euros, but that 800,000 euros would be deducted in 'fees'.

I had another job brewing, too, one that had not come out in the press – as manager of 1860 Munich. Once upon a time, 1860 Munich had been a big club, one of those that had started the German Bundesliga. In recent years, though, the team had been struggling and they were now languishing in the second division. The goal was to get back into the top flight.

The club had a new owner, Jordanian businessman Hasan Ismaik, whom I knew. I had travelled to Abu Dhabi to meet him and talk about the Munich job. He wanted to give it to me, but I was not sure that the Germans on the club's board were equally convinced that I was the right man for the job. One thing I learned from my time in Mexico was never to take a job where you were not really wanted.

Finally, I got an official invitation from Ukraine and went to Kiev just before Christmas to talk about managing their national team. I would not be celebrating Christmas with the family this time. Johan and Amana were in Bangkok. Lasse was there, too. He had met a Thai woman. I met with representatives of the Ukrainian FA. It was a big job and I wanted it. Ukraine had done poorly in the World Cup qualifiers so far. They were in the same qualifying group as England. Their chances of reaching the World Cup in Brazil were slim, but they still existed. I asked for a contract spanning the European Championship in France in 2016, but the FA thought I was too expensive. The job went to a domestic coach instead, Mikhail Fomenko. I went to Panama to celebrate Christmas with Yaniseth.

On 16 January 2013, the English FA celebrated its 150th anniversary. All previous England managers were invited to a big event in London and I accepted. With time, my reputation in England had improved, I felt. Many people, in hindsight, realised that my England record was not that bad compared with what later managers had been able to achieve. With each failed championship result, the expectations for England among both the supporters and the media had been scaled down considerably. When England went out on penalties in the quarter-finals of the 2012 Euros, most people thought that the team – and my friend Roy Hodgson, who had taken over as England manager just a month before the tournament – had done as well as anyone could have hoped.

I have never liked the kinds of events where you stand around chit-chatting. That has never been my strength, but it was nice to see my old friends David Dein, Adrian Bevington and Michelle Farrer again. I had a good relationship with most people at the FA. The event was full of foot-ball dignitaries. I exchanged a few words with Sir Bobby Charlton, but otherwise, I preferred to keep to the side.

At one point, Fabio Capello came up to talk to me in Italian. Capello had abruptly left the England job before the Euros. He claimed that he had done it as a matter of principle when the FA forbade him to appoint John Terry, who was involved in a racism controversy, as team captain. I suspect that Fabio saw it more as an excuse to leave England. Now he had taken the job as Russia manager. We talked for ten minutes. Mostly it was Fabio who talked. He spoke about his new job and how things were in Moscow. He asked nothing about me.

I also talked to Owen Hargreaves. He had been without a club since leaving Manchester City the summer before. I asked if he would be interested in playing in Dubai, but Owen was not sure. All his injuries seemed to have depleted him. He was mentally spent, which was a shame, because Owen was still only 31 years old. At his best, during the 2006 World Cup, he was a world-class player. Tord loved Hargreaves. I did, too.

The reason I asked Owen if he would be interested in coming to Dubai was that I had been offered a job there, as sporting director of the club Al-Nasr. It had not come out yet. I had travelled to Dubai before coming to England to meet the people at the club. It sounded interesting, but I had not yet accepted the job. In the papers, they were writing that I was going to Munich. That rumour was confirmed when suddenly 1860 Munich announced on its homepage that it was a done deal and I was Munich's new manager. The problem is, it was not true. I had not accepted the position. It was very strange how they could say publicly that I had accepted it. Maybe it was not a mistake. Maybe politics were behind it.

The next morning, a director of the club, Robert Schäfer, came to London to meet with me. According to him, it was a misunderstanding that had led to my appointment being officially announced. The club hoped that I would take the job. But it was unclear what exactly my job would entail. There was talk of sharing the head-coaching job with the German coach who had been made caretaker manager, Alexander Schmidt. I was not interested in that. It would only lead to problems. I decided to say no to the job and instead move to Dubai, in the United Arab Emirates.

● ● ●

Everything is new in Dubai, and that includes the football. When I became a football coach in Degerfors in 1976, the United Arab Emirates had existed as a country for just five years. The UAE Pro League did not start until 2008. I had been coaching football for over thirty years.

I had signed an eighteen-month deal as technical director of Al-Nasr. I had not taken the job to retire as a coach, as had been my intention when I went to Notts County. Some people thought I went to Dubai for the money, but that was not true, either. My salary was going to be 700,000 dollars a year, a long way from what I had been making at the height of my career. The truth was simpler – I just wanted to work.

My job was to analyse all aspects of the footballing operations at the club, from the senior team through to the youth sides, and see what could be improved. Al-Nasr, like most clubs in the country, had big resources to invest in football. What they lacked was know-how and long-term planning. They wanted to win, now; or, rather, the sheikh who owned the club wanted to win now. All clubs were owned by wealthy sheikhs, who in the end were all related to each other. Ours was His Highness Sheikh Hamdan Bin Rashid Al Maktoum. He was also the finance minister of the country. He was not present when I was introduced to the media but I was promised that I would meet him as soon as possible. The sheikh did not come to the games, but I was assured that he followed closely what was happening with the club. He wanted to win a title, they told me.

The manager of the senior team was Walter Zenga, my old goalkeeper from Sampdoria. Zenga had managed Al-Nasr since 2011 and in the 2011/12 season the team had finished third in the league, which was a very good result. It meant qualification for the Asian Champions League. This season things had not gone so well. The team was fifth in the league when I came to the club. The higher-ups were not happy with Zenga and word had it that the idea was to fire him and let me take over as head coach. I advised them against that. It was similar to Notts County. I did not want to come in and start firing people. Zenga was a tough and sometimes sullen man, but he also had strong coaching skills. He deserved a chance to turn things around.

My office was located in Al-Maktoum Stadium, the club's home ground. The name plate outside my door said 'guest'. When I got there on the first day, sometime before lunch, no one was there. The work schedule in Dubai differed markedly from what I was used to. For most people at the club, the working day started in the afternoon. It had to do with the heat. Training began around five o'clock during the winter months, when the temperature was still pleasant, but as the season went on, the hotter it would get. During the summer, the average temperature in Dubai hovered around forty degrees Celsius, and the team had to train at eleven o'clock at night.

The Arab players all had similar names, such as Mohammed, Ibrahim and Rashid, and learning who was who was not easy. From my office I could see them arriving at the stadium. They went right past my window. So I asked Islam, the club's Egyptian secretary, to give me a sheet of paper with the photos and names of all the players. Each time a player went past the window, I could check his name and try to memorise it.

Each team was allowed to have four foreign players, three from any country and one from the rest of Asia. The same rules applied in all the Asian leagues. At Al-Nasr we had two Brazilians. One of them, Léo Lima, was a midfielder who had once played for Porto in Portugal. He was the team's best player, but Zenga had trouble finding his true position. Usually, Lima played as a defensive midfielder. I suspected that it was not his best position. He had a tendency to dribble and hold on to the ball too long to be a defensive midfielder.

I quickly established a routine. I came to the office at around 2.30 p.m. I might have a meeting with an agent or people from the club. I was on the technical committee. At five o'clock, I sat up in the stands and watched the first team train. I was itching to get down on the field. That is where I wanted to be. Zenga was probably not entirely comfortable with having me there as an observer every day. After that, I went to watch the youth teams on the training pitches next to the stadium. At eight o'clock the day was over and I went home.

It took a long time to find a home. For more than a month I lived in the JW Marriott Marquis hotel. It had seventy-two floors and was said to be the tallest hotel in the world. The tallest building in the world, Burj Khalifa, was in downtown Dubai. I looked at an apartment there, but it was too expensive, and the windows could not be opened. I didn't like that. It felt stuffy.

Eventually, I rented a two-bedroomed apartment on the twenty-seventh floor of Oasis Beach Tower, an apartment complex located near the beach in the Marina District. It had a balcony overlooking the artificial island shaped like a palm tree, and in the distance you could see Burj Al Arab, the sailboat hotel. There was a lot of life and commotion in the area with plenty of tourists from England and Scandinavia. Housed on the ground floor of the building was an Italian restaurant, Frankie's, which became my favourite place to eat. It all reminded me of the hotel suite I'd had in Manchester. I liked it from the start in Dubai.

● ● ●

Interest in football was huge in Dubai. The problem was the same as in Thailand – people were more interested in the English Premier League than in local clubs. Maybe 500 people showed up for our home games. The stands were mostly empty, every game. It was the same with other clubs. All the games were broadcast on television, but I am not sure how many viewers they attracted.

What the league was missing was a big name. Many clubs, among them Al-Nasr, had spent a lot of money bringing older players from Europe to the Gulf. The season before, striker Luca Toni, who had won the World Cup with Italy in 2006, had played for Al-Nasr. It had not worked out. Most of the clubs had grown tired of washed-up stars who were more interested in one last paycheck than in playing hard and helping their teams. The league's biggest star was Asamoah Gyan, a relatively young forward from Ghana, who played for the top team, Al Ain. Gyan scored bucketloads of goals, but even he failed to draw big crowds.

One name was guaranteed to stir up interest in football in the United Arab Emirates – David Beckham. David had left LA Galaxy. He was 38 years old and most people probably expected him to retire. My idea was to try to lure him to Dubai to start a football academy. I contacted David's agent to see if it would be possible. The agent said that David was definitely interested in coming to Dubai, but not just to start an academy. He also wanted to play.

It was exactly what the league needed. With David Beckham at Al-Nasr, we would fill the stadium for every game. I was convinced that David still had a lot to give. He would not say he wanted to continue playing if that was not the case. I explained to the club that we had the possibility of bringing the biggest name in football to Al-Nasr but, to my surprise, my suggestion received a lukewarm response. The club thought it would be too expensive. The answer was no. David went to Paris St Germain where he became a success and was part of the team that won the French league.

● ● ●

At Al-Nasr, the first team was up and down. Good performances were followed by real stinkers. Mostly, Zenga played a 4-3-3 formation, but we didn't have good enough wingers for that. Lima's best position was still unclear, and the team's other foreigners were not good enough. In the Champions League group games, we lost every match. Other members of the technical committee all thought that Zenga had to go. I warned them that it would be a mistake to sack him now. Clubs in the UAE kept firing their coaches. It was a big problem. My advice was to wait, at least until the season was over, before they made changes.

However, major changes were certainly necessary, not least on the youth side. Al-Nasr had an extensive youth programme with Under-15, Under-17 and Under-19 teams. Every day I sat and watched the training sessions and it became clear pretty quickly that half of the youth coaches were not good enough and should be replaced. More training pitches were desperately needed, and some social and economic problems required solutions. Most players in the youth teams came from poorer families and I was told that some of the younger players were taking drugs to keep their energy up.

It would be a challenge to build up the club from scratch, and I was not sure that they really had the long-term perspective required to succeed. A lot of it was up to the owner and his willingness to finance the restructuring. No one seemed sure of his true intentions for the club. Several months had passed and I still had not met him personally.

It was my job to look for possible replacements for Zenga. Two Premiership Managers were both interested, as was Roland Andersson. Roland had been assistant coach for the Swedish national team and had long coaching experience in Saudi Arabia. He would fit in well in Dubai. When I suggested Roland to the club's management, though, they were not convinced. They wanted a bigger name. Did I not want to take over the head-coaching job myself?

● ● ●

In early May 2013, with only a few weeks of the Premier League season left, it was announced that Sir Alex Ferguson would retire as Manchester United manager at the end of the season. I had a hard time believing that it was true. Ferguson was on his way to winning a thirteenth championship title with the club. He was 71 years old and had nothing left to prove. Still, I had been convinced that he would never leave football. How could he? Football was his everything.

A week later, David Beckham announced that his playing career had come to an end. Immediately, journalists began calling me for comments. They wanted to know what my best memory was of David. I said it was probably the free kick against Greece.

I was in London at the time – I had come to testify in one of the civil trials against Samir Khan – and I stayed in my own apartment. Nancy had finally gone, four years after our agreement stipulated that she should move out. In January, when I was in London for the FA anniversary, my lawyers and I had met with Nancy for a mediation hearing. After twelve hours of discussion, Nancy refused to accept a deal. Since then she had grown ever more desperate. She needed money. Eventually, she had

357

accepted a new agreement. She would get the house in Italy and £175,000 from the sale of the apartment in London. On 30 April 2013, she had finally moved out.

The apartment was hardly in good condition. Much of the furniture was missing and she had taken all the kitchen equipment with her. The heating was turned off. The apartment was dirty. The kitchen was really dirty. I wondered how Nancy could have lived like that? She always demanded that everything should be spotless. It almost seemed as though she had secretly rented out the place. But, frankly, I didn't care. I was just happy to have her out of there.

●　●　●

Three years had also passed since I sued Samir Khan for financial fraud. After repeated postponements, one of the cases against him was to be held in Reading, an hour's drive from central London. This was the case brought by the liquidator of Pier 24. The day before, my lawyers from the firm Onside Law and I had gone through what would happen at the trial. Samir Khan's wife, Sarah, had, according to the lawyers, agreed to let me have whatever assets she had left. But Samir would not give up. He was determined to fight on.

The trial was held in the judge's office. When we came into the room, Samir Khan was sitting at a table. Another man was sitting next to him. The lawyers had brought several boxes of papers and evidence with them, which they put on the table. I sat on a chair at the side. I would not testify on that first day. The judge was a tough lady. She ordered the man who was sitting next to Samir to leave the room. He did not have permission to be there. Samir had no lawyer. He would represent himself in court.

The trial was due to last for four days. On the first day, the case against Samir was presented. The judge had read the stacks of documents. I sat and listened to the lawyers explaining how Samir had embezzled my money. They talked about Southsea and all the rest. I said nothing, I just listened, hour after hour. Samir also listened. He looked like a broken man. But maybe it was just a façade. He used to be very polished. When the day was over, we went back to London.

The next day we were back at the judge's office. Now it was Samir's turn to prove his innocence. I was to answer questions but that is not what happened. Before the day's hearing started, Samir agreed to bankrupt himself. He had no money to pay me what he owed so this was my best hope of recovering a fraction of what he'd taken from me. And with that, everything was over. The lawyers were very happy. They said it was a great result in the circumstances. We left Samir and travelled back to London. It did not feel like a great result.

● ● ●

I was supposed to fly back to Dubai after that. We had one game left before the league season was over. I would meet the club management and discuss what to do before the next season. The team had struggled towards the end. The club had still not decided what to do about Zenga. Chances were that he would stay.

It was a dilemma for me. I had convinced the club not to get rid of Zenga. At the same time I had been asked to find a new coach. During my London stay I had met with Roberto Di Matteo, who had won the Champions League with Chelsea in 2012 but been fired since then. He wanted to come to Dubai but he was probably going to be too expensive.

359

The club could decide to keep Zenga. If so, they wanted me to stay as his boss. I didn't think that would work, or that Zenga would accept it.

There was another alternative. Before going to London, I had received another job offer, as head coach of the Chinese team Guangzhou R+F. The salary would be double what I was earning in Dubai but, more importantly, they were offering a coaching job. I wanted to get back to coaching. The more training sessions and the more games I watched from the stands in Dubai, the more convinced I had become that I needed to be on the football pitch. I was no administrator. The problem was that I had a year left on my contract with Al-Nasr, and I felt a strong loyalty to the club. They had been good to me all along. They wanted me to stay in Dubai.

The Chinese, however, wanted me to go directly from London to China to sign the contract. Johan, who had been involved in the negotiations with the Chinese, said I should definitely go directly to China. Lasse called and said the same. Pini had also become involved. He said that if I went to Dubai, I would risk losing the China job.

But it was my decision.

It was cold and rainy in London when I took the taxi to Heathrow airport. I checked in, got on the plane and flew off.

EPILOGUE

The motorway through Guangzhou is elevated, which means we are travelling high above the tops of the trees. A month and a half has passed since I came to China. The street life flies by us below. We never need to stop or even slow down, despite driving through the heart of a city of more than twelve million residents. We just keep going.

From London, I flew back to Dubai. I didn't want just to leave the job. The club had treated me perfectly. I liked it in Dubai. But I wanted to get back to the football pitch. I am a football coach. At Al-Nasr, they understood that. We parted as friends. I felt I had accomplished what I went there to do. I had set up the football school and the academy, given my advice about the senior team and how the club could be developed. Now it was up to them to move forward.

● ● ●

The first December snow had just fallen in Björkefors when I started telling my story. I was without a job. Now, eight months later, I am sitting in a car in China on my way to train my new team. It has taken me a lot longer than I had expected to go through my story. The job has been much bigger than I had expected. I have never stopped to think back about my life before.

In Värmland, we don't talk much about ourselves. We are kind and polite, but we seldom reveal our true emotions – a character trait that has helped me in my professional life. In my career I have said only what is necessary, and left my emotions out of it. But things work differently in the world outside.

I suppose it is no coincidence that I started the story by recounting the time I visited Nisse Liedholm at his vineyard. I understand now why Liedholm asked me for help in finding a team to coach, even just a youth team. He could not let go of football. He had spent a lifetime on the football pitch, but he was still not satisfied. If Liedholm, the legend, was not satisfied, is it possible ever to be satisfied as a football manager? Now, twenty years later, I know the answer to that question.

The other day I read the manuscript of my book from start to finish for the first time. My life. I was surprised by the emotion that swept over me when I got to the end. I felt depressed. Yaniseth and Alcides had returned to Panama after visiting me in China. It was late in the afternoon and I took my bicycle and cycled along the Pearl River, which flows through Guangzhou. It was beautiful. Where had the years gone? My children? Friends? The women? Time? It hurt to think back.

● ● ●

All my life I have kept diaries in which I have written down what I have done and where I have been each day. To help me remember my story, I wanted to go through those diaries and so I asked my brother to send them to me. He did not know where I was going to be, so he sent them to my lawyers in London. When I came to China, I asked my lawyers to send the diaries here and now they are stuck in Chinese customs.

My mother kept a diary, too. Lasse found one in my parents' house at Björkefors, which dated back to 2002. Underneath each date, my mother had written: 'Sven-Göran called.'

Each day I called home. Each day my mother wrote it down in her diary. I had never thought much about those calls. They were not about anything important. I would tell my parents where I was and where I was going after that. My mother would tell me about the weather in Sweden and if Lasse had come over for coffee that day. But the important thing was not what was said.

I understand that my mother found all the newspaper gossip about the women a burden. She wrote that down. I told my parents not to read all that garbage, but still they did. 'I feel sorry for you, my son,' my mother wrote in her diary on 22 April 2002, after the Ulrika business had come out. 'But stay strong, it will pass.'

She had difficulty sleeping. She lay awake at night and worried. She did not want to say anything to me. One day my dad said to me that he wouldn't mind reading about the football, too, not just the women. My mother got mad. She thought that was mean of him, even though she was the one who had wanted him to talk to me about the women stories.

As for me, I don't regret anything. I have given everything for football. There is no other way. The price I have paid for my success is high but I have never asked myself if it was worth it. Others have also had to pay a price for my success, not least my family. I left Anki for football. I could not always be there for my children. It was difficult for my brother to live in my shadow. My parents suffered quietly. At the same time, I believe they are all living pretty happy lives today. Perhaps I had something to do with that as well?

I should have made different decisions when it came to my finances but money was never important to me. I was born poor and maybe I will die poor, but I know I have lived and will continue to live a good life in between. I should never have trusted Samir Khan but I know that I also have myself to blame for being so gullible. Still, I cannot understand how a legal system like Britain's can be so slow. Imagine if I worked the same way in football. I would not have got far.

The other day we put Björkefors up for sale. If my finances had been better, I may not have decided to sell it. It feels a bit melancholy. I made Björkefors what it is but it has not been the same since my mother died. My father does not want to live there any more and my children will never want to live there permanently. I don't want to live there permanently. The summers are beautiful, but the winters are long. Besides, there is only one place where I belong.

● ● ●

I still believe that I am one of the world's greatest football managers. You have to believe that, otherwise you might as well give up. I know I am a better manager now than I was when I won the UEFA Cup with Gothenburg. It would be strange otherwise. I have managed a dozen teams on four different continents since then. Experience is one of the most important tools in a football manager's arsenal.

The other day I was thinking about the catastrophic first season I had with Roma. I was 36 years old and believed I knew everything. The teams I had managed before, in Sweden and Portugal, won title upon title. I was not afraid to take over a team that the season before were a missed penalty away from being crowned champions of Europe. I had my footballing philosophy and I was convinced that it would generate the same results there as it had with my previous teams. What I didn't understand was that Roma was different. It was a team full of superstars. Still, I tried to change them. Change everything. I suppose I trusted myself more than my players and that is why things went the way they did.

There is nothing more difficult for a football manager than to admit failures and mistakes. It is a sign of weakness. I would much rather point out that I have won seventeen titles than the fact that I have not won a single one since Lazio. England was a failure. In 2006, we should have reached the final. Our team was good enough. There was no team better than us. If we had reached the final, would we have won it? I have never approached a game thinking I would not win it. Still, I don't lose any sleep over England. I know I did a good job.

I have been lucky in my career. I was lucky when Tord called and asked if I wanted to come to Degerfors. What would have happened if he had not done that? What would have happened if they had not called me from IFK Gothenburg? But when you are given the opportunity, you must deliver the goods. In football, you are quickly exposed if you just talk garbage. I think that is the difference between football and business.

Football coaching is different today compared to when I started. You have to be able to handle players, coaches and owners, but also sponsors and the media. New training methods and new philosophies emerge, yet much stays the same. How you handle people as a coach remains the same, what you do to make a player feel comfortable, how you explain things in the best possible way. The players must know what they should do on the football pitch. After that, it is up to them. In the end, the best players win.

● ● ●

The training ground is located far outside the city. The drive takes an hour. The club wants to build a new training ground, but the problem is finding the land for it. Everything is already bought up. Everywhere you look in Guangzhou, enormous skyscrapers and apartment complexes are rising up.

A contruction company, R+F, owns the team. The two owners of the company, Zhang Li and Li Sze Lim, bought the club two years ago. I have been to visit them in their offices on the top floor of one of the skyscrapers in the city. Very impressive. They have huge resources and ambitions for the club. Football is something new to them. If we do well, it will help the company, but they want to see results before they invest too much money. The first goal is to qualify for the Asian Champions League.

I use my time in the car to go through today's training session with my assistant coach, Roger Palmgren. Our South African fitness coach, Divan Augustyn, is also travelling with us. Some of the players are unhappy that they have to do some extra physical work. I promise Divan that I will talk to them before the first session of the day. Physical conditioning is very important. Many of the players were in poor shape when we came to the club.

We arrive at the hotel that is our base and I shake hands with all the people working there. This is important. After that, I go to my room. All the players and coaches have a room at the hotel where they can change and shower and rest between training sessions. Most of the Chinese players live at the hotel, while the foreign players live in the city. My room is a suite, but it is not very fancy.

The room next to mine belongs to Yakubu, our big goalscorer – the same Yakubu I had on loan at Leicester. He and I have a good understanding. He came to Guangzhou R+F a year ago. In his debut last seaon, against Guangzhou Evergrande, he scored the only goal of the match. Evergrande still won the league. This year, they are on top again. The team is managed by my old friend Marcelo Lippi. I met him the other day. This is the first time he has taken a job outside Italy. He loves it in China.

The coaching staff gather in the dining hall forty-five minutes before the first training session. We are about ten people, among them my Chinese assistant manager, Li Bing. His title is actually team leader, but I use him as an assistant coach. I also have an interpreter, Julio, who is a fun-loving Chinese guy. I suppose he has a real name in Chinese. We have another interpreter, Ricardo, who can translate into Portuguese for our two Brazilian players. I lead the meeting. We have a few minor things to cover. Nothing complicated.

To get to the training pitches, you have to walk along a narrow trail that zigzags through a grove. I follow our three goalkeepers. It is warm and humid, but a nice little walk. We go through an opening in the fence and step on to the first training pitch. There are three pitches, arranged lengthways, with the short ends against each other. I have never seen that before. The fitness coaches have put out cones and balls on the middle pitch, and pulled the goals closer so that we can play small games, three-on-three and four-on-four.

It is almost eleven o'clock when we gather on the pitch. I want to talk to the players before we get started. I understand that the last few days have been hard work, I tell them. I understand that they are tired. But it is important to follow the conditioning programme we have set up. I don't want to hear any complaints. It is their job as footballers to train hard. I say a couple of sentences at a time, waiting for the interpreter to translate. The whole speech takes about two minutes.

Divan takes care of the warm-up. He does a lot of core strength exercises, which is good. We try to use the ball as much as possible, even during the physical training. After that we move on to small-game play. The skies have darkened and we have been playing for just a few minutes when it starts to rain. It feels good. In the heat, the rain is a release.

Roger and I are standing together, watching the play. The tempo is fast. Things have been looking better and better. The last game we won 4–1 at home to Hangzhou Greentown. Zhang Li, one of the owners, was there. He came out on the pitch to congratulate me afterwards. Our two Brazilians, Davi and Rafael, have played better recently. We have also signed a new Australian centre back, Eddy Bosnar. I am convinced he will do a good job for us.

When training is over on the pitch, the players move into the gym next door for the extra physical work. Soon, lunch will be served. This afternoon we are doing another session. We are going to play the full field. I stay on the pitch to do some interval training on my own. The rain is falling harder now. It does not bother me. On the contrary, it feels wonderful. I don't want to stop. I run another leg. A little farther this time.

INDEX

PHOTO CREDITS